THE ECONOMY

PATRON

TUN DR MAHATHIR MOHAMAD

Editorial Advisory board

CHAIRMAN
Tan Sri Dato' Seri (Dr) Ahmad Sarji bin Abdul Hamid

MEMBERS OF THE BOARD
Tan Sri Dato' Dr Ahmad Mustaffa Babjee
Prof. Dato' Dr Asmah Haji Omar
Puan Azah Aziz
Dr Peter M. Kedit
Dato' Dr T. Marimuthu
Ms Patricia Regis
Tan Sri Dato' Dr Wan Mohd Zahid Mohd Noordin
Dato' Mohd Yusof bin Hitam
Mr P. C. Shivadas

The Encyclopedia of Malaysia was first conceived by Editions Didier Millet and Datin Paduka Marina Mahathir. The Editorial Advisory Board, made up of distinguished figures drawn from academic and public life, was constituted in March 1994. The project was publicly announced in October that year, and eight months later the first sponsors were in place. In 1996, the structure of the content was agreed; later that year the appointment of Volume Editors and the commissioning of authors were substantially complete, and materials for the work were beginning to flow in. By early 2007, 13 volumes were completed for publication. Upon completion, the series will consist of 16 volumes.

The Publishers wish to thank the following people for their contribution to the first seven volumes:
Dato' Seri Anwar Ibrahim,
who acted as Chairman of the Editorial Advisory Board;
and
the late Tan Sri Dato' Dr Noordin Sopiee
Tan Sri Datuk Augustine S. H. Ong
the late Tan Sri Zain Azraai
Datuk Datin Paduka Zakiah Hanum bt Abdul Hamid
Datin Noor Azlina Yunus

EDITORIAL TEAM

Series Editorial Team

PUBLISHER
Didier Millet

GENERAL MANAGER
Charles Orwin

PROJECT COORDINATOR
Marina Mahathir

EDITORIAL DIRECTOR
Timothy Auger

PROJECT MANAGER
Martin Cross

PRODUCTION MANAGER
Sin Kam Cheong

DESIGN DIRECTORS
Annie Teo
Yusri bin Din

EDITORIAL CONSULTANT
Vivien Stone

EDITORS
Azrina Abdul Karim
William Citrin
Kiri Cowie
Fong Min Yuan

ASSISTANT EDITOR
Lee Li Lian

DESIGNERS
Muamar Ghadafi bin Ali
Theivani A/P Nadaraju

Volume Editorial Team

EDITORS
Chuah Guat Eng
William Citrin
E. Ravinderen Kandiappan
Deborah Koh Leng Hoon
Nolly Lim
Ridzwan Othman

ASSISTANT EDITOR
Chang Yan Yi

DESIGNERS
Lawrence Kok
Muamar Ghadafi bin Ali
Yusri bin Din

EDITORIAL CONSULTANTS
Colin Chang
Assoc. Prof. Dr Eddie Chiew Fook Chong
Carolyn Lim Siew Choo
Datuk Zainal Aznam Yusof

ILLUSTRATORS
Chai Kah Yune
Jackie Chin
Eva binti Mohd Ali
Lee Sin Bee
Lim Joo
Tan Hong Yew
Terng Kong Hwee

SPONSORS

The Encyclopedia of Malaysia was made possible thanks to the generous and enlightened support of the following organizations:

- DRB-HICOM BERHAD
- MAHKOTA TECHNOLOGIES SDN BHD
- MALAYAN UNITED INDUSTRIES BERHAD
- MALAYSIA NATIONAL INSURANCE BERHAD
- MINISTRY OF EDUCATION MALAYSIA
- NEW STRAITS TIMES PRESS (MALAYSIA) BERHAD
- TRADEWINDS CORPORATION BERHAD
- PETRONAS BERHAD
- UEM WORLD BERHAD
- STAR PUBLICATIONS (MALAYSIA) BERHAD
- SUNWAY GROUP
- TENAGA NASIONAL BERHAD

- UNITED OVERSEAS BANK GROUP
- YAYASAN ALBUKHARY
- YTL CORPORATION BERHAD

PNB GROUP OF COMPANIES
- PERMODALAN NASIONAL BERHAD
- NCB HOLDINGS BERHAD
- GOLDEN HOPE PLANTATIONS BERHAD
- SIME DARBY BERHAD
- MALAYAN BANKING BERHAD
- MNI HOLDINGS BERHAD
- PERNEC CORPORATION BERHAD

Malaysian Quality of Life Index, 1990–2004

Source: Economic Planning Unit

Legend: 1990 (base year) — 2004

- Public safety -21.5%
- Transport and communications 18.1%
- Environment -0.3%
- Working life 22.1%
- Family life 4.2%
- Education 15.9%
- Income and distribution 8.0%
- Housing 18.9%
- Social participation 6.6%
- Health 18.1%
- Culture and leisure 21.2%

Note: The Malaysian Quality of Life Index is an aggregate measure of the quality of life using 42 indicators, representing 11 components of life. Between 1990–2004, the overall Malaysian quality of life increased by 10.9%.

Student enrolment in public educational institutions

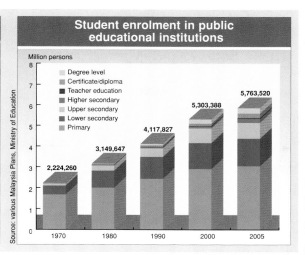

Source: various Malaysia Plans, Ministry of Education

Million persons

Legend:
- Degree level
- Certificate/diploma
- Teacher education
- Higher secondary
- Upper secondary
- Lower secondary
- Primary

Values: 1970: 2,224,260; 1980: 3,149,647; 1990: 4,117,827; 2000: 5,303,388; 2005: 5,763,520

Mean monthly household income, 2004
Population, 2005
Development Composite Index, 2005

Note: The Development Composite Index is based on 16 indicators. The average Development Composite Index for Malaysia is 100.0.
¹Includes Putrajaya
²Includes Labuan

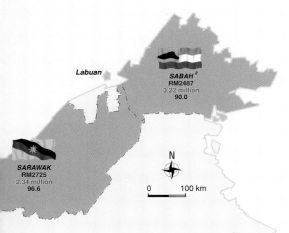

Labuan

SABAH ²
RM2487
3.22 million
90.0

SARAWAK
RM2725
2.34 million
96.6

0   100 km

Source: various Bank Negara Annual Reports, Department of Statistics

Gross exports and imports by product (RM million)

Products	1970	1980	1990	2000	2005
Exports					
Agriculture	2813	12,249	17,904	22,913	37,421
Rubber	1724	4618	3026	2571	5787
Saw logs	630	2622	4042	2489	2465
Palm oil	258	2605	4412	9948	19,036
Sawn timber	201	1352	3063	3020	4051
Other	-	1052	3361	4885	6082
Minerals	1323	9485	14,512	26,800	52,321
Tin	1013	2505	902	435	935
Petroleum	203	6710	10,642	14,241	28,508
Iron ore	107	270	-	-	-
LNG	-	-	2634	11,300	20,790
Other	-	-	334	824	2088
Manufactured goods	630	6108	46,830	317,937	429,873
Others	366	349	376	5657	14,173
Total	**5132**	**28,191**	**79,622**	**373,307**	**533,788**
Imports					
Consumption goods	853	4733	12,682	17,372	24,600
(Food, beverages and tobacco, consumer durables, other)					
Investment goods	1401	7142	29,856	47,064	60,734
(Machinery, transport equipment, metal products, other)					
Intermediate goods	1901	11,253	36,040	230,611	308,335
(For manufacturing, construction, agriculture, petroleum, other)					
Imports for re-export	92	407	541	6309	21,862
(Tin ore and natural rubber)					
Dual use goods	-	-	-	6391	11,308
(Motor spirit, passenger motor cars, other)					
Others	-	-	-	4679	7171
Total	**4247**	**23,535**	**79,119**	**312,426**	**434,010**

Source: various Bank Negara Annual Reports, Department of Statistics

Employment by sector and unemployment rate

Source: various Economic Reports, Bank Negara Annual Reports

Million persons / %

Legend:
- Government services
- Services
- Construction
- Manufacturing
- Mining and quarrying
- Agriculture, forestry and fisheries
- Unemployment rate

Values: 1970: 2,944,000 (8.0%); 1980: 5,135,659 (5.3%); 1990: 6,685,000 (4.5%); 2000: 9,274,600 (3.1%); 2005: 10,894,800 (3.5%)

Trade balance, 2005

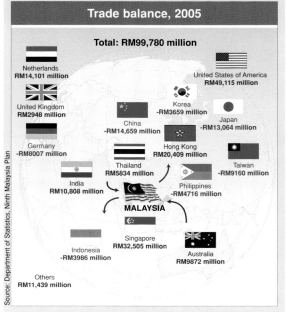

Total: RM99,780 million

- Netherlands RM14,101 million
- United States of America RM49,115 million
- United Kingdom RM2948 million
- Korea -RM3659 million
- Japan -RM13,064 million
- China -RM14,659 million
- Germany -RM8007 million
- Hong Kong RM20,409 million
- Thailand RM5834 million
- Taiwan -RM9160 million
- India RM10,808 million
- Philippines -RM4716 million
- MALAYSIA
- Singapore RM32,505 million
- Indonesia -RM3986 million
- Australia RM9872 million
- Others RM11,439 million

Source: Department of Statistics, Ninth Malaysia Plan

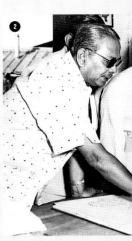

1. Workers at an electronics factory. Electrical and electronic products were the leading industry within the manufacturing sector in 2005.

2. Prime Minister Tunku Abdul Rahman (left) and other officials inspecting plans for the Kemendore Land Development Scheme in Melaka in 1960.

3. Prime Minister Dato' Seri Dr Mahathir Mohamad (second from left) at the 20th anniversary of the Look East Policy in 2002.

4. A Bank Bumiputra advertisement, c. 1966, showing a variety of Bumiputera workers. The bank was established in 1965 specifically to provide credit facilities to the Bumiputera community in order to increase their participation in the Malaysian economy.

5. Consolidating latex tapped from rubber trees. In 2005, natural rubber prices hit a 17-year high as a result of demand from China's automotive

industry and the high price of synthetic rubber. Malaysian exports of natural rubber totalled RM5.79 billion in 2005.

6. The JARING network monitoring centre. JARING was the country's first Internet Service Provider, bringing the internet to Malaysia in 1992. In 2000, it offered broadband internet access.

7. Prime Minister Dato' Seri Dr Mahathir Mohamad launching the Japanese version of a book about the Malaysia Incorporated policy in 1995.

8. Aerial view of PETRONAS's Petroleum Industry Complex in Kertih, Terengganu. The Forbes Global 500 ranked PETRONAS first in terms of return on revenue and assets in the petroleum refining industry in 2005.

ECONOMIC DEVELOPMENT

The structure of the Malaysian economy has changed from one based on agriculture to one focused on manufacturing and services. This has been the result of deliberate economic policies developed and implemented by the government since Independence. The nation's pre-World War II economy was almost completely dependent on the export of two primary commodities, rubber and tin. The large-scale planting of oil palm began in the 1960s, and Malaysia gradually became the world's largest producer of palm oil. In the 1970s and the 1980s, the development of a lucrative oil and natural gas industry contributed significantly to the nation's economic development. Since 1987, it has been the manufacturing sector that has been spearheading the growth of the economy, and from the late 1990s onwards, the focus has been on the services sector and knowledge-based industries.

As a mixed economy, Malaysia has elements of a free market economy but with government direction. The most influential economic policy to date has been the New Economic Policy, introduced by the government in 1971 to reduce ethnic imbalances, eliminate poverty and improve the economic status of the Bumiputera.

In the 1980s, Malaysia sought to emulate the economic success of Japan and other East Asian countries. To this end, the Look East Policy was adopted to replicate in Malaysia the work ethic of these successful economies. This policy was followed by the Malaysia Incorporated concept which stressed the importance of cooperation between the public and private sectors in order to ensure rapid economic growth and national development. To complement these policies, the government launched the Privatization Policy in 1983.

Privatization was intended to facilitate economic growth, relieve the financial and administrative burden of the government, reduce the government's presence in the economy, decrease public spending and allow market forces to govern economic activities and improve efficiency. The policy was also integral to the government's strategy of realizing active participation by Bumiputera in the corporate sector.

In 1991, the aim of Vision 2020, namely, to achieve developed nation status by that year, was announced. The framework for this was laid out in the National Development and National Vision Policies.

In 2002, the government launched the K-economy Master Plan. The master plan articulated the means of developing a knowledge-based economy to advance the country's economic growth.

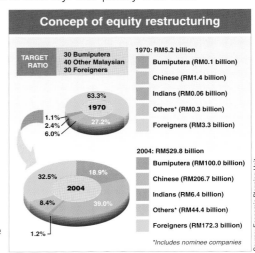

Concept of equity restructuring

TARGET RATIO
30 Bumiputera
40 Other Malaysian
30 Foreigners

1970: RM5.2 billion
- Bumiputera (RM0.1 billion)
- Chinese (RM1.4 billion)
- Indians (RM0.06 billion)
- Others* (RM0.3 billion)
- Foreigners (RM3.3 billion)

1970
63.3%
27.2%
1.1%
2.4%
6.0%

2004: RM529.8 billion
- Bumiputera (RM100.0 billion)
- Chinese (RM206.7 billion)
- Indians (RM6.4 billion)
- Others* (RM44.4 billion)
- Foreigners (RM172.3 billion)

2004
32.5%
18.9%
39.0%
8.4%
1.2%

*Includes nominee companies

Source: Economic Planning Unit

Economic planning and growth

The government uses planning to achieve economic growth. Social and political considerations have always been part of economic development. Careful five-year economic planning ensures coherence in policy making and social stability, providing the foundation for economic growth. As a result of government policies, Malaysia has become one of the most successful developing countries in the world.

Deputy Prime Minister and Minister of National and Rural Development Tun Abdul Razak being briefed on the First Malaysia Plan by planning officers and state engineers in the National Development Operations Room, 1966.

Planning for growth

Development planning has been a function of the government since the 1950s with the preparation of the First Malaya Plan, 1956–60. In 1961, the Economic Planning Unit (EPU), part of the Prime Minister's Department, was created to formulate policies and strategies for socioeconomic development and evaluate their achievements.

Development plans are based on long, medium, and short-term planning horizons. With the exception of the First Outline Perspective Plan, which was for a 20-year period, the long-term or Outline Perspective Plans each cover a period of ten years, and focus on broad economic directions and strategies in the national development agenda over the long term.

The medium-term plans are the five-year Malaysia Plans (which are reviewed in the middle of each five-year cycle). These facilitate the operation of the Outline Perspective Plans. They set macro- economic growth targets and allocate public sector funds for programmes. Annual budgets by the Ministry of Finance and the EPU ensure the effectiveness of the medium- and long-term plans. Short-term monetary and financial development is monitored by Bank Negara Malaysia (see 'Monetary policy and Bank Negara Malaysia').

Between 1957 and 1970, development policy was aimed at promoting growth with a strong emphasis on the export market. Although the economy grew

Timeline of the economic plans

First Outline Perspective Plan 1971–1990

New Economic Policy 1971–1990

Import-Substitution 1958–1968

Export-Orientation 1969–1985

First Malaya Plan 1956–1960	Second Malaya Plan 1961–1965	First Malaysia Plan 1966–1970	Second Malaysia Plan 1971–1975	Third Malaysia Plan 1976–1980	Fourth Malaysia Plan 1981–1985
Increased economic growth in order to raise income per capita and standards of living. Emphasized rural development.	Raised economic output to protect living standards through economic diversification and development of products other than rubber.	Addressed the four main socioeconomic problems: heavy dependence on exports of rubber and tin, high rate of population growth, uneven distribution of income and low level of human resources.	Established political will and capacity to realize New Economic Policy objectives of eradicating poverty and restructuring society to foster national unity. The end of the plan coincided with the worldwide recession of 1974–75.	A period of recovery. The role of public enterprises was enlarged in order to achieve the New Economic Policy objectives via regional development, modernization of agricultural sector and expansion of labour-intensive manufacturing.	The global recession in the early 1980s caused a general slowdown in the economy. The role of the private sector in the implementation of the New Economic Policy was highlighted.

Prime Minister Dato' Hussein Onn (right) proposing the Fourth Malaysia Plan to the Dewan Rakyat (House of Representatives) in 1981.

RIGHT: Covers of the Malaysia Plans.

First Malaysia Plan

HIGHLIGHTS SECOND MALAYSIA PLAN

Rancangan Malaysia Ketiga 1976–80
RANCANGAN UNTUK PERPADUAN NEGARA

RANCANGAN MALAY KEEMPAT 1981-1985

1955   1960   1970   1980

rapidly, at an annual rate of six per cent, socio-economic imbalances between the ethnic groups led to the 1969 racial riots.

The launch of the New Economic Policy in 1971 was the most significant policy change in Malaysian history (see 'New Economic Policy: 1971–1990'). Apart from socioeconomic goals, the overriding aim was national unity. To achieve its goals, two strategies were adopted: reducing poverty across all races, and restructuring society to correct economic imbalances.

The Vision 2020 plan was launched in 1991. It articulated what Malaysia should achieve by 2020, and affirmed the government's commitment to the development of human capital and to raising the standard of living to that of a developed nation (see 'Balanced growth: 1991 onwards').

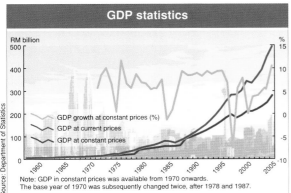

GDP statistics

RM billion / %

- GDP growth at constant prices (%)
- GDP at current prices
- GDP at constant prices

Note: GDP in constant prices was available from 1970 onwards. The base year of 1970 was subsequently changed twice, after 1978 and 1987.

Source: Department of Statistics

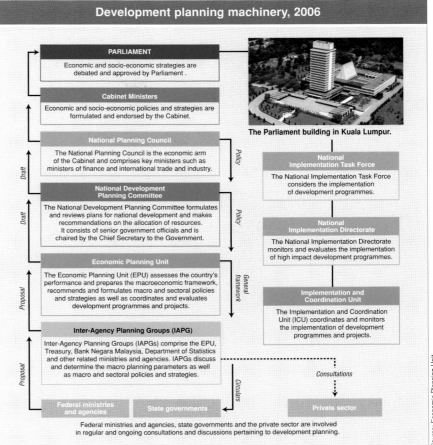

Development planning machinery, 2006

PARLIAMENT
Economic and socio-economic strategies are debated and approved by Parliament.

Cabinet Ministers
Economic and socio-economic policies and strategies are formulated and endorsed by the Cabinet.

National Planning Council
The National Planning Council is the economic arm of the Cabinet and comprises key ministers such as ministers of finance and international trade and industry.

National Development Planning Committee
The National Development Planning Committee formulates and reviews plans for national development and makes recommendations on the allocation of resources. It consists of senior government officials and is chaired by the Chief Secretary to the Government.

Economic Planning Unit
The Economic Planning Unit (EPU) assesses the country's performance and prepares the macroeconomic framework, recommends and formulates macro and sectoral policies and strategies as well as coordinates and evaluates development programmes and projects.

Inter-Agency Planning Groups (IAPG)
Inter-Agency Planning Groups (IAPGs) comprise the EPU, Treasury, Bank Negara Malaysia, Department of Statistics and other related ministries and agencies. IAPGs discuss and determine the macro planning parameters as well as macro and sectoral policies and strategies.

Federal ministries and agencies | **State governments**

The Parliament building in Kuala Lumpur.

National Implementation Task Force
The National Implementation Task Force considers the implementation of development programmes.

National Implementation Directorate
The National Implementation Directorate monitors and evaluates the implementation of high impact development programmes.

Implementation and Coordination Unit
The Implementation and Coordination Unit (ICU) coordinates and monitors the implementation of development programmes and projects.

Consultations

Private sector

Federal ministries and agencies, state governments and the private sector are involved in regular and ongoing consultations and discussions pertaining to development planning.

Draft — Policy — Policy — Proposal — General framework — Proposal — Circulars

Source: Economic Planning Unit

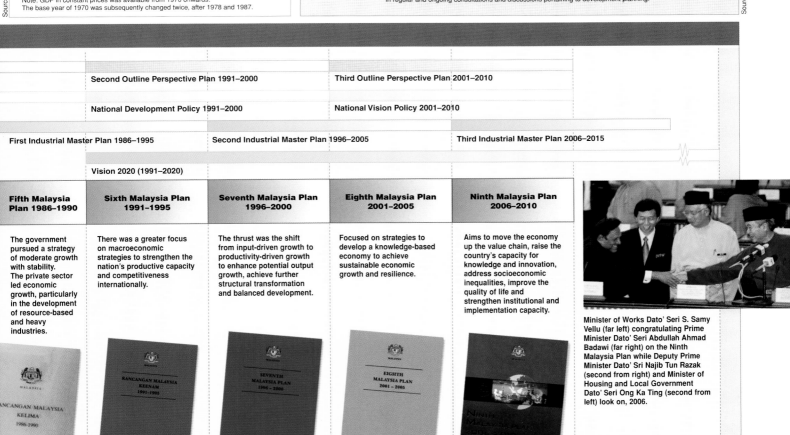

| Second Outline Perspective Plan 1991–2000 | Third Outline Perspective Plan 2001–2010 |

| National Development Policy 1991–2000 | National Vision Policy 2001–2010 |

| First Industrial Master Plan 1986–1995 | Second Industrial Master Plan 1996–2005 | Third Industrial Master Plan 2006–2015 |

Vision 2020 (1991–2020)

Fifth Malaysia Plan 1986–1990	**Sixth Malaysia Plan 1991–1995**	**Seventh Malaysia Plan 1996–2000**	**Eighth Malaysia Plan 2001–2005**	**Ninth Malaysia Plan 2006–2010**
The government pursued a strategy of moderate growth with stability. The private sector led economic growth, particularly in the development of resource-based and heavy industries.	There was a greater focus on macroeconomic strategies to strengthen the nation's productive capacity and competitiveness internationally.	The thrust was the shift from input-driven growth to productivity-driven growth to enhance potential output growth, achieve further structural transformation and balanced development.	Focused on strategies to develop a knowledge-based economy to achieve sustainable economic growth and resilience.	Aims to move the economy up the value chain, raise the country's capacity for knowledge and innovation, address socioeconomic inequalities, improve the quality of life and strengthen institutional and implementation capacity.

Minister of Works Dato' Seri S. Samy Vellu (far left) congratulating Prime Minister Dato' Seri Abdullah Ahmad Badawi (far right) on the Ninth Malaysia Plan while Deputy Prime Minister Dato' Sri Najib Tun Razak (second from right) and Minister of Housing and Local Government Dato' Seri Ong Ka Ting (second from left) look on, 2006.

1990   2000   2010   2020

Public sector, private sector

As a mixed economy, Malaysia combines elements of a market economy characterized by free enterprise and a planned economy with government participation. The private sector constitutes the principal source of employment and growth, and private sector efficiency is the key justification for privatization. The Malaysia Incorporated concept embodies the public–private partnership that underpins the economy.

Prime Minister Dato' Seri Dr Mahathir Mohamad (second from left) at the launch of the 'Framework for Malaysia Incorporated and Privatisation Towards National Productivity' in 1983.

The public sector

Prior to 1971, the government's involvement in the economy was limited to the provision of infrastructure, social services and the regulation of private sector activities. Under the New Economic Policy (NEP), however, government participation increased significantly (see 'New Economic Policy: 1971–1990'). Since then, the government has played an essential economic and developmental role in several other respects.

The government functions as the national development strategist, undertaking planning on the national level for individual sectors as well as the entire economy. Management of the early commodities-based economy, industrialization and the transition to a knowledge economy have been carried out by the government.

The government also establishes and maintains the country's institutional, legislative and regulatory framework. In doing so, it has consistently maintained a pro-private sector posture, always striving to maintain a business and investment climate that is conducive to the growth of the private sector. To achieve socioeconomic objectives, the government indirectly influences—via public policy—aspects such as the composition, location, ownership and employment of the private sector, but minimal direct controls are exercised over private enterprises. The government has been mindful of the need to shield infant industries from foreign competition until they can hold their own; it has been equally mindful of the dangers of overprotection.

In terms of macroeconomic management, the government's objectives include formulating a judicious mix of fiscal and monetary policy, with a view to promoting growth and controlling inflation (see 'Monetary policy and Bank Negara Malaysia'). Invariably, it is also the government that formulates macro-level responses to challenges and threats to the economy, such as those posed by the Asian financial crisis of 1997 (see 'Malaysia's innovative response to the financial crisis'). Direct government involvement in industry and commerce has paved the way for private sector participation and eventual leadership.

The private sector

Aided by the pro-private sector policies of the government, the private sector has grown in depth

The Look East Policy and Malaysia Incorporated

Prime Minister Dato' Seri Dr Mahathir Mohamad (right) visiting a factory in Korea in the early 1980s to study the Korean patriotism, discipline, good work ethics, competent management system and close cooperation between the Korean government and its private sector.

In the early 1980s, Malaysia pursued a Look East Policy. Various aspects of Japan, South Korea and Taiwan's business cultures and practices were adopted. One key aspect which Malaysia sought to emulate was the harmonious relationship between the public and private sectors. The private sector was viewed as the public sector's partner in growth because the prosperity of the private sector would in turn benefit the public sector through corporate taxation.

On 25 February 1983, Prime Minister Dato' Seri Dr Mahathir Mohamad introduced Malaysia Incorporated, a concept which would underpin the creation of a new relationship between the government and the private sector whereby both parties would strive cooperatively towards national development.

At the conceptual level, Malaysia Incorporated required both the private and public sectors to recognize that they shared common corporate goals, and that they should therefore work together in a symbiotic relationship to their mutual benefit. Malaysia was to be viewed as a 'company' owned by both the government and the private sector. On a practical level, it meant that the economy had to be deregulated and the government machinery made more efficient, responsive and open in order to spur private investment and business growth, which in turn would result in greater tax revenue and more funds for socioeconomic development.

While it is difficult to directly link the Malaysia Incorporated policy to concrete economic developments, within five years of its launch there was a marked increase in private investments. By 1990, private investments amounted to more than 60 per cent of total investments.

Public and private sector cooperation

Trade missions
The government has initiated a number of trade missions to forge business links with both developed trading partners and non-traditional markets. Involving public sector officials and leading private sector entrepreneurs, these missions have promoted trade and Malaysian investments in developing economies.

Malaysian Business Council (MBC) and National Economic Action Council (NEAC)
With the establishment of the NEAC in 1998 as a consultative body to the Cabinet to deal with the Asian financial crisis, the MBC, which had functioned in a similar capacity, ceased operations. The NEAC advises the government on economic issues and comprises top civil servants and representatives from the corporate sector and associations.

Smart Partnership
Events held since 1995, such as the Langkawi International Dialogue, aim to promote better understanding between the public and private sectors, facilitate profitable ventures between local and foreign businesses, and link the country to the rapid technological advancements made in various fields around the world.

Prime Minister Dato' Seri Abdullah Ahmad Badawi (centre) with the major sponsors of the Global 2004 Langkawi International Dialogue.

and breadth. Virtually all manufacturing, agricultural, mining, construction and other commercial activities are conducted by the private sector. Hence, private enterprises constitute the major source of employment and output growth. The importance of the private sector is also apparent in its contribution to employment, consumption expenditure and investment expenditure. Indeed, the growth of the private sector has been crucial to the success of government socioeconomic policies, which are premised on the idea of equitable distribution of wealth in the context of an ever-expanding economy.

Privatization is one development through which the public sector and the public at large have benefited from the efficiency and productivity of the private sector. In the process of implementing the NEP, the state established a large number of statutory bodies. This involved a high level of public capital formation. In the early 1980s, this resulted in an increase in the development budget and a considerable deficit in the federal budget. With the expansion of public services, the number

of public sector employees grew disproportionately large, and emoluments became the single largest item of Federal Government operating expenditure. In addition, government agencies suffered from slow decision-making, low efficiency and poor overall performance.

Malaysia was one of the first countries in the world to privatize and, after the successful privatization of several projects between 1983 and 1987, plans were made to draw up a programme for more systematic implementation in order to sustain the policy's success. In 1991, the Privatization Master Plan was released by the Economic Planning Unit to chart the future course of privatization.

Aerial view of Johor Port, privatized in 1995.

The steps towards privatization

In the process of implementing the New Economic Policy (NEP), the state established a large number of statutory bodies (non-financial public enterprises), wholly owned enterprises and joint ventures, which involved a high level of public capital formation. In the early 1980s, this resulted in an increase in the development budget and a considerable deficit in the federal budget which had to be financed by borrowings from foreign sources.

Privatization was conceived as a solution to the burgeoning public sector and its inefficiencies. Furthermore, privatization was in line with the government's overall policy of free enterprise. Since privatization enabled the transfer of government interests in commercial and industrial enterprises to the Bumiputera business community, it was seen as an effective way to increase Bumiputera participation in the corporate sector and thereby meet one of the objectives of the New Economic Policy. Since the launch of the Privatization Policy in 1983, a large number of public enterprises have either been commercialized, corporatized or privatized.

Commercialization
Commercialization is the first stage of the privatization process and public enterprises operate in a business-like environment before being transformed into corporatized entities, then full-fledged commercial entities.

Corporatization
At the corporatization stage, several changes take place. First, there is a change in legal status of the entity from a department or statutory body to a company governed by the Companies Act 1965. Second, a transfer of assets and liabilities occurs. Third, bureaucratic administration is replaced by commercial management. Clear financial and operational performance targets are introduced along with commercial accounting methods. Centralized production-oriented decisions are replaced with consumer and market-driven ones; similarly, the

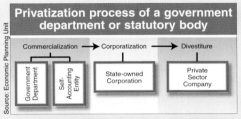

mindset of employees is changed to be more businesslike and market-driven. Although a corporatized entity operates on commercial lines, the government owns all the equity.

Privatization
Privatization is the transfer to the private sector of government interests, investments and responsibility for providing goods and services that are traditionally within the state's domain. The government disengages itself from direct involvement in providing goods and services so that it can resume its traditional role as economic planner and regulator of the private sector. Privatization represents a shift from public to private sector driven growth.

Methods of privatization which have been used include Build–Operate–Transfer, Build–Operate–Own, Build–Lease–Transfer, Build–Transfer, land swap, sale or equity and/or assets, lease of assets, management buy out, management contract and corporatization.

Privatization process of a government department or statutory body

Commercialization → Corporatization → Divestiture

Source: Economic Planning Unit

Prime Minister Dato' Seri Dr Mahathir Mohamad (centre) at the launch of Tenaga Nasional Berhad (TNB) in 1990.

Efficiency and productivity of selected entities

Entity (and year privatized)	Before privatization	After privatization (2000)
Tenaga Nasional Bhd (1991) Revenue generated	RM3.3 bil	RM14.3 bil
Johor Port Bhd (1995) Average container throughput (TEUs)	128,556	659,181
Telekom Malaysia Bhd (1990) Direct exchange lines per employee	36	183
North South Expressway (PLUS) (1989) Travelling time from north to south of Peninsular Malaysia	15.4 hours	7.5 hours

Source: Economic Planning Unit

Privatization achievements, 1983–2005

Total privatized projects –existing projects –new projects	490 346 144
Jobs eliminated from government payroll	113,220
Savings –capital expenditure	RM153.6 billion
Proceeds from sale of government equity and assets	RM24.2 billion
Market capitalization as at 31 October 2005	RM171.4 billion
Percentage of total Bursa Malaysia capitalization	24.4%

Source: Economic Planning Unit

Privatized projects by sector, 1983–2005

4.1%	Mining and quarrying	11.2%	Finance, real estate and business services
6.5%	Agriculture and forestry	11.4%	Wholesale, retail trade, hotel and restaurant
7.6%	Government service	12.0%	Transport, storage and communications
8.4%	Electricity, gas and water	14.3%	Manufacturing
9.2%	Other services	15.3%	Construction

Source: Economic Planning Unit

The Federal, state and local governments in the economy

The government is instrumental in developing the nation. Administrative power in Malaysia is shared between the Federal Government and the 13 states. While the bulk of state revenue is derived from state sources, development funding primarily comes from the Federal Government. Local authorities are the third tier of the government, and have their own revenue streams.

Workers marking the completion of the first phase of drilling for the Stormwater Management and Road Tunnel (SMART) flood diversion project, 2004. The project will cost the Federal Government more than RM1.9 billion.

Source: Economic Report 2005–2006

Federal Government finance, 2005

	RM million
Revenue	106,304
Operating expenditure	97,744
Current surplus	8561
Gross development expenditure	30,571
Direct expenditure	28,839
Gross lending	1732
Loan recoveries	3250
Net development expenditure	27,321
Overall deficit	-18,761
Sources of financing	
Net foreign borrowings	-3503
Net domestic borrowing	12,700
Change in assets	9564

Source: Economic Report 2005–2006

State government consolidated finance, 2005

	RM million
Revenue	11,606
State sources	8460
Federal grants	3086
Federal reimbursements	60
Operating expenditure	6584
Current surplus	5022
Development expenditure	5205
Development fund	4776
Water supply fund	429
Loan recoveries	15
Net development expenditure	5190
Overall balance	-168
Sources of financing	
Net federal loans	275
Change in assets	-107

Source: Economic Report 2005–2006

Local government consolidated finance, 2005

	RM million
Revenue	5031
Own sources	3906
State and federal grants	1125
Federal reimbursements	-
Current expenditure	3901
Current surplus	1130
Net development expenditure	1795
Overall balance	-665
Sources of financing	
Net federal loans	-6
Net state loans	-3
Change in assets	674

Powers of the Federal and state governments

The Federal Government has overarching powers despite the tradition of state autonomy. The Federal Government has authority over external affairs, defence, internal security, law, federal citizenship, finance, commerce, industry, communications, transportation and other matters.

The Federal Government possesses all the powers necessary to carry out effective development policies in the states and controls the limited independent development activities of the states. The power to tax, borrow, lend, and spend lies primarily with the Federal Government.

The states have power over issues concerning the Islamic religion, land, agriculture, forestry and local government. However, state governments possess minimal sources of independent revenue and are heavily dependent on Federal Government grants and budget allocations.

Generally, the principal source of state revenue is federal grants based on state population and road mileage. However, in 2004, petroleum and forestry royalties, land premium and taxes as well as profits and dividends from investment contributed about 57.6 per cent of state revenue. Other sources of

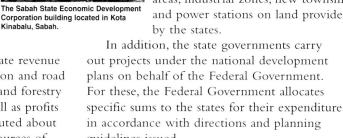

The Sabah State Economic Development Corporation building located in Kota Kinabalu, Sabah.

revenue include fees from licences and permits, rents as well as sales of goods and services. States can only borrow with the consent of the Federal Government or Bank Negara Malaysia.

Federal and state development efforts

The states are at different levels of economic and social development; they differ widely in terms of area and their natural and human resources.

The Federal Government is, amongst other things, responsible for improving the economic and social wellbeing of all sectors of the population, redressing rural–urban imbalances, and promoting the integration of the states and people of Malaysia. In this respect, the Federal Government undertakes major projects such as the building of infrastructure (ports, roads and airports), agricultural areas, industrial zones, new townships and power stations on land provided by the states.

In addition, the state governments carry out projects under the national development plans on behalf of the Federal Government. For these, the Federal Government allocates specific sums to the states for their expenditure in accordance with directions and planning guidelines issued.

Presidents of local councils admiring cheques for annual grants received from the Federal Government in Petaling Jaya, 1999.

A low-medium cost housing project undertaken by the Selangor State Development Corporation (Perbadanan Kemajuan Negeri Selangor or PKNS) to help achieve the state government's 'Zero Squatter 2005' target.

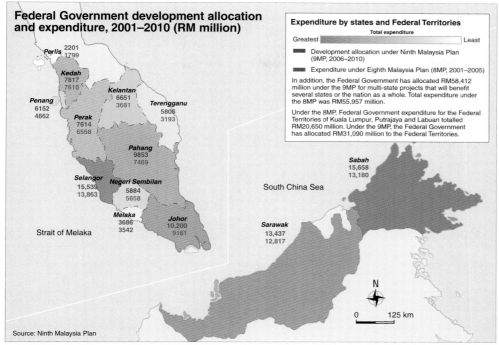

Federal Government development allocation and expenditure, 2001–2010 (RM million)

Perlis 2201 / 1799
Kedah 7817 / 7610
Penang 6152 / 4862
Kelantan 6651 / 3681
Perak 7614 / 6558
Terengganu 5806 / 3193
Pahang 9853 / 7469
Selangor 15,539 / 13,863
Negeri Sembilan 5884 / 5658
Melaka 3686 / 3542
Johor 10,200 / 9161
Sabah 15,658 / 13,180
Sarawak 13,437 / 12,817

South China Sea
Strait of Melaka

N

0   125 km

Source: Ninth Malaysia Plan

Expenditure by states and Federal Territories

Total expenditure
Greatest ——————————————— Least

Development allocation under Ninth Malaysia Plan (9MP, 2006–2010)

Expenditure under Eighth Malaysia Plan (8MP, 2001–2005)

In addition, the Federal Government has allocated RM58,412 million under the 9MP for multi-state projects that will benefit several states or the nation as a whole. Total expenditure under the 8MP was RM55,957 million.

Under the 8MP, Federal Government expenditure for the Federal Territories of Kuala Lumpur, Putrajaya and Labuan totalled RM20,650 million. Under the 9MP, the Federal Government has allocated RM31,090 million to the Federal Territories.

Government services

By virtue of the Local Government Act 1976, local governments are required to provide services to the community. These include environmental (e.g. trimming trees), public health (e.g. fogging) and cleaning services; enforcement and licensing; the provision of public amenities (e.g. children's playgrounds); social services; and development.

Facilities and services provided by the local government: public playgrounds (top), cleaning (middle) and fogging services (bottom).

The nature and objective of state-level agencies differ from state to state. In terms of implementation, it is the state economic development corporations (SEDC) that play a pivotal role in the overall development. SEDCs spearhead Federal Government financed projects as well as state-driven development programmes. Established as trust corporations, the SEDCs, which were established from the late 1960s onwards, have undertaken projects that range from tourism and industry to housing and land development. The SEDCs have been instrumental in the development of industrial estates (see 'Industrial Areas'), and in the promotion of the Bumiputera Commercial and Industrial Community (BCIC, see 'New Economic Policy: 1971–1990').

Local governments or authorities

Local governments operate as a third administrative tier beneath the Federal and state governments. Local governments operate under the exclusive jurisdiction of their respective state governments, except those of the Federal Territories, which fall under the jurisdiction of the Federal Territories Ministry.

A local government's revenue consists of assessment rates, rents, licence fees, car parking charges, planning fees, compounds, fines, interests and other tax revenue payable to the local authority.

Non-traditional funding undertaken by state and local governments

The Shah Alam Stadium, opened in 1994, has played host to international and local sporting events, major concerts, cultural shows and large outdoor displays.

Spatial development

Re-zoning of areas and conversion of land from agricultural to residential or industrial use enables state and local authorities to impose higher assessment rates. Some Federal Land Development Authority (FELDA) settlements have been converted into residential, commercial, and industrial areas. Large-scale rezoning has been carried out in Selangor and Perak.

Investment schemes

Through their subsidiaries, state economic development corporations (SEDCs) engage in a variety of business ventures, such as industrial development, to attract local and foreign investment. The states of Johor,

User-charged facilities

Most state and local authorities impose a charge on the use of public facilities such as sports stadiums, parking spaces, community halls, recreational parks and of slaughterhouses. Charges tend to be relatively low because of the general perception that the government is responsible for providing social services.

Pahang, Sarawak and Selangor are particularly active in this area. Several of their subsidiaries are listed on the Bursa Malaysia.

Tourism

Tourism contributes to the income of most state governments, which undertake initiatives to develop hotels, resorts, theme parks, historical sites, natural attractions and shopping facilities.

Tithes (zakat)

With Muslims forming a majority of the population, tithes are a potential source of revenue for state governments. Vigorous awareness campaigns have been initiated by state government agencies to improve the rates of collection. Since tithes are distributed to the poor, they help to reduce the state's expenditure on social welfare.

Privatization schemes

Privatization projects are undertaken through the contracting out of public services to the private sector to stimulate competition between firms. This results in a more efficient provision of services, and allows state and local governments to eventually reduce operating costs. It also enables state and local governments to minimize manpower requirements.

The Department of Hawkers and Small Businesses of the Kuala Lumpur City Hall is responsible for the licensing of hawkers in the city. Licence fees are a source of revenue for the Kuala Lumpur City Hall.

The economy: 1957–1970

Initiatives were introduced in the years after Independence to diversify the economy through industrialization and the development of a more varied agricultural sector, but tin and rubber continued to dominate. The economy expanded, but by the end of the 1960s serious socioeconomic imbalances had emerged, primarily in the form of divisions in which ethnicity correlated with economic function and level of income.

Rubber: Between 1957 and 1970, rubber was the premier industry of Malaysia in terms of employment, export and foreign exchange earnings.

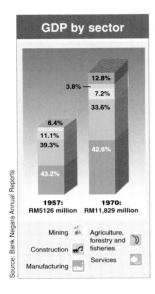

GDP by sector

1957: RM5126 million
- 43.2%
- 39.3%
- 11.1%
- 6.4%

1970: RM11,829 million
- 42.6%
- 33.6%
- 7.2%
- 3.8%
- 12.8%

Mining · Construction · Manufacturing · Agriculture, forestry and fisheries · Services

Source: Bank Negara Annual Reports

Foundations

In the post-Independence years there were strong arguments for diversifying the economy away from tin and rubber. Tin deposits were gradually depleting. The country had lost its position as the world's leading producer of natural rubber to Indonesia, there was increasing competition from synthetic rubber, and world market prices were frequently destabilized by periodic releases from the United States' rubber stockpile.

Continued dominance of rubber and tin

Efforts to diversify the economic base included the adoption of an import-substituting industrialization policy (see 'Industrial policies and plans'), but rubber and tin remained the twin pillars of the economy. The pattern of rubber- and tin-dominated production and trade had lacked diversification, but had nevertheless brought about a standard of living that was fairly comfortable by Asian standards.

Economic activity continued to be dualistic in nature with the advanced, export-oriented sectors co-existing with a low-productivity, subsistence agriculture sector. The former consisted of an economy which revolved around the urban-based, entrepôt trade activities of Penang and Singapore; the latter was composed of the rural-based, peasant economy of rice cultivation, fishing and mixed farming.

In addition to being prime export earners, the plantation and mining industries benefited the economy in many ways.

They lent themselves easily to taxation, and by their very activities monetized the urban, and much of the rural, economy, thereby increasing tax collection. Government revenues from tin mining and rubber plantation activities made possible the building of railways, roads and bridges and contributed to the expansion of urban centres.

Socioeconomic imbalances

On the other hand, the continued emphasis on rubber and tin in the post-Independence years led to significant imbalances in regional and ethnic development. First, most of the tin mines and rubber plantations were located away from the concentrations of Malay settlements along the coasts and lower reaches of the main rivers. Second, most rubber- and tin-related activities were found on the west coast of the Peninsula, resulting in lopsided geographical development that neglected the east coast of the Peninsula where the population was predominantly Malay. Third, there was uneven development in favour of urban areas, where the Malays were under-represented.

Furthermore, the influx of Indian and Chinese immigrant workers who were required in the rubber estates and tin mines respectively had created an increasingly plural society. In 1957, Malays comprised 50 per cent of the population, Chinese accounted for 37 per cent, Indians made up 11 per cent and other ethnic groups constituted two per cent. The Malays were mainly engaged in subsistence farming in rural areas, the Chinese in tin mining and commerce in urban areas, and the Indians in

Selected indicators for 1960–1970

	Early 1960s	Late 1960s–1970
GDP average annual growth rate	6.3% (1960–65)	5.5% (1966–70)
Unemployment rate	6.0% (1962)	8.0% (1970)
Income earned by richest 20% of population as percentage of total (Malay Peninsula)	48.6% (1957–58)	56.0% (1970)
Income earned by poorest 40% of population as percentage of total (Malay Peninsula)	15.9% (1957–58)	11.2% (1970)

Source: Various Malaysia Plans

Development milestones

1. Constructed between 1958 and 1963, the Klang Gates dam and water supply scheme served to supply water to an estimated population of 370,000 in Kuala Lumpur and Petaling Jaya. The largest of its kind in Malaysia at that time, it cost RM4.5 million.

2. Prime Minister Tunku Abdul Rahman Putra marking the launch of the Malayan Microwave Trunk System by making the first trunk call to Singapore in 1959.

3. The Yang di-Pertuan Agong Tuanku Syed Putra Al-Haj Ibni Syed Hassan Jamalullail (second from right) on a inspection of the RM125-million Cameron Highlands hydro-electric project in 1960.

4. Minister of Rural Development Tun Abdul Razak looking through Negeri Sembilan's Red Book of rural development projects, c.1970.

5. Minister of Communications Tun Sardon Haji Jubir (second from right) and Minister of Works Tun V. T. Sambanthan (middle) on a site inspection of the Subang International Airport, 1964.

Using the 'special rights' of the Bumiputera enshrined in the Constitution, the government implemented measures designed to assist the Bumiputera in key aspects of economic life. These measures included subsidies, preferential treatment in securing licences and franchises, quotas for employment and university places, and loans and grants to develop business enterprises and purchase equity shares.

The most significant form of state intervention was its direct participation in commercial and industrial undertakings. The NEP period saw the creation of hundreds of non-financial public enterprises (NFPEs), for example, the Urban Development Authority (UDA) and PETRONAS. The NFPEs became vehicles through which the NEP's objectives were achieved, first by nurturing profit-oriented projects and then by selling them to private-sector Bumiputera organizations.

Restructuring in terms of equity participation was also achieved through other means, notably through two entities: Perbadanan Nasional Berhad (PERNAS, now known as Tradewinds Corporation

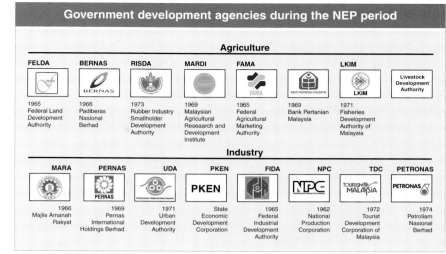

Government development agencies during the NEP period

Berhad) and Permodalan Nasional Berhad (PNB). PNB was tasked with establishing and maintaining a sound portfolio of investments in companies, most of which would then be transferred to the Bumiputera through unit trust schemes such as Amanah Saham Nasional (ASN) and Amanah Saham Bumiputera (ASB).

Key NEP agencies

To provide opportunities and avenues for Bumiputera to participate in commercial activities, trust agencies such as Majlis Amanah Rakyat (MARA), state economic development corporations (see 'The Federal, state and local governments in the economy'), the Pilgrims' Management and Fund Board (LTH, see 'Islamic Financial Services'), Perbadanan Nasional Berhad (PERNAS) and Permodalan Nasional Berhad (PNB) were established.

Permodalan Nasional Berhad

Incorporated as a wholly owned subsidiary of Yayasan Pelaburan Bumiputra (Bumiputra Investment Foundation or YPB) in 1978, Permodalan Nasional Berhad (PNB or the National Equity Corporation) became a pivotal instrument of the NEP to promote share ownership in the corporate sector among the Bumiputera, and develop opportunities for suitable Bumiputera professionals to participate in the creation and management of wealth.

Through PNB, shares acquired in major Malaysian corporations from an initial grant provided by YPB were transferred to a trust fund, and sold to the Bumiputera in the form of smaller units. PNB manages the national unit trust scheme (Amanah Saham Nasional Berhad) to ensure that shares are retained, resulting in the cultivation of the habit of saving, and the development of entrepreneurship and investment skills by the Bumiputera. As of 2005, there were eight unit trust funds and two listed property trust funds managed by PNB. Four of the eight were open to all Malaysians. There were 665,000 non-Bumiputera investors holding five billion units in 2005.

With total managed funds of more than RM72 billion in 2005, PNB was the country's leading investment institution with a diversified portfolio of interests that included unit trusts, institution property trusts, property and asset management.

Unit and real estate investment trusts managed by Amanah Saham Nasional Berhad in 2006.

Perbadanan Nasional Berhad

Incorporated in 1969 with a paid-up capital of RM116.2 million, Perbadanan Nasional Berhad (PERNAS or the National Corporation) was entrusted with the task of increasing the participation of Bumiputera in employment and management as well as ownership of the nation's economic sector. Its greatest triumph in realizing the NEP objectives was achieved in early 1981 when it transferred 13 profitable companies to PNB at cost price. PNB paid RM350 million for companies which were worth more than RM1 billion. In 1979, PERNAS changed its name to PERNAS International Hotels and Properties Berhad when PNB became its largest shareholder. It was listed on the Kuala Lumpur Stock Exchange in 1990, and in 1996, it changed its name again, to PERNAS International Holdings Berhad, to reflect the expanded nature of its activities. In July 2004, it was rebranded as Tradewinds Corporation Berhad (TCB) as the majority of its shares were now held by the private sector and not PNB. TCB is involved in a wide range of business activities, its four core interests being hotels, property investment, plantations and manufacturing. The majority of these businesses were acquired as a result of the privatization of PNB assets from 1996 onwards. As of May 2005, TCB had a paid-up capital of RM623 million and its total assets exceeded RM4 billion.

MARA headquarters in Kuala Lumpur, c. 1966.

Majlis Amanah Rakyat (MARA)

In 1965, the Bumiputera Economic Congress was held to find a means to increase Bumiputera participation in trade and commerce. As a result, MARA or the Council of Trust for the Indigenous People was established as a statutory body in 1966. In 2006, it is an agency of the Ministry of Entrepreneur and Co-operative Development. Its objective is to encourage, guide, train and assist the Bumiputera in participating actively in commercial and industrial activities in order to create a Bumiputera Commercial and Industrial Community.

Over the years, MARA has assisted Bumiputera entrepreneurs set up their businesses by providing financial and technical support. Universiti Teknologi MARA (UiTM) and MARA colleges have been established to increase the number of Bumiputera in the fields of commerce, accountancy and information technology to meet the industry demands. The German Malaysian Institute, a joint venture with the German government, is a centre for advanced skills training in production technology and industrial electronics, specializing in mould, tool & die, mechatronics, process instrumentation and control and electronics and information technology.

Balanced growth: 1991 onwards

The National Development Policy of the 1990s maintained the New Economic Policy's thrust of socioeconomic restructuring, but shifted the focus from quantitative targets to qualitative ones. Poverty eradication efforts focused on hardcore and relative poverty. Vision 2020, launched in 1991, targeted the achievement of 'fully developed nation' status by the year 2020.

The NEP and NDP compared		
	New Economic Policy 1971–1990	**National Development Policy 1991–2000**
Poverty	General strategy to eradicate poverty.	Emphasis on hardcore poverty and relative poverty.
Equity restructuring	Quantitative targets set for greater Bumiputera participation in the economy.	Qualitative development of an active Bumiputera Commercial and Industrial Community. No quantitative goals were specified.
Roles of the private and public sectors	Equity restructuring was public-sector driven.	Equity restructuring was private-sector driven.
Focus of development efforts	Emphasis on physical and financial resources.	Emphasis on human resources, science and technology, and sustainable development.

The MAPEN I and II reports.

National Economic Consultative Councils

The National Economic Consultative Councils (MAPEN I and II) were established by the government in 1989 and 1999 respectively to provide a forum for citizens to voice their opinions on the achievements or otherwise of the New Economic Policy and thereafter, the National Development Policy.

MAPEN I had 150 council members while MAPEN II had 154. Council members were hand-picked by the government and were representative of the various races, occupations and political inclinations in the country.

Prime Minister Dato' Seri Dr Mahathir Mohamad delivering the opening speech of MAPEN II in Kuala Lumpur, 1999.

Planning for the 1990s

In 1989, as the New Economic Policy (NEP) approached the end of its 20-year planning period, the government formed the National Economic Consultative Council (Majlis Perundingan Ekonomi Negara or MAPEN I) to review the achievements of the NEP and to draft a plan for the post-NEP period. Two key policy documents were subsequently formulated.

In March 1991, MAPEN I's report, 'Malaysia: The Way Forward (Vision 2020)' was made public. Then in May 1991, the government announced the start of the National Development Policy. The principles of sustainable development in the protection of the environment took on a more prominent role in economic planning.

The National Development Policy (1991–2000)

The National Development Policy (NDP) formed the basis for the Second Outline Perspective Plan (1991–2000). Building on the thrust of the NEP, the NDP continued to emphasize growth with equity. Under the NDP, however, the objective was to achieve a more balanced form of development, which required shifts in focus: from quantitative goals to qualitative achievements, and from reliance on the public sector to reliance on the private sector in the equity restructuring process.

The focus of the NDP was on qualitative aspects of the policy's implementation, with the ultimate aim being self-sufficiency on the part of the Bumiputera. Renewed efforts to develop an active Bumiputera Commercial and Industrial Community concentrated therefore on promoting entrepreneurial competence and efficiency. Human resource development focused on equipping the Bumiputera with the necessary skills to manage their own businesses and finances as well as to qualify for higher-level management positions in modern corporations. At the same time, Bumiputera businessmen were encouraged to acquire hands-on experience through apprenticeship programmes and by becoming active partners in joint ventures with non-Bumiputera businessmen.

The NDP also continued to address the issue of poverty. Although the nation as a whole had

Covers of the Second and Third Outline Perspective Plans which contain the National Development and National Vision Policies respectively.

progressed under the NEP, pockets of poverty continued to exist: 143,100 households (four per cent of the total) were classified as hardcore poor in the Household Income Survey 1990. Under the NDP, initiatives were undertaken to reduce poverty in both rural and urban areas, irrespective of race. These initiatives focused on both hardcore poverty and relative poverty.

Results of the NDP

The Second National Economic Consultative Council (MAPEN II) was formed in August 1999 to review the NDP. In November 2000, MAPEN II presented its report. It was found that the economy had grown at an average rate of 6.7 per cent per annum from 1991 to 2000, nearly achieving the seven per cent target for the Second Outline Perspective Plan period despite the financial crisis in 1997. The government had formed the National Economic Action Council (NEAC) on 7 January 1998 to make recommendations to arrest the worsening economic situation and revitalize the economy. (see 'Malaysia's innovative response to the financial crisis').

The private sector contributed significantly to economic development during the NDP period. Poverty was reduced by half and significant progress was achieved in restructuring employment. Only the percentage of Bumiputera corporate equity ownership declined below the 1990 level due to increased foreign ownership.

The first meeting of members of the National Economic Consultative Council in 1989.

NATURAL RESOURCES AND AGRICULTURE

Natural resources and agriculture have played a major role in the development of Malaysia. The sectors have contributed to GDP, export earnings, employment and have provided raw materials to the industrial sector. Before manufacturing gained momentum in the 1970s, Malaysia was largely an agriculture-based economy. At its high point in 1955, the natural resources and agricultural sectors (which include rubber, oil palm, and petroleum; activities related to food, fishing and livestock; and mining) contributed as much as 53.2 per cent of GDP and 61 per cent of employment.

Malaysia has gained international prominence in natural resources and agriculture in a number of ways, notably as the world's largest exporter—at various points in time—of natural rubber, tin, palm oil and pepper. Where oil palm and natural rubber are concerned. Malaysia leads in the research and development of cutting-edge agricultural technologies. Although the sectors contributed only 14.9 per cent of GDP and 13.3 per cent of employment in 2005, Malaysia remains a leading producer and exporter of natural resources and agricultural produce including palm oil, natural rubber, cocoa, pepper, oil and gas, timber and tin.

Challenges facing the natural resources and agricultural sectors have been numerous. Competition has come not only from other low-cost producers, but also from the invention of synthetic substitutes. Meanwhile, as the nation has continued to undergo a structural shift from an agriculture-based economy to one based on manufacturing and services, competition for labour resources and foreign direct investment among these sectors intensifies. As a result, Malaysian plantation companies have resorted to diversifying their interests and investing in neighbouring countries, where labour and suitable land are more readily available.

To address the challenges faced by these sectors, government policies have been introduced to modernize and increase efficiency in production through greater use of automation and information and communication technology (ICT), to upgrade the quality of products, expand the range of end uses, encourage vertical integration between upstream production and downstream manufacturing and to step up global marketing.

Under the Ninth Malaysia Plan (2006–10), RM11.43 billion has been allocated to the agricultural sector, which will be revitalized to become one of the main engines of economic growth. The emphasis will be on large-scale commercial production, the wider application of modern technology and ICT, the production of high-quality and value-added products, harnessing the potential of biotechnology, and increasing the participation of entrepreneurial farmers and a skilled workforce.

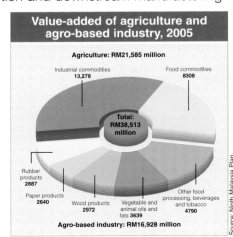

Value-added of agriculture and agro-based industry, 2005

Agriculture: RM21,585 million

Industrial commodities 13,278

Food commodities 8308

Total: RM38,513 million

Rubber products 2887

Paper products 2640

Wood products 2972

Vegetable and animal oils and fats 3639

Other food processing, beverages and tobacco 4790

Agro-based industry: RM16,928 million

Source: Ninth Malaysia Plan

Agricultural policies and institutions

In addition to facilitating the growth of individual agricultural sub-sectors such as palm oil and fisheries, agricultural policies since 1957 have also sought to fulfil broader objectives such as rural development and equitable growth. The National Agricultural Policies have fostered the development of a modern and dynamic agricultural sector that is strategically linked to domestic as well as international markets.

Agricultural production, 2005

Industrial commodities	('000 tonnes)
Rubber	1124.0
Crude palm oil	14,961.0
Palm kernel oil	1868.0
Sawlogs ('000 cubic metres)	21,334.0
Cocoa	28.0
Food commodities	
Padi	2400.0
Pepper	19.1
Pineapple	407.6
Fruits	1586.9
Vegetables	771.3
Coconut	602.0
Fisheries	
Marine (fish landings)	1325.0
Aquaculture	250.0
Livestock	
Beef	28.5
Mutton	1.5
Pork	209.0
Poultry	980.1
Eggs	443 .0
Milk (million litres)	41.1
Miscellaneous	
Tobacco	14.0
Flowers ('000 stalks)	126.4

Source: Ninth Malaysia Plan, Ministry of Agriculture and Agro-Based Industry, Ministry of Plantation Industries and Commodities

Early promotional efforts

Under the New Economic Policy (1971–90), efforts were made throughout the 1970s to promote agricultural diversification, reduce rural poverty and increase the Bumiputera share of agricultural income. Public enterprises bought over large plantation houses from their foreign, mainly British, owners. Large-scale land development and resettlement schemes transformed significant numbers of impoverished farmers into smallholders who grew not only rubber and oil palm, but also rice and other commercially viable crops (see 'Rural and regional development').

Nevertheless, the production and income of smallholders remained low as a result of structural and logistical factors. Later constraints to growth in the agricultural sector were attributable to the success of the country's industrialization policies which led to increased and competing demands for water, land and human resources. At the same time, civil and customary (*adat*) laws governing land matters were promulgated to protect and preserve native lands, for instance the Malay Reservations Enactments and the Aboriginal Peoples Act, which ensured that designated parcels of land remained in the ownership of Malays and Orang Asli respectively.

The need for a coordinated approach to development led to the formulation in 1984 of the First National Agricultural Policy (NAP1).

Land laws

All matters relating to land are under the jurisdiction of the respective state governments. Key legislation includes the National Land Code 1965, Irrigation Areas Act 1953, Forest Act 1984, Fisheries Act 1985, Environmental Quality Act 1974, Land Conservation Act 1960, Sabah Land Ordinance 1930 and Sarawak Land Code 1958.

The National Land Code 1965 established a uniform system of land laws.

The National Land Code was enacted to unify land administration throughout the country. Related matters such as forestry, agriculture and mining are also under the state's purview.

The National Land Council (NLC) (comprised of Federal and State representatives) formulates national policies 'for the promotion and control of the utilization of land for mining, agriculture, forestry or any other purpose'. The Federal and state governments implement these policies and may consult the NLC with respect to any matter relating to the utilization of land, any legislation dealing with land or the administration of any such legislation. State governments have extensive powers over drainage and related matters such as land improvement, soil conservation, protection of wild animals, birds, national parks, drainage and irrigation and rehabilitation of land subject to soil erosion.

The National Agricultural Policies (1984–2010)

Between 1984 and 1991, the government through NAP1 pursued expansionary policies on export crops, in particular oil palm and cocoa. Investments in infrastructure, institutional building and new land development were made to enhance these crops in order to earn foreign exchange, create employment and income earning opportunities as well as reduce poverty. Attention was also paid to problems of uneconomic farm size, non-remunerative crops and low productivity among smallholders.

This era also witnessed the rapid expansion of the manufacturing sector, which reduced the relative importance of the agricultural sector.

The overall development of the agricultural sector was beset with problems such as labour shortages, rising wages and increasing competition for land from other uses.

Part of the Muda irrigation scheme in Kedah, the Pedu Dam allowed double-cropping of *padi*.

Agricultural development projects

In 1965, the Muda Irrigation Project was implemented in Kedah and Perlis to enable double cropping of *padi* in the country's largest granary area. In 1972, the Muda Agricultural Development Authority (MADA) was formed to operate and maintain the physical infrastructure of the area, achieve the nation's aim of self-sufficiency in rice production, as well as integrate the production, marketing, credit, research and agro-based downstream processing facilities necessary to accelerate the development of farmers. MADA prevented the exploitation of farmers by middlemen by purchasing rice directly from farmers at a guaranteed minimum price at all times. MADA further assisted farmers by negotiating fair prices from suppliers of fertilizers and farm machinery. The Kemubu Agricultural Development Authority (KADA) was formed in Kelantan in 1972 for a similar purpose.

With the success of MADA and KADA, Integrated Agricultural Development Projects (IADPs) were developed throughout the country in the late 1970s, and intensified in

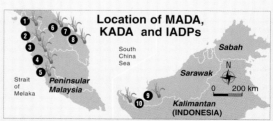

Location of MADA, KADA and IADPs

(1) Muda Agricultural Development Authority (MADA) (2) Penang (3) Kerian-Sungai Manik (4) Seberang, Perak (5) Northwest Selangor (6) Kemubu Agricultural Development Authority (KADA) (7) Kemasin-Semerak (8) Ketara-Besut (9) Kalaka-Saribas (10) Samarahan

the 1980s. Each of these projects is implemented by a lead agency, supported by other complementary agencies. Project management units onsite coordinate other functionally related agencies of the Ministry of Agriculture at the federal, state and district levels. The aim of IADPs is to improve the standard of living and welfare of the farming communities.

Forest conservation

In accordance with the Federal Constitution, forestry is a state matter and the state governments have complete jurisdiction over their respective forest resources. The Federal Government provides technical advice on forest management and development, undertakes research and education, and promotes industrial development of wood-based industries and trade.

The Forest Enactment and Rules for administering forests were established by the Federated and Unfederated Malay States in the early 1930s and were replaced by the National Forestry Act in 1984. The Act was amended in 1993 to provide for stiffer penalties for illegal logging. The Interim Forestry Policy, first formulated in 1952, was officially adopted as the National Forestry Policy in 1978 and revised in 1993.

At the Second Ministerial Conference of Developing Countries on Environment and Development in 1992, Malaysia declared that she would try to maintain at least 50 per cent of her land area permanently under forest cover.

As of 2006, out of a land mass of 32.2 million hectares (mha), 19.52 mha remains under tree cover. This makes Malaysia one of the most forested countries in the world. Under the Ninth Malaysia Plan (2006–10), the government has allocated RM251.5 million to forest management.

Apart from stringent restrictions imposed on logging under the National Forestry Policy, other steps taken to ensure sustainable forests include the introduction of reduced impact logging techniques such as heli-logging in Sarawak and the skyline system in Sabah. Logged-over areas are replanted with fast growing timber species such as *Acacia mangium, Eucalyptus,* and *Albizia falcataria*. The Ministry of Natural Resources and Environment and the Ministry of Agriculture and Agro-based Industries have

cooperated to encourage agroforestry—the cultivation of commercial timber plantations—among smallholders. To facilitate the regeneration of forests, a 5000-hectare tree seed centre has been established in Bintulu, Sarawak, while a Model Forest project covering 183,000 hectares has been initiated in Bentong, Pahang. Research continues on the alternative use of plantation crops such as rubber and oil palm wood and fibres as raw material for wood-based industries.

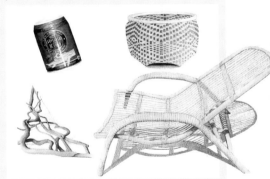

Above: Reduced-impact logging practices include the use of environmentally friendly machinery such as anti-vibration chainsaws and directional felling which ensures that trees fall in the path of least damage to their surroundings.

Above right: Timber being extracted using the skyline system which minimizes damage to the environment. This was first introduced in Sabah in 1996 under the Malaysian-German Sustainable Forest Management Project in a 100,000-hectare forest reserve within the Deramakot and Segaliud Lokan Forest Reserves.

Left: Details of selected trees are entered in a forester's database to monitor their growth.

and tertiary processing are clustered in the Peninsula. To ensure sufficient supply of timber for local wood-based industries, a total ban on the export of logs has been imposed on Peninsular Malaysia since 1985. In Sabah, log exports are subject to high royalties and domestic log utilization quotas. Exports of rubberwood sawn timber has been banned since 2005. During the Second Industrial Master Plan (see 'Industrial policies and plans'), the Malaysian Timber Council set up timber depots throughout the country to manage the supply of timber and source it from other countries.

Among wood-based activities, furniture manufacturing has grown into a leading industry. Malaysia was the world's tenth largest furniture exporter in 2005, and the export value of furniture was RM7 billion. To assist manufacturers, ten 'furniture villages' equipped with the necessary infrastructure for manufacturing and research and development were set up between 1996 and 2000. To provide skilled labour, three timber technology training centres and an institute are in operation.

Challenges to the industry

Malaysia practises a forest management system which dates back to 1910, and continued efforts to manage on a sustainable yield basis have brought the country recognition from timber organizations worldwide.

The industry is currently facing two challenges: the anti–tropical timber campaign, and timber certification or eco-labelling. Environmentalists have lobbied against the import and use of tropical timbers, alleging that harvesting contributes to worldwide environmental degradation. The issue has also been linked to that of the encroachment on the rights of forest-dwelling native tribes.

Traditional forest products

While timber remains the dominant product of the forest, bamboo, rattan and nipah palm are also widely used. Some plants have medicinal properties: *tongkat ali* is reputed to be an effective aphrodisiac and *kacip fatimah* is used in traditional medicine to prevent pre- and post-natal ailments.

Clockwise from top: drink containing *tongkat ali*, rattan basket and chair, and the *tongkat ali* root.

Compliance with the chain-of-custody standards qualifies timber product manufacturers or exporters to receive the Certificate for Chain-of-Custody from MTCC.

Exports of major timber products, 2005

Total: RM 21.5 billion

- Builders' carpentry and joinery 5.4%
- Fibreboards 5.1%
- Mouldings 3.2%
- Others 5.5%
- Wooden and rattan furniture 27.4%
- Saw logs 11.5%
- Sawn timber 16.0%
- Plywood 25.9%

Source: Malaysian Timber Council

Logging in Kelantan. Timber from over 60 species of trees is exported from Malaysia. In 2005, exports of saw logs and sawn timber generated RM2.5 billion and RM3.4 billion respectively.

Oil and gas

The petroleum industry is a major contributor to Malaysia's economic growth and industrialization. The oil and gas sector also acts as a conduit for foreign direct investment and a source of foreign exchange earnings and job creation. The country's substantial gas reserves, larger than those of oil, provide a platform for the sustainable development of natural gas for use in both the domestic market as well as in the form of liquefied natural gas (LNG) for export. PETRONAS, the national petroleum corporation, has played a vital role in rapidly transforming the country's oil and gas sector into a dynamic and integrated industry.

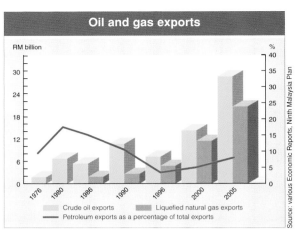

Oil and gas exports

Source: various Economic Reports, Ninth Malaysia Plan

The first oil well located at Canada Hill, Miri, Sarawak. It was drilled by the Anglo-Saxon Petroleum Company in 1910.

Reserves and economic contribution

Malaysia's continental shelf is divided into six major sedimentary basins: the Malay, Penyu, Sarawak, Sabah, Northeast Sabah and Southeast Sabah. Petroleum is currently being produced from the Malay, Sarawak and Sabah Basins, where the composition of the seabed provides conducive conditions for extraction.

As of 1 January 2006, Malaysia's crude oil reserves were estimated to stand at 5.25 billion barrels and natural gas reserves at 87.95 trillion standard cubic feet. Although the contribution of the petroleum sector to the national economy in absolute terms has risen, its share has declined since the mid-1980s due

to Malaysia's economic diversification efforts. Crude oil export earnings in 2005 amounted to RM28.5 billion with countries in the Asia Pacific region being the key export destinations. Export revenue from liquefied natural gas (LNG) in 2005 amounted to RM20.8 billion, with Japan, South Korea and Taiwan as the three largest importers.

Upstream activities

Exploration, development and production of oil and gas comprise the activities of the upstream sector of the petroleum industry. Commercial operations began in 1910 when the Anglo-Saxon Petroleum Company, the forerunner of the present Sarawak Shell Berhad,

Major oil and gas activities

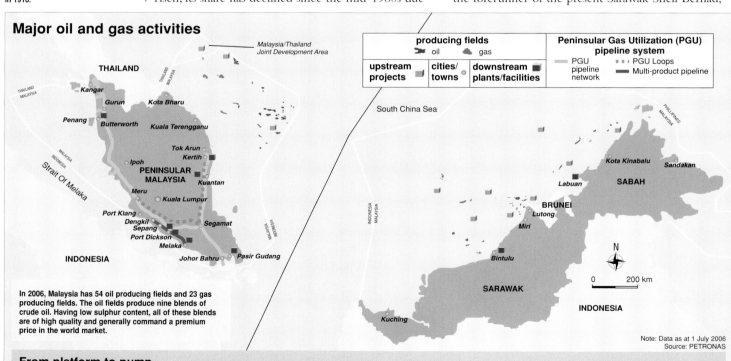

In 2006, Malaysia has 54 oil producing fields and 23 gas producing fields. The oil fields produce nine blends of crude oil. Having low sulphur content, all of these blends are of high quality and generally command a premium price in the world market.

Note: Data as at 1 July 2006
Source: PETRONAS

From platform to pump

PETRONAS's Baronia platform off the coast of Sarawak where wells are drilled into the ocean bed to obtain crude oil.

Refinery in Kertih, Terengganu. Crude oil is processed at refineries into various commercial petroleum products.

From refineries, petrol is transported in tankers to service stations.

In 2006, PETRONAS has over 700 service stations in Malaysia and the largest share of the domestic market for petroleum products.

struck oil in the town of Miri, marking the start of the Malaysian petroleum industry. Exploration efforts shifted offshore in the 1950s, and oil was discovered in two areas off the coast of Sarawak in 1962. Other finds followed in rapid succession. In Peninsular Malaysia, petroleum exploration began in 1968 and the first oil field was discovered in 1971.

For the year which ended on 31 March 2006, Malaysia's petroleum production stood at an average of about 700,000 barrels of crude oil and 960,000 barrels of oil equivalent of natural gas per day.

Downstream activities

Downstream petroleum activities include oil refining, marketing and distribution of petroleum products, trading, gas processing and liquefaction, gas transmission pipeline operations, petrochemicals manufacturing and marketing and shipping.

Currently, there are five oil refineries in the country with a combined refining capacity of about 557,300 barrels per day (bpd). These include the 88,000-bpd Esso refinery and the 155,000-bpd Shell refinery, both located in Port Dickson, and three refineries owned and operated by PETRONAS through its subsidiaries, two in its refinery complex in Melaka and one in Kertih, Terengganu with a combined refining (including condensate splitting) capacity of 314,300 bpd.

The active pursuit of Malaysia's Natural Gas Development Master Plan has led to growth in the LNG and petrochemical sectors as well as the shift to natural gas as a cleaner source of energy and the development of related infrastructure and technological applications. Key examples include the implementation of the Peninsular Gas Utilization (PGU) project which serves as the backbone of the nation's gas supply system, the Natural Gas for Vehicles (NGV) programme through which NGV-dispensing facilities are made available at selected PETRONAS service stations located in high-density traffic areas, and the gas district cooling (GDC) system whereby natural gas is used as an energy source to produce chilled water for air conditioning and for co-generation in an integrated energy system. The GDC system is currently used in the Kuala Lumpur City Centre, the Kuala Lumpur International Airport and Putrajaya.

Future outlook

At the current level of reserves and production rate, Malaysia's oil and gas reserves are expected to last for about 20 and 34 years respectively. To ensure more sustainable energy development, renewable energy has been included as the fifth fuel under Malaysia's Five-Fuel Diversification policy, the first four fuels being oil, gas, hydro and coal (see 'Utilities').

Nevertheless, the oil and gas industry is expected to continue to play an important role in contributing to the further industrialization and economic growth of Malaysia through investment promotion, technology transfer and generation of revenue and foreign exchange earnings.

PETRONAS

The shape of PETRONAS's logo represents an oil drop and a typographic 'P'.

Petroliam Nasional Berhad, commonly known by the acronym PETRONAS, is Malaysia's national petroleum corporation. Incorporated on 17 August 1974 under the Companies Act 1965, it is wholly owned by the Malaysian Government. It is vested with the entire ownership and control of the petroleum resources in the country under the Petroleum Development Act 1974.

The company first exported crude oil in 1975, and moved rapidly to expand its operations. PETRONAS Carigali was set up to undertake exploration and production activities in 1978 and made its first oil discovery, the Dulang oilfield off the Terengganu coast, in 1982. PETRONAS entered the petroleum retail business in 1979 with three skid-tank stations and opened its first service station in Kuala Lumpur in 1981.

Since then, PETRONAS has grown and transformed from being a mere regulator and manager of Malaysia's petroleum resources into an integrated international oil and gas company, ranked among the 500 largest corporations in the world by *Fortune Global*.

The Peninsular Gas Utilization project, which started in 1984 and was completed in 1997, comprises more than 2500 kilometres of main and lateral pipelines.

PETRONAS's LNG Complex in Bintulu, Sarawak has a total capacity of about 23 million tonnes per annum, making it the world's largest LNG production facility at a single location.

National Petroleum Policy

Subsequent to the passing of the Petroleum Development Act in 1974, the National Petroleum Policy was formulated in 1975. The policy aims at regulating the oil and gas industry in order to achieve the country's economic development goals. It addresses several issues, which include ensuring adequate supply for domestic consumption, Malaysian equity participation, promoting foreign investment and sustainable development of oil and gas resources.

The establishment of PETRONAS, through the Petroleum Development Act 1974, has streamlined the ownership, management and control of oil and gas resources and activities in Malaysia.

The Ministry of International Trade and Industry (MITI) as well as the Ministry of Domestic Trade and Consumer Affairs (MDTCA), through the Petroleum Regulations of 1974 (amended in 1975 and 1981), are vested with powers to regulate all downstream activities. MITI is responsible for the issuance of licenses for the processing and refining of petroleum and the manufacture of petrochemical products, whilst MDTCA issues licenses for the marketing and distribution of petroleum products.

Foreign oil companies

Prior to the oil crisis in the early 1970s, foreign oil companies in Malaysia operated under a concession system. Large areas were made available to foreign oil companies and these companies paid small royalties and taxes to the government. The oil crisis in 1973 led to the promulgation of the Petroleum Development Act 1974 and the formation of a national petroleum company, PETRONAS.

At present, oil and gas exploration, development and production activities in Malaysia are carried out through Production Sharing Contracts (PSCs) between PETRONAS and a number of international oil and gas companies, including its wholly-owned subsidiary, PETRONAS Carigali Sdn Bhd.

PETRONAS signed its first group of PSCs in 1976 with Esso Production Malaysia Inc, Sarawak Shell Berhad and Sabah Shell Petroleum Company. In 1985, PETRONAS revised its PSC terms to allow for accelerated cost recovery and improved sharing ratios of profit for contractors. To promote exploration of deeper offshore areas, PETRONAS introduced the 'deepwater' PSC in 1993. In 1997, PETRONAS instituted a PSC based on the 'revenue-over-cost' concept to encourage additional investment in Malaysia's upstream sector as well as promote the development of smaller and marginal oil fields. Foreign oil companies in Malaysia include ExxonMobil, Shell, Nippon Oil, Murphy Oil Corporation, Amerada Hess, Talisman, Newfield and others.

Yang di-Pertuan Agong Tuanku Ismail Nasiruddin Shah Ibni Sultan Zainal Abidin (second from right) visiting Shell's and Esso's Port Dickson oil refineries in 1966.

Food production

Apart from tropical fruits, pork, poultry and eggs, most of the country's food is imported. Attaining acceptable levels of self-sufficiency is an ongoing concern, while long-term policies are geared towards the development of a dynamic food sector that can eventually cater to both domestic and foreign demand.

Farmers in Seberang Prai, Penang, using a transplanting machine to plant seedlings. Malaysia produces about 65 per cent of its *padi* requirements. The largest *padi* growing region is Muda in Kedah with 97,257 hectares of *padi* area.

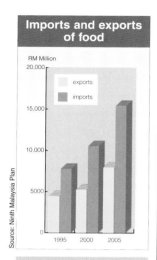

Imports and exports of food

RM Million

- exports
- imports

Source: Ninth Malaysia Plan

Fruits

Malaysia is a net importer of fruits and fruit products. In 2005, imports of fruits totalled RM694.9 million, while exports amounted to RM471.9 million. In 2006, over 40 types of fruits are being cultivated. Most are grown on a small-scale basis except banana, pineapple, star fruit, guava and watermelon which are cultivated on a commercial basis for domestic and export markets. These fruits, along with jackfruit, mango and papaya, have also been identified for promotion as they are non-seasonal, have short gestation periods and potential for downstream processing.

A worker plucking guava at a plantation in Sitiawan, Perak. The fruit's economic importance lies in its superior nutritional content, ease of cultivation, and versatility in processing and canning.

Food policy

Malaysia has allocated considerable sums under various development plans to increase food production. Various incentives and subsidies have been extended to encourage food production especially after the mid-1980s. Nevertheless, Malaysia remains a net importer of food, with imports increasing over the years. In 2005, Malaysia's food import bill came to RM15.4 billion while food exports amounted to RM8 billion.

Since the 1980s, Malaysia has carried out development projects aimed at reducing imports of food and related products. In particular, the planting of cash crops as import substitutions, and the growth of food processing industries have been encouraged.

The aim to make Malaysia a *halal* food hub was first promulgated in the Second Industrial Master Plan. In 2005, the global demand for *halal* food was estimated to be US$445 billion. Malaysia's *halal* certification is already recognized by the Muslim world and various centres nationwide have been dedicated to *halal* food production.

Rice

Rice is the staple food of Asia, and Malaysia is no exception. Traditionally, rice has been cultivated in Malaysia using customary methods in small, widely scattered areas. However, irrigation projects and the establishment of Integrated Agricultural Development Projects (IADPs) in the 1970s and 1980s transformed most rice planting in Malaysia from a traditional endeavour to a modern, large-scale production industry (see 'Agricultural policies and institutions').

As of 2005, most of the rice was produced by the eight major granary areas totalling 210,500 hectares. These areas are irrigated areas of Muda, Kemumbu, Kemasin-Semarak, Ketara, Penang, Krian-Sungai Manik, Seberang Perak and northeast Selangor. *Padi* production is on the rise mainly due to an increase in the area planted as well as improvements in cultivation practices.

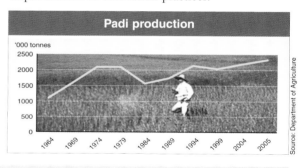

Padi production

'000 tonnes

Source: Department of Agriculture

Livestock

Government officials inspecting a cattle-rearing project in Kampung Sungai Tas, Kedah.

The rapid increase in livestock production in Malaysia in the 1970s was due to a number of factors. The expansion of the animal feed industry, through both local and foreign private investment, in turn encouraged the growth of poultry and pork production. Malaysia is self-sufficient in both products, and exports the excess to other countries in Southeast Asia. Self-sufficiency levels (SSLs) for poultry and eggs are 121 and 113 per cent respectively. Cooperation between foreign and local investors has enabled the introduction of advanced production technology. Another factor that led to the rapid development of the livestock industry is the ability to vertically integrate the industry. Integrated production is best shown by Kentucky Fried Chicken Malaysia Berhad, a franchise which produces poultry meat and is also involved in the production of parent stock, processing and marketing to fast food chains and retail outlets.

Production of beef and mutton has not advanced as rapidly as that of poultry and pork—production of the former is mainly by smallholders diversifying their agricultural activities. The integration of livestock rearing in oil palm and rubber plantations has contributed to the high growth of beef and mutton production between 1995 and 2004. Beef and mutton production relies quite heavily on government subsidies as imports are much cheaper than locally produced meat.

In 2005, for beef, mutton and milk, SSLs were only 23, 8.3 and 5 per cent respectively. Beef was mainly imported from India and Australia, while mutton and milk came from Australia and New Zealand.

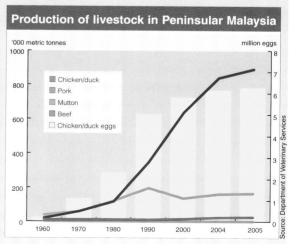

Production of livestock in Peninsular Malaysia

'000 metric tonnes

million eggs

- Chicken/duck
- Pork
- Mutton
- Beef
- Chicken/duck eggs

Source: Department of Veterinary Services

The objective of Malaysia's policy on rice has always been to achieve self-sufficiency. This goal has not been reached as Malaysia still imports rice at an average of 20 to 35 per cent of its total consumption needs. Malaysia has never enjoyed a comparative advantage in rice production vis-à-vis other rice-growing countries, especially Thailand and Indonesia. Production costs are between 15 to 20 per cent higher in Malaysia compared to those in Thailand. The difference between the retail cost of locally produced and imported rice ranges from 11 to 70 per cent. On economic grounds alone, it would cost much less to import rice. However, rice is a strategic commodity, so the objective of self-sufficiency in rice has been rigorously pursued. The threat of a supply shortage and the desire to reduce food imports have contributed to efforts of increasing rice production. In 2005, the self-sufficiency level (SSL) of rice was 72 per cent.

Efforts to reduce imports of rice as well as reducing per capita intake of rice have shown encouraging results. While production of rice has remained stable for the period 1997 to 2005, per capita rice consumption has decreased from 102.2 kilograms in 1985 to 86.9 kilograms in 1995, and 82.8 kilograms in 2005.

Export earners

The value of exports in 2005 for cocoa beans and products was RM50 million, while pepper exports totalled RM120 million. Uncertainties in world demand and prices have contributed to the declining production of cocoa.

Smallholders account for most of the production of pepper, which increased from 13,000 tonnes in 1995 to 24,000 tonnes in 2000 as a result of better farm management, but declined to 19,100 tonnes in 2005.

Other cash crops

Cash crops are grown to help farmers diversify their agricultural activities and as a source of extra income. The main cash crops planted include maize, groundnuts, tapioca, sweet potato and yam.

Areas of cultivation of these crops have remained stable for the period 1995 to 2004, partly due to the fact that these crops are cultivated on a smallholder basis and also due to the lack of market and price incentives. Maize has the largest planted area of these crops, while groundnuts have the smallest.

A pepper farm in Sarawak. Once the world's largest producer of pepper, in 2005, Malaysia was the world's fifth largest producer. Sarawak accounts for 95 per cent of the pepper produced.

The ubiquitous Yeo's canned drink, Babas' curry powder and Adabi food mix are locally manufactured and certified *halal*.

Import substitution and food processing

Historically, Malaysia has been a net importer of food products despite the government's effort to increase production. The financial crises of the 1980s and 1997 showed Malaysia's vulnerability to food shortages in the face of global economic downturns.

To help reduce imports of food products and to ensure adequate supply of strategic food products, the government has increased research and development, provided incentives for the setting up of small- and medium-scale industries to promote 'value added' activities and offered incentives such as tax relief to increase downstream processing of food products.

The development of the local food processing industry has also been spurred by changes in the population structure and consumption patterns. Modern lifestyle and higher incomes have increased the demand for ready-to-serve and fast food items. The introduction of franchised food chains in particular has increased the demand for local inputs, especially of processed poultry, beef and fish.

Exports of processed food contributed 60.5 per cent of food exports in 2005. The major exports were cocoa and cocoa preparations (RM1.7 billion), cereals and flour preparations (RM818.6 million), margarine and shortenings (RM610.9 million) and processed seafood (RM525.5 million). Food processing comprised 9.9 per cent of the total manufacturing output.

Fishing and aquaculture

All Malaysian states border the sea, and fishing is an important activity of the coastal people in each of them. Nevertheless, the number of people involved in the fishery sector has declined significantly since 1966.

Malaysia is surrounded by three seas—the South China Sea, the Strait of Melaka and the Sulu Sea—and within its Exclusive Economic Zone (EEZ), some 138,700 square kilometres are suitable for trawling and deep sea fishing. In 1991, it was estimated that Malaysia had 453,900 metric tonnes of harvestable fish stock within the EEZ, but this has declined rapidly due to overfishing and the destruction of natural breeding grounds, caused partly by the felling of mangrove forests and partly by marine pollution. Fisheries, however, attained a self-sufficiency level of 91 per cent in 2005. The National Agricultural Policy aims to further develop deep-sea fishing in order to supplement growth in the sector, especially in the provision of food supply and the processing of fish-based products for both domestic consumption and export.

A fish farm in Kenyir Lake, Terengganu. Output in the fisheries sector was 1.53 million tonnes in 2005.

Harvesting tiger prawns reared by FELCRA Agro Industry in Juru.

The potential of aquaculture is also to be further explored. Aquaculture comprises activities such as fish and prawn breeding and shellfish culture. Aquaculture products such as seaweed, surimi and ornamental fish are high value-added activities mainly targeted for the export market. Although still an infant industry, aquaculture grew by 17.4 per cent per annum from 2003 to 2005. In 2005, prawn farming was the major activity followed by freshwater fish and marine fish farming. Malaysia is one of the leading tiger prawn producers in the world. There are about a million hectares of water bodies, comprising disused mining ponds, rice fields, reservoirs, lakes, lagoons and mangrove swamps, which are suitable for aquaculture. In the Peninsula, the most suitable water resources are concentrated on the west coast. Two man-made lakes, the Kenyir and Pergau, in Terengganu and Kelantan respectively, provide additional resources. In Sabah and Sarawak, the coastal areas are rich in mangrove swamps, which cover an area three times larger than those in Peninsular Malaysia. These resources will be further supplemented by the reservoir which will be created by the Bakun dam in Sarawak.

Science and technology in the agricultural sector

By utilizing science and technology, the agricultural sector has increased the quantity and improved the quality of its products. Of the various government agencies involved in promulgating the use of science and technology in agriculture, the Malaysian Agricultural Research and Development Institute (MARDI) is the key agency.

MARDI investments for research in some SITC* divisions, 1996–2005

Fish, crustacians, molluscs and preparations	RM1.73 million
Feeding stuff for animals	RM6.76 million
Vegetables and fruits	RM17.58 million
Live animals, meat and meat products, and milk and eggs	RM20.46 million
Cereals and cereals preparations	RM33.48 million

Note: * SITC is the Standard International Trade Classification

Source: MARDI

Top: A MARDI research officer at work in Kuala Lumpur, part of a research team which is trying to delay the papaya's ripening process and render it virus resistant.

Above: The Tudor-styled cottage at MARDI's Agro-Technology Park in Cameron Highlands, Pahang.

Introduction of science and technology

For much of the period following Independence, agricultural research in Malaysia was heavily concentrated on a single commodity, rubber. Only in the late 1960s did the country begin to develop its research capabilities in other export commodities and domestic crops when research institutions such as the Malaysian Agricultural Research and Development Institute (MARDI) were established. From then on, science and technology was more widely utilized in agriculture.

The establishment of statutory research organizations has enhanced downstream activities and the value-added of commodities beyond just improving yields and crop management systems. The Rubber Research Institute of Malaysia (RRIM), established in 1925, was subsequently merged with other rubber related agencies to form the Malaysian Rubber Board (MRB or Lembaga Getah Malaysia) (see 'Rubber'). Research has shown that constituents of latex possess medicinal and pharmaceutical properties. In 1979, the Palm Oil Research Institute of Malaysia (PORIM) was established, and later, the Malaysian Palm Oil Board (MPOB) (see 'Palm Oil'). Novel palm oil products include vitamin E and palm diesel.

Golden Langkawi musk melon grown using the fertigation system.

Impact of science and technology

Through the use of science and technology, the agricultural sector has progressed and modernized. The sector has experienced increased crop yields, safer food supplies and improved farming and environmental practices.

More than 31 varieties of *padi*, such as Setanjung and Pulut Siding, have been developed by MARDI. After its introduction in 1985, MR 84 was widely planted in Malaysia until the year 2000. Thereafter, new varieties of *padi* were developed. An example is the MR 219 which matures in 105 days (10 to 15 days less than earlier varieties) and is more disease resistant. Since the debut of MR 219, the nation's rice self-sufficiency level has risen to more than 70 per cent, thus reducing the import of *padi*. These new varieties are grown in more than 90 per cent of the national production area or granary (see 'Agricultural policies and institutions'). Similarly, the introduction of Eksotika I and II papaya and Josapine and Maspine pineapples has boosted the local fruit industry.

Technological advancements in post-harvest handling of horticultural produce and food processing technologies have also been made. There are now new techniques for the management of agricultural resources such as soil, water and genetic diversity. Machines, tools and implements developed have made certain agricultural operations less hazardous and less labour- and time-consuming.

Key applications of science and technology

The world's first commercial pineapple hybrid

The advent of the Josapine pineapple has given the fresh pineapple industry a major boost. Its attractive looks, appealing aroma and sweet golden yellow flesh are strong selling points. Resistant to the 'blackheart' disorder, it can easily be exported in refrigerated containers. Work on hybridization to produce the Josapine pineapple first started in Pontian, Johor in 1984. MARDI officially released it on 5 August 1996. The name 'Josapine' reflects the cross between the Johor and Sarawak cultivars. It is the first pineapple hybrid in the world which has been successfully commercialized. Demand from local consumers and the potential for export have resulted in a significant increase in its cultivation.

The Josapine pineapple.

Eksotika I and II—Malaysia's flagship papaya

Papayas, before Eksotika, had inconsistent yields. Their relatively large fruit size made them cumbersome to handle and to serve. Papayas used to be grown for domestic consumption and exports were insignificant. In 1972, MARDI started a backcross breeding program to improve papayas. The Sunrise Solo from Hawaii was crossed with a local cultivar, the Subang 6. Subsequent progenies underwent a series of self-pollination and backcrossing to the Sunrise Solo. In 1987, the result of this process was released as Eksotika I. Another hybrid, Eksotika II, was released in 1991.

The Eksotika papaya has significantly boosted the Malaysian fruit industry, particularly in the generation of export earnings. In 2004, Eksotika generated about RM36 million or 42 per cent of total export earnings of fruits. As a result of science and technology in papaya breeding, Malaysia is the second largest exporter of papayas (24 per cent) in the world after Mexico in 2006.

Eksotika papayas.

The farming of vegetables under rain-shelters has enabled year round production of vegetables such as cabbage and cauliflower according to market demand. The technology used involves minimal or no use of pesticides, thus producing quality, safe vegetables. Fertigation is the method of applying fertilizer directly to the root; plants are individually irrigated with complete and balanced fertilizer solutions. The effective modified atmosphere (MAP) system has made it possible for flowers to retain their freshness even after a long duration, allowing for lower-cost, large-volume exports by sea. In poultry, the introduction of designer eggs such as the Omega-3 has resulted in the production of 100,000 such eggs per day or 36.5 million eggs per year in 2005.

MARDI Director-General Dr Abdul Shukor Abdul Rahman showing off the range of agro-food products developed by the agency in 2006.

Omega-3 eggs are nutritionally enhanced with Omega-3, fatty acids and vitamin E.

In the biotechnology sector, development of transgenic crops to produce crops with higher yields, resistance to pests, disease and adverse conditions, as well as improved quality, is underway. Plant tissue culture technology for fruits, flowers, ornamental plants, vegetables, herbs, cereals, industrial and cash crops has been developed to enhance the production and availability of disease-free, true-to-type and quality planting materials. Science has also made possible the development of sol-gel pesticide biosensors, diagnostic kits for antibiotic residue in poultry, the creation of super-microbes and probiotic solutions for healthy living.

Government agencies spearheading use of science and technology

The application of science and technology in agriculture is spearheaded by agencies linked to the agro-plantation and agro-food sectors. These agencies include research institutions, universities and government departments.

In the agro-plantation sector, three commodity boards, the MPOB, the MRB, and the Malaysian Cocoa Board conduct research on Malaysia's principal export commodities under the auspices of the Ministry of Plantation Industries and

Commodities. The Forest Research Institute Malaysia (FRIM) based in Kepong, Kuala Lumpur, administered by the Ministry of Natural Resources and Environment, is considered a world leader in tropical forest research.

In the agro-food sector, MARDI is the largest public agency and the principal agricultural research agency participating in research both locally and internationally. Its science and technology endeavours cover various areas including food crops such as fruits and vegetables; industrial crops like rice, sweet potato and kenaf; animal breeding and husbandry; sustainable agriculture; post-harvest handling and food processing. Plant, animal and food biotechnology, mechanization and automation, and biodiversity are new research areas in 2006. While the basic and emerging technologies are researched at MARDI's headquarters in Serdang, Selangor, base technologies, technology transfer and commercialization activities are conducted at MARDI's 29 regional research stations.

Other government agencies that advocate the application of science and technology in agriculture include the Veterinary Research Institute under the Department of Veterinary Services, which is based in Ipoh, Perak. This agency focuses on three primary areas: animal diseases, technology and product development, which includes vaccine production. The Fisheries Research Institute is headquartered in Penang and focuses on the management of marine resources, aquaculture, aquatic ecology, biotechnology, fish products and fish diseases. The Malaysian Institute for Nuclear Technology Research (MINT) works on agro-technology and biosciences at its Selangor-based laboratories.

While agricultural research and development in Peninsular Malaysia is conducted by federal research and development institutes, this is not the case in Sarawak and Sabah. There, the respective state level departments of agriculture, forestry and fisheries have their own research units that cater for their particular research and development needs.

TOP AND ABOVE: MARDI developed *Badorlin* hairsheep and *Brakmas* cattle. The former breed can adapt well to tropical environments and have better weight gain and lower mortality rates than indigenous sheep. The latter is a medium-sized breed suitable for oil palm plantations.

Rice	• Direct seeded new rice varieties MR219, MR220, aromatic rice varieties MRQ50, MRQ74 (Maswangi). • Sealed technology for commercial storage of milled rice. • Rice fertilizer technology (FERTO). • Smart organic fertilizer and Zeo-*padi*.	**Herbs**	• Aromatic products from herbs. • Integration of herbs within rubber ecosystems. • Extraction of essential oils.	
Fruits	• Durian varieties MDUR78, MDUR79 and 88. • Regulation of flowering and fruiting and high-density planting of mango. • Integrated management of insidious fruit rot (IFR) in mango. • The 'all green' watermelon. • New variety of Sapodilla, the *Ciku Mega*. • Improved variety of pomelo, the *Melomas*. • Disease free oranges for commercial production. • Exporting fruits by sea.	**Livestock**	• Beef cattle: Brakmas and Charoke. • Beef cattle-oil palm integration system. • New goat breed—Boer goats. • Bioprocessed Palm Kernel Cake (PKC). • Closed-house system for broiler chickens. • Oil Palm Frond (OPF) total mix feed. • Nutriblok-multipurpose feed supplement for ruminants.	Starfruit cultivated under a netted structure.
		Food processing	• Convenience foods and army rations. • Mechanized food production—machines for production of *ayam percik, lemang, rempeyek* and *satay*.	
Vegetables	• Protected cultivation of vegetables. • Organic farming. • Use of fertigation technique.	**Biotechnology**	• Rapid detection kit for organophosphate residues. • Transgenic crops such as rice, pineapple and papaya. • Fibre optic biosensor for pesticide residues. • Production of mycelium-bound lipase.	Vegetables grown under a rain-shelter.
Floriculture	• New orchid hybrids. • Nursery seedling posting media. • Cyclic night-lighting technology for chrysanthemum production.			

A sensor measures the temperature in a greenhouse where strawberries are being cultivated.

1. Robotic arms at work in a PROTON plant in Tanjung Malim, Perak. In 2005, there were six motor vehicle manufacturers, nine assemblers and 50 franchise holders in Malaysia.

2. A construction site in Kuala Lumpur. The construction industry accounted for less than five per cent of GDP in 2004, but is a strong growth stimulant because of its links with related manufacturing industries such as the electrical, machinery and metal industries.

3. A Malaysian Agricultural Research and Development Institute (MARDI) researcher propagating plants using tissue culture. Biotechnology, in particular agricultural, healthcare and industrial biotechnology, is expected to generate RM270 billion in revenue and create 280,000 jobs by 2020.

4. Malaysia Smelting Corporation's smelting complex in Butterworth, Penang was established in 1902. In 2004, 33,740 tonnes of tin metal were produced in Malaysia.

5. One of two Slurry Shield boring machines used in the Stormwater Management and Road Tunnel (SMART) project, the longest tunnel project in Malaysia. Construction on the 9.7-kilometre tunnel below Kuala Lumpur city centre began in January 2003.

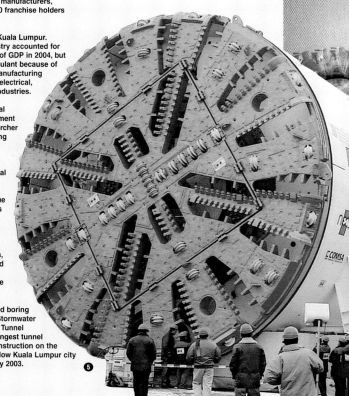

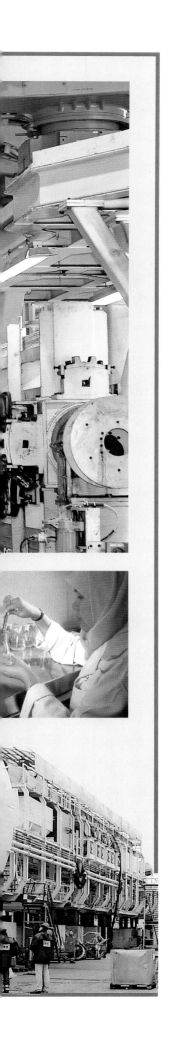

THE INDUSTRIAL SECTOR

Malaysia's economic development since the Industrial Master Plan (IMP) in 1986 has been so rapid that the country has been classified as a newly industrialized economy. The prime engine of growth has been the manufacturing sector, which in 2005 accounted for 31.4 per cent of GDP, 28.7 per cent of employment and 80.5 per cent of total exports at RM430 billion.

Malaysia's record of outstanding growth in this sector has been the result of an industrialization programme that dates back to the Pioneer Industries Ordinance 1958, Investment Incentives Act 1968 and the Industrial Coordination Act 1975. Since 1958, the industrialization strategy has undergone several distinct phases as a result of the policies formulated in response to changing internal and external circumstances. The first phase was based on a policy of import-substitution. This phase lasted until the end of the 1960s when, owing to the limited size of the domestic market, the initial growth spurt began to taper off, and subsequently there were rising levels of unemployment and social unrest. In the 1970s, the objective was to attract foreign direct investments, and growth through labour-intensive and export-oriented industries was seen as a solution.

In the early 1980s, measures were taken to widen and deepen the industrial base through the development of import-substituting heavy industries, resulting in the 1983 'national car' project. In 1986, the IMP was launched, and in the 1990s, a new transitional phase began with the launch of IMP2 (1996–2005) which emphasized the development of clusters of inter-related, capital-intensive, high value-added and high-technology industries. The 1990s also saw the construction of mega projects such as the Kuala Lumpur International Airport and the Sepang Formula 1 circuit.

The new emphasis of industrial policy, as enshrined in IMP3 (2006–20), is on biotechnology. This new growth area is expected to spearhead the next phase of the country's journey towards full industrialization by the year 2020. Another key aspect is the development of dynamic industrial clusters and small and medium enterprises (SMEs) to encourage strategic alliances in high value-added and high-tech industries.

The evolution of the industrial sector has brought about dramatic developments in society. Production assembly jobs created by the electrical, electronics and textiles industries enabled record numbers of women to participate in the labour force. Later, in the 1990s, rapid industrialization led to labour shortages and the introduction of large numbers of foreign workers. Industrial development did not merely create a new landscape of firms and factories, but it resulted in new patterns of urbanization, and with it, new lifestyles and socioeconomic trends.

Prime Minister Dato' Seri Abdullah Ahmad Badawi (left) chairing the National SME Development Council's first meeting at Putrajaya in 2004. Minister of Housing and Local Government Dato' Seri Ong Ka Ting (right) and Bank Negara Malaysia Governor Tan Sri Dr Zeti Akhtar Aziz (second from left) were among those present.

Industrial policies and plans

The rapid transformation of the country from its agricultural roots to an industrial economy involved the implementation of various government policies and plans which shaped and stimulated industrial development.

Minister of Commerce and Industry Dr Lim Swee Aun (left) making an inspection tour of a rubber manufacturing factory in Klang, 1963.

Import-substitution (1958–1968)

Like many developing countries initiating the first phase of industrialization, Malaysia pursued an import-substitution strategy. This involved the provision of various incentives, including tariff protection, to encourage the development of local industries, particularly for the manufacture of simple consumer products such as canned food and beverages for the domestic market.

In 1958, the Pioneer Industries Ordinance was introduced. It provided generous tax relief and tariff protection to selected industries. To further encourage industrialization, in 1960, the government established the Malayan Stock Exchange (see 'Financial markets') to mobilize private capital for industrial development, and Malaysian Industrial Development Finance Berhad (MIDF) to finance viable new industrial projects (see 'Small and medium enterprises'). By the late 1960s, it was apparent that the import-substitution policy was unable to encourage industries to make fuller use of domestic raw materials as its main objective was to substitute imported final consumer goods. The limited domestic market and lack of emphasis on technological development and performance standards further hampered the success of the policy. Moreover, import-substitution, as it was implemented, did not protect domestic manufacturers. Instead, it indirectly favoured foreign interests. By locating just their final assembly locally, not only were foreign interests able to escape import tariffs, they were also able to avoid the transfer of richer and more meaningful technology to local hands.

Industrial growth stagnated towards the end of the 1960s as the low technology import-substitution industries approached saturation. In 1968, there was a policy shift towards export-oriented industrialization. The Investment Incentives Act 1968, which broadened the scope of incentives for industrial development, was also introduced.

Export-orientation (1968–1980)

In contrast to import-substitution, export-orientation was premised on the idea that industrialization was best driven by the export sector. Where import-substitution relied on import tariffs, export-orientation emphasized the creation of a favourable climate for exporters. Key initiatives therefore included tax and non-tax incentives for exporters, and the provision of infrastructure for export activities.

In 1971, export processing or free trade zones were set up under the Free Trade Zone Act of 1971. Companies enjoyed tax holidays, exemptions from import and export duties, unrestricted and tax-free remittances of profits and dividends within these enclaves. To allow firms outside free trade zones to enjoy similar benefits, the Customs Act of 1967 was amended to permit the establishment of licensed manufacturing warehouses.

In order to rationalize industrial development and provide direction on the type of industries which would be promoted, the Industrial Coordination Act (ICA) was introduced in 1975. Under the ICA, manufacturing licences were issued upon compliance with guidelines on equity ownership and employment structure, in accordance with the New Economic Policy (see 'New Economic Policy: 1971–1990').

By 1980, Malaysia had become a major exporter of electrical and electronic goods. Textiles, textile products and wood products were also significant contributors to export earnings. The share of manufactured goods in gross exports, which had stagnated between eight and 12 per cent during the 1960s, increased to nearly 20 per cent at the end of the 1970s. The export-orientation industries were characterized by labour-intensive processes, and while they generally contributed positively to growth, employment and the trade balance, they involved a high level of imported content and foreign investment.

More import-substitution

In the midst of the country's general policy of export-orientation, the government made another significant foray into import-substitution. The initiatives this time focused on heavy industries, seen as critical for national strategic interests. The acquisition of relevant technology was regarded as a means of achieving greater depth in the industrial sector. Steel, automotive, and cement

TOP AND ABOVE: Advertisements for Bata shoes and F&N carbonated drinks, c.1958. Consumer products such as these were the focus of the import-substitution strategy.

BELOW: Advertisement on the perks of investing in the Pelepas Free Zone in Johor.

Pelepas FREE ZONE
Asia's fast-growing Free Zone within a thriving logistics hub

10 REASONS TO INVEST IN PELEPAS FREE ZONE

1. Competitive operational costs 2. Full tax exemption on all activities within Pelepas FREE ZONE 3. Located within the award-winning Port of Tanjung Pelepas, enhancing your logistics costs savings 4. Green Lane Concept with minimal inspection and documentation of all cargo movements 5. No fund repatriation, currency or personnel recruitment quota restrictions 6. No customs formalities for all FREE ZONE activities 7. Modern facilities and efficient services 8. 100% foreign ownership of equity allowed for approved activities 9. Vast reserve of prime land for future expansion of operations 10. Just 15 minutes to Singapore via the SecondLink

Come visit us and discover for yourself even more reasons why you REALLY should set up operations here.

industries were set up, and protective barriers legislated around them (see 'Heavy industry').

The Promotion of Investments Act 1986 was introduced to replace the Investment Incentives Act 1968. It also broadened the scope of incentives to promote small- and medium-scale enterprises (SMEs), as well as tourist and hotel projects.

The Industrial Master Plan (1986–1995)

From 1986 onwards, industrialization was structured and directed by the Industrial Master Plans (IMPs). It was recognized that the long-term competitiveness of the industrial sector, in terms of both light and heavy manufacturing, required continued integration with export markets. Hence, all three IMPs have emphasized the strategy of export-orientation. Past policies to promote export-orientation industries were rearticulated, with particular emphasis on resource-based industries and diversification of non-resource-based industries and selected heavy industries. Foreign investment was encouraged through deregulation and the simplification of investment procedures.

The measures taken led to rapid growth as well as new challenges. The demands of the burgeoning industries placed heavy pressures on infrastructure. Most significantly, a shortage of labour emerged, in particular of technically skilled labour, which hindered progress towards higher value-added production stages. Higher labour costs not only reduced the competitiveness of Malaysian goods, but also hampered Malaysia's ability to attract foreign direct investment.

Other challenges emerged. Entrepreneurial effort had until then focused overwhelmingly on generating investment and exports. With some exceptions, such as the palm oil processing sub-sector, little attention was paid to technological content and the development of linkages with the domestic economy. Manufacturing operations were shallow, tending towards a broad range of products within a similar stage of production and lacking the depth of the vertically integrated manufacturing that characterized mature, world-class competitors. Malaysia's industrial growth was being generated by increased inputs of capital and labour, rather than by productivity gains through technical innovation.

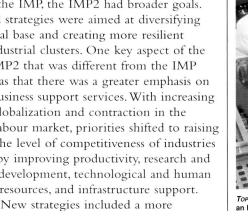

IMP3 aims to improve the productivity of the three main sectors—manufacturing, services and agriculture.

The Kentucky Fried Chicken food processing plant at Port Klang opened in 1990, and was the most modern such plant at the time with a capacity to process 45,000 chickens per day for local sale and export.

In 1995, the manufacturing base was still heavily dominated by the electrical and electronic products sub-sector. Similarly, the principal markets remained the United States, Singapore, Europe and Japan, which together accounted for about three-quarters of Malaysia's total manufactured exports. The need for new products and markets became increasingly evident.

The Second Industrial Master Plan (1996–2005)

To sustain growth and to address the issues and challenges facing the manufacturing sector, the government formulated the Second Industrial Master Plan (IMP2).

Unlike the IMP, the IMP2 had broader goals. Policies and strategies were aimed at diversifying the industrial base and creating more resilient industrial clusters. One key aspect of the IMP2 that was different from the IMP was that there was a greater emphasis on business support services. With increasing globalization and contraction in the labour market, priorities shifted to raising the level of competitiveness of industries by improving productivity, research and development, technological and human resources, and infrastructure support. New strategies included a more effective role for SMEs in the industrial mainstream, increased reverse investments (Malaysian entrepreneurs investing overseas), the development of non-traditional markets, and the development of vertically integrated value-added chains and industrial clusters.

The Third Industrial Master Plan (2006–2020)

The Third Industrial Master Plan (IMP3) contains strategies to enhance the competitiveness of the manufacturing and service industries. Its focus is to generate new sources of growth, besides developing SMEs and upgrading the agricultural sector.

Particular areas addressed by the IMP3 include innovation and linkages between manufacturing-related services, the potential of biotechnology, research and development, adoption of information and communications technology, logistics infrastructure, industry clusters, participation of local suppliers and service providers in the global supply chain, and upgrading the skills of the workforce.

TOP: Production of lead frames at an ICT company in Bayan Lepas, Penang. The electrical and electronics industry was the largest contributor to the country's manufacturing output, exports and employment in 2006.

ABOVE: Worker engaged in the sealing lids manufacturing process at a Globetronics Technology Berhad facility. In 2005, the electrical and electronics industry contributed 55 per cent of Malaysia's exports.

Value-added of the manufacturing sector, 2005	
Total value-added:	**RM82,394,000,000**
Resource-based	**43.7%**
Vegetable, animal oils and fats	4.4%
Other food processing, beverages and tobacco	5.8%
Wood products including furniture	3.6%
Paper and paper products, printing and publishing	3.2%
Industrial chemicals including fertilizers and plastic products	12.2%
Petroleum products including crude oil refineries and coal	6.4%
Rubber processing and products	3.5%
Non-metallic mineral products	4.5%
Non-resource-based	**54.2%**
Textiles, wearing apparel and leather	2.2%
Basic metal industry	0.8%
Metal products	4.9%
Manufacture of machinery except electrical	4.2%
Electronics	28.0%
Electrical machinery	1.2%
Transport equipment	12.9%
Others	**2.1%**

Source: Economic Planning Unit

Manufacturing

From the 1970s onwards, the economy underwent significant change, with manufacturing replacing agriculture as the engine of growth. While manufacturing encompasses a broad range of activities, one industry in particular has dominated the sector: electrical and electronic products. In addition to driving GDP growth, manufacturing has also had a major impact on trade and employment.

Manufactured exports, 2005	
Total value: RM429.87 billion or 80.5% of total gross exports	
RESOURCE-BASED	
Food	2.0%
Beverages & tobacco	0.4%
Wood products	2.1%
Paper and paper products	0.5%
Petroleum products	3.9%
Chemicals and chemical products	6.9%
Rubber products	1.6%
Non-metallic mineral products	0.7%
NON-RESOURCE-BASED	
Textiles, clothing and footwear	2.4%
Manufactures of metal	4.0%
Electrical and electronic products	65.8%
Transport equipment	1.6%
OTHERS	8.1%

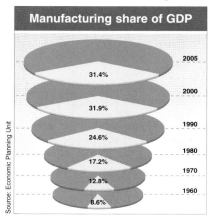

The rise of manufacturing

As an activity, manufacturing denotes the manufacture of any product, regardless of whether it is snack food or complex hi-tech electronic equipment. Where statistical records are concerned, heavy industries are frequently included, but in terms of issues they are often discussed separately (see 'Heavy industry').

Manufacturing in the 1950s was not a significant sector; in 1955, it contributed only eight per cent to GDP, and existed largely to support the tin and rubber sectors. It was when these commodities began facing challenges—competition from synthetic rubber, rapid depletion of tin deposits and declining commodity prices—that manufacturing became a priority. The subsequent changes in the manufacturing sector reflected the country's evolving industrialization policies, namely, the adoption of the import-substitution strategy, and the subsequent shift to export-orientation (see 'Industrial policies and plans').

Between 1970 and 1990, the manufacturing sector grew at ten per cent per annum, out-performing other economic sectors such as agriculture and services. High growth rates were also recorded in the 1990s, except for 1998 when manufacturing growth contracted as a result of the Asian financial crisis (see 'Malaysia's innovative response to the financial crisis'). As a result of this growth, manufacturing recorded a significant increase in its share of GDP, from 12.8 per cent in 1970 to 31.4 per cent in 2005. In general, the trend of Malaysia's GDP growth has been consistent with the growth of the manufacturing sector, with growth rates exceptionally high when export-

TOP AND ABOVE: Workers at a soap factory, c. 1960s. Iris Technology's plant at Technology Park Malaysia, Kuala Lumpur, manufactures contact and contactless smart cards.

In the 1950s, key industries were linked to rubber and tin. Other industries—such as food processing, beverages, tobacco, soap, furniture, printed materials, metal products and glass bottles—catered to local demand which flourished due to an increasing population and growing national income. Industries supplying the construction sector also grew with the construction boom

orientation was emphasized, first in the 1970s, and then during the second half of the 1980s and in the 1990s under the Industrial Master Plans. This implies that there is a strong positive correlation between manufacturing output growth, exports and GDP growth rates. Even when the real exchange rate appreciated in the early 1980s, causing Malaysian exports to become less competitive while import costs decreased, the government continued to emphasize manufacturing to provide overall dynamism to the economy.

Manufacturing has had a significant impact on key aspects of the economy such as employment and trade. Two industries in particular have emerged as major sub-sectors: textiles, and the electrical and electronics sub-sector.

Manufacturing and employment

A total of about three million people were employed in the manufacturing sector in 2005, compared with just 251,939 people in 1970.

Manufacturing has played an important role in overall employment creation. Between 1995 and 2000, for example, the sector accounted for 41.7 per cent or 530,000 of the new jobs created. In the 1970s, the industry groups that created significant employment opportunities were food, footwear, other apparel and made-up textile goods, wood and wood products, general engineering and machinery and equipment. In 2005, the key job-creating sectors were electrical and electronic products, wood and wood products, rubber products and the textile industry. Small and medium enterprises (SMEs) were the largest source of employment.

Manufacturing and trade

In 1971, manufactured goods comprised only 11.9 per cent of total exports. By 2005, they

Manufacturing share of GDP

2005 — 31.4%
2000 — 31.9%
1990 — 24.6%
1980 — 17.2%
1970 — 12.8%
1960 — 8.6%

Manufacturing employment

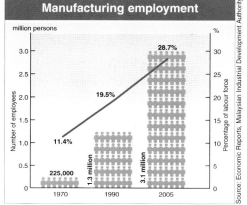

million persons

11.4% — 225,000 (1970)
19.5% — 1.3 million (1990)
28.7% — 3.1 million (2005)

| 1957 | 1970 | 1980 | 1990 | 2000 |

The artwork provides a snapshot of the key industries over the years.

that followed World War II. Nevertheless, manufacturing remained insignificant compared to agriculture.

Following the adoption of import-substitution, the main industries at the end of the 1960s were those producing consumer goods for domestic consumption, such as food, wood products, chemicals and rubber products. The export-oriented policy adopted from 1968 to 1986 resulted in export-led industries such as textiles and apparel and the electrical and electronics sector becoming the key industries, with resource-based industries such as food, rubber and wood industries losing ground.

The promotion of heavy industries in the early 1980s (see 'Heavy industry') led to increased production by automobile factories, steel mills, petrochemical and cement plants.

Industries targeted for development by the Industrial Master Plans

Resource-based	Non-resource-based
• Food processing • Rubber, palm oil, and wood • Chemical and petrochemical • Non-ferrous metal products • Non-metallic mineral products	• Electrical and electronics • Transport equipment • Machinery and engineering products • Ferrous metal • Textiles and apparel

accounted for 80.5 per cent of Malaysia's exports. The composition of manufactured exports also experienced substantial change consistent with the shifts in industrial orientation. The electrical and electronics sub-sector has experienced the fastest growth in exports.

Export earnings boomed during the second half of the 1970s. In 1981, however, they fell by almost four per cent as a result of the global recession. Prices of major export items such as rubber, petroleum, manufactured goods and palm oil declined sharply. At the same time, rising wages made the export-oriented manufacturing sector less competitive.

Manufacturing also influenced the country's import structure. In the 1960s, import–substitution resulted in both a decline in imports of consumer goods, and an increase in imports of intermediate goods, such as machinery and other inputs required by the fledgling import–substitution industries. Subsequent export-orientation policies and the second round of import–substitution increased the need for imported intermediate inputs. In the early 1980s, this increase in imported intermediate inputs, coupled with weak export performance, resulted for the first time in a balance of payments problem in Malaysia. The current account turned modestly negative in 1980, then extremely negative in 1981 and 1982. Imported intermediate inputs continued to grow, reaching 78.9 per cent of total imports by 2004. About 45 per cent of imported intermediate inputs consist of parts and accessories used in the electrical and electronics industry (see 'Industrial policies and plans').

In 2005, ASEAN, the United States, Japan and China were Malaysia's top four trading partners for manufactured exports. The bulk of the exports consisted of electrical and electronic goods.

Electrical and electronics sector

Within three decades beginning in 1970, this sector dominated the manufacturing industry in terms of both manufacturing output and exports. Its rapid growth was spearheaded by the general growth of the manufacturing sector in the 1970s and 1980s. Despite the subsequent promotion of heavy and resource-based industries, the sector continued to dominate the scene.

Electrical and electronics exports, 2005

Source: Malaysian Industrial Development Authority

42.8%   38.1%   10.4%   8.7%

- Electrical products
- Electronic components
- Industrial electronics
- Consumer electronics

In 2005, the total value of electrical and electronics exports was RM282.8 billion representing 65.8 per cent of total exports of manufactured products. There were 1385 companies in operation with investments of RM72.2 billion, providing more than 548,000 jobs amounting to 18.3 per cent of the total employment in the manufacturing sector.

Textiles and apparel

In 2005, the industry was the seventh largest manufacturing export earner, accounting for 2.4 per cent of exports of manufactured goods. Yarn, woven fabrics and clothing were the main exports.

Before the 1990s, the industry was one of the dominant sectors of the economy. In the early 1980s, it was the second largest contributor, after the electrical and electronics industry, in terms of the nation's manufacturing output, export earnings and employment.

During the mid-1990s, other export-oriented industries such as electrical and electronics, chemicals and chemical products, wood and wood products overtook the industry in importance. Being traditionally dependent on labour,

Workers at a textile factory. Textiles and apparel were one of the 12 sub-sectors identified for development under the Industrial Master Plans.

the industry has lost out to countries where cheap labour is abundant. The largest threat to date is China, currently the world's top textiles and apparel producer. With the phasing out of the Multi Fibre Arrangement in 2005, the industry began to be subject to more intense competition in the quota-free world market.

Industrial areas

Industrial areas in Malaysia exist in various forms, the most common being industrial estates, free zones, specialized industrial estates and technology parks. While they differ in strategic intent and purpose, they are all essentially sites designed to cater to the needs of industries and to promote industrialization.

Operators at one of BCM Electronic's assembly line at Kulim Hi-Tech Park.

Rationale

Prior to the creation of industrial areas in Malaysia, manufacturers tended to set up operations in locations that had easy access to raw materials, labour, basic utilities and transportation infrastructure. Uncoordinated development resulted in a disorganized landscape, with industrial activities sometimes infringing on residential, recreational and ecological areas.

In this respect, industrial areas provide a solution in the form of zoning. They also enable economies of scale and scope to be achieved in the provision of industrial infrastructure, services and other resources. Industrial areas offer enterprises an environment with relatively low set-up and operational costs but high potential for developing linkages with supporting industries, making them an effective means of attracting capital investment.

Because industrial estates create concentrations of human activity and settlement, they are also a means by which planners can encourage a redistribution of population in favour of less developed areas. Industries have been encouraged by specific incentives to locate their operations in less developed areas; this has resulted in a wider dispersal of industrial areas and more diversified regional industrialization.

Early sites

Malaysia's first 'packaged' industrial site was in Petaling Jaya. Following the passage of the Pioneer Industries Ordinance in 1958, which offered incentives for industrial investment, the Petaling Jaya Authority leased out 121.4 hectares of former rubber plantation land, subdivided into industrial lots. The project was an immediate success, with all the lots taken up and 80 factories operating by 1960. The industrial area had grown to 283.3 hectares by 1965.

In the wake of Petaling Jaya's success, new industrial sites were set up in other major urban areas: Mak Mandin (Penang), Tasek (Perak), Larkin and Tampoi (Johor) in 1962, followed by Batu Tiga and Shah Alam (Selangor) and Senawang (Negeri Sembilan) in 1968.

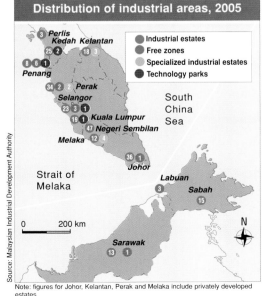

Distribution of industrial areas, 2005

- ● Industrial estates
- ● Free zones
- ● Specialized industrial estates
- ● Technology parks

Perlis
Kedah Kelantan
Penang
Perak
Selangor
Kuala Lumpur
Negeri Sembilan
Melaka
Johor
Strait of Melaka
Labuan
Sabah
South China Sea
Sarawak

0   200 km

Source: Malaysian Industrial Development Authority

Note: figures for Johor, Kelantan, Perak and Melaka include privately developed estates.

Categories of industrial areas

Industrial estates

A significant number of industrial estates in Malaysia are developed by public sector agencies, for instance the State Economic Development Corporations (see 'The Federal, state and local governments in the economy'), and the Regional Development Authorities. Private sector industrial estates are developed by private property developers, and are often part of ambitious planned townships containing a mix of residential, commercial and recreational zones as well as industrial areas.

Aerial view of the Shah Alam Industrial Estate, Selangor.

Technology parks

With the drive towards high technology in the late 1980s, the concept of specialized industrial estates was extended to technology parks. A key function of technology parks is to provide the physical infrastructure required in order for hi-tech industries to operate. In addition, technology parks place special emphasis on creating an environment conducive to innovation, the dissemination of ideas and the development of the most critical resource in high-tech activities: human capital. Technology parks provide a place for like-minded companies and individuals to undertake research and development, design and engineering, and marketing of technology. They also function as focus points in the hi-tech industry's efforts to attract venture capital.

The earliest technology parks were Kulim Hi-Tech Park (Phase 1 and 2) in Kedah, Technology Park Malaysia at Bukit Jalil in Kuala Lumpur, and Bayan Lepas Technoplex in Penang. The Bukit Jalil facility is considered part of the Multimedia Super Corridor (MSC), which itself can be seen as a larger technology park dedicated to the development of multimedia products and services.

In the mid-1990s, the Selangor State Development Corporation (PKNS) with the assistance of Malaysian Technology Development Corporation Sdn Bhd (MTDC) and Standards and Industrial Research Institute of Malaysia (SIRIM) embarked on developing a world-class technology park—the Selangor Science Park 1 (SSP1). The first science park in Malaysia, it is located on 193.6 hectares of land in Kota Damansara, Petaling Jaya, and is specially designed for production plants and supporting industries, with easy access to research and development institutes, universities and technical training centres. Companies investing in the SSP1 have the option to access various venture capital funds from the state of Selangor's investment arms, while SIRIM offers product testing, research and development support and international recognition and certification for quality systems. MTDC, the national venture capital and technology transfer organization, offers business support services, technological development and manufacturing consultancy. The aim is to attract a cluster of companies with the latest state-of-the-art technologies to SSP1.

Benefits of industrial estates

The early industrial estates offered fully developed sites with utilities, good transportation links and long-term leases of land with titles. These early industrial estates were conceived as projects from which firms' development costs were to be recovered through adequate return on invested capital. They generally did not entail the use of direct subsidies, which is a characteristic of free zones.

Deputy Prime Minister Tun Abdul Razak cutting the ribbon to declare the Batu Tiga Industrial Estate, Selangor, open in 1968.

Free zones

Towards the end of the 1960s, industrial policy shifted from import substitution to export orientation (see 'Industrial policies and plans'). A major initiative of Malaysia's early export-oriented industrial regime was the passage of the Free Trade Zone Act of 1971, and the subsequent opening up of free trade zones, or export processing zones. Free trade zones are known today as free industrial zones, or simply free zones (FZ).

FZs are specifically designated industrial areas where imported machinery, raw materials and semi-finished goods may enter duty-free because they are to be processed on-site, and then re-exported. In Malaysia, FZs were established to achieve four objectives: employment creation, promotion of exports to ease balance of payments deficits, encouragement of technology transfer and promotion of growth-enhancement activities.

Manufacturing companies that were already in operation before the availability of FZs, but fulfilled all export and operational criteria under the Free Trade Zone Act, were designated as licensed manufacturing warehouses (LMW), a status which offered similar tariff exemptions and incentives as FZs. LMW status was also granted to firms that found the locations of available FZs impractical. LMW status thus effectively extended the benefits of FZs to all qualifying manufacturing concerns within the country.

Brochure from Kuala Lumpur International Airport (KLIA) free zone. Because of their focus on export-oriented industries, free zones are often sited close to transport hubs, such as Bayan Lepas International Airport in Penang and KLIA in Sepang.

ABOVE: Technology Park Malaysia is a comprehensive centre for research and development activities related to knowledge-based industries.

LEFT: Kulim Hi-Tech Park, set up at a cost of RM1.2 billion, was officially opened in 1996, and was the country's first high technology park. Located in southern Kedah, it is the silicon wafer fabrication centre of Malaysia. Companies located there include Silterra Malaysia Sdn Bhd and Infineon Technologies Kulim Sdn Bhd, which together account for investments of more than RM10 billion as of 2006.

A brochure on Selangor Science Park 1 (SSP1). Companies located in SSP1 enjoy a host of financial incentives such as pioneer status, investment tax allowance and research and development incentives. Grants may also be given by the Federal Government to local small and medium industries. A company with pioneer status is granted partial exemption from the payment of income tax.

Selected SIEs and their specializations

SIE	Specialization
Pengkalan II, Perak	furniture, foundry
Serkam, Melaka	halal food
Tanjung Kling, Melaka	shoes and textile
Sungai Gadut, Negeri Sembilan	wood-based industries
Gebeng III, Pahang	petrochemicals
Tanjung Gelang I and II, Pahang	petrochemicals

Specialized industrial estates (SIEs)

The latter half of the 1980s saw an emphasis on synergistic linkages that enhanced industrial efficiency and innovation. It was noted that the benchmarks of industrial excellence seldom existed in a vacuum. Rather, a successful industry or enterprise was usually to be found operating within a wide, complex community of manufacturers, suppliers, suppliers' suppliers, competitors and other service providers. The government realized that the rate of technological innovation and development could be accelerated through the concentration of such a mutually supportive set of industries in a single physical location. This concept became the basis for the many specialized industrial estates that have been established throughout the country for electronics, wood furniture, chemicals, oil and gas, and pharmaceuticals.

RIGHT: Brochure promoting Rawang Technology Park.

Heavy industry

Several early ventures in heavy industry, primarily in steel manufacturing, were undertaken during the 1960s and 1970s. On the whole, however, the private sector did not invest significantly in large-scale heavy industry because of the large capital requirements, long gestation periods and relatively unattractive returns involved. It was thus left to the government to spearhead this diverse industry, with the establishment of HICOM in the 1980s.

Worker in a steel mill in Hulu, Selangor. As of 2005, Malaysia had five fully integrated steel mills.

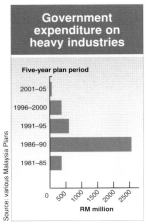

Government expenditure on heavy industries

Five-year plan period

(Bar chart, RM million, x-axis: 0, 500, 1000, 1500, 2000, 2500)

- 2001–05
- 1996–2000
- 1991–95
- 1986–90
- 1981–85

Source: various Malaysia Plans

During the Fifth Malaysia Plan 1986–1990, the government emphasized heavy industry as a means of building the long-term capacity for economic growth.

Strengthening the industrial base

In the late 1960s, the nation changed its focus to export-oriented manufacturing (see 'Industrial policies and plans'). By the end of the 1970s, however, the initial growth spurt in manufacturing had begun to taper off. The industrial sector was too heavily concentrated on electronics and textiles; and the share of Bumiputera ownership in 1980 was, at 12.4 per cent, far below the 30 per cent target of the New Economic Policy (NEP) (see 'New Economic Policy: 1971–1990'). It became clear that Malaysia would need to widen and strengthen its industrial base. At this point, the development of heavy industries was proposed as the logical next step in the evolution of Malaysian industrialization.

Venturing into heavy industries

Malaysia ventured into heavy industries for several reasons. First, developing her own heavy industries would enable Malaysia to not only replace some of the heavy industrial inputs that were being imported, but also widen and deepen the existing industrial base. Second, linkages would be created between core industries and their ancillary small- and medium-sized industries. Third, heavy industries would entail the transfer of technology, in particular, sophisticated and complex processes that would significantly advance the nation in terms of technology. Fourth, heavy industries could be used as a vehicle for achieving NEP targets and reducing regional economic imbalances.

With these goals in mind, Malaysia embarked on a significant heavy industries initiative in the early 1980s, introducing a policy of import-substitution for these industries, which then coexisted with the overall industrial policy of export promotion.

Owing to the strategic importance of heavy industries, and to the fact that these ventures were extremely large-scale and capital-intensive in nature, the government itself undertook the heavy industrialization programme. Its first step was the establishment of Heavy Industries Corporation of Malaysia Berhad (HICOM). In the 1990s, the government began developing aerospace and other hi-tech industries that would further broaden the industrial base and lead the nation into a phase of hi-tech industrialization.

DRB-HICOM Berhad (Diversified Resources Berhad–Heavy Industries Corporation of Malaysia Berhad)

HICOM was incorporated on 27 November 1980 to identify, plan, initiate, invest in, implement and manage selected heavy industrial projects. Although wholly owned by the government, HICOM was established under the Companies Act 1965 to give it the operational flexibility of a private enterprise.

Manufacture and assembly of the HICOM Perkasa truck is carried out by Malaysian Truck and Bus Sdn Bhd, a joint venture between DRB-HICOM and Isuzu.

Its establishment and the implementation of its early projects marked Malaysia's first major foray into heavy industry.

During its first four years, HICOM initiated six projects: the manufacture of cement, iron and steel, the national car (see 'The automotive and motorcycle industry'), small motorcycle engines, and general-purpose engines. By 1987, however, HICOM's projects had fallen on hard times and saddled the government with huge debts.

In 1988, after a managerial and organizational restructuring that coincided with the recovery of the overall economy, HICOM began to expand. It was renamed HICOM Berhad in December 1993, and by the time it became a public listed company in early 1994, it had 22 subsidiaries and 31 associated companies.

DRB was incorporated on 28 August 1990 to restructure Imatex Berhad, a property development company; its other ventures included the manufacture and assembly of monocoque buses and Pinzgauerall-terrain vehicles. DRB was also awarded the contract for the privatization of the automated inspection of commercial vehicles. A joint venture was formed in 1994 with PROTON to develop, manufacture and

DRB-HICOM

LEFT: Logo of DRB-HICOM.

ABOVE: Die-casting. HICOM Diecastings Sdn Bhd supplies aluminium diecast parts to the automotive, motor-cycle and other related industries.

sell PROTON cars. In 1995, Modenas, the national motor-cycle company, was set up by DRB. In November 1995, a privatization cum restructuring exercise took place, followed by a merger and consolidation exercise which saw the birth of the DRB-HICOM Group.

In 2006, DRB-HICOM Berhad is the single largest integrated automotive company in the country with interests in property development and construction and services. In 2005, its profit before taxation amounted to just under RM277 million.

Major industries

Cement, steel and iron

The cement, steel and iron industries produce essential inputs for the construction sector. In the mid-1990s the cement industry, comprising six integrated plants and four grinding plants, operated at almost maximum capacity due to demand from large-scale construction projects such as the Kuala Lumpur International Airport (KLIA), the Kuala Lumpur City Centre (KLCC) and Putrajaya.

Even though the steel industry started back in the 1960s, Malaysia still has to import steel products, particularly flat products that are required by the automobile, electrical and high technology industries. In 1994, about 90 per cent of the requirements of these products were imported. Most of the iron and steel products locally produced are for domestic consumption, except round bars and rods which are exported to a few markets in the region.

The Malaysian steel industry grew strongly in the two years following the Asian financial crisis to record a consumption level of 6.9 million metric tonnes in 2000. As of 2006, the industry is still dominated by domestic investors. The main raw materials for steel making are scrap metal, direct reduced iron and hot briquetted iron.

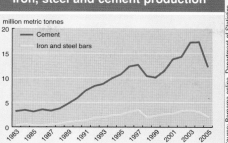
Iron, steel and cement production

million metric tonnes

— Cement
— Iron and steel bars

Source: Bernama online, Department of Statistics

Rolling of steel slabs into plates at Lion Plate Mills in Kemaman, Terengganu.

The YTL–Pahang Cement factory in Bukit Sagu, Pahang.

Aerospace

The aerospace industry is still in its infancy. In the Seventh Malaysia Plan (1996–2000), a market niche was identified in the manufacture of small aircraft, production of aircraft parts and components and the development of avionic and services-related industries. A high-technology centre for the manufacture of aircraft components has been established in Melaka. In 2006, there were two light aircraft assemblers (one government owned), seven component manufacturers and 28 establishments involved in maintenance, repair and overhaul activities.

Malaysia's first satellite, Malaysia East Asia Satellite (MEASAT), was launched in 1996 and marked Malaysia's entry into the field of space-age communications. The country's first earth-imaging satellite, TiungSAT-1, was launched by Astronautic Technology (M) Sdn Bhd (ATSB) from the Baikonur Cosmodrome, Kazakhstan on 26 September 2000. In 2004, the country's second microsatellite, RazakSAT, successfully completed the Flight Model-Manufacturing Readiness Review (FM-MRR) in Daejeon, South Korea. Part of the manufacturing and component installations of RazakSAT have been done in Malaysia, as will the final integration process for all of the satellite's components. RazakSAT is due to be launched in 2007.

Manufacture of aircraft composites by Asian Composites Manufacturing Sdn Bhd. The company is the sole supplier of fixed trailing edge panels for Boeing.

Poster featuring MEASAT, Malaysia's first satellite.

A Caterpillar wheel loader shovelling fruit bunches at a palm oil mill.

Machinery and equipment

The machinery and equipment industry developed from the needs of the mining, construction and agricultural sectors. It is of strategic importance due to its usage in other sectors. Malaysia manufactures machinery and equipment, along with components and parts. With the rapid growth of the manufacturing sector over the last three decades, the industry has expanded to produce a diverse range of machinery such as automation equipment for the semiconductor industry, blow moulding machines, pressure vessels, conveyors and conveyor systems, cranes, power and hydraulic presses, welding machines, filling and packaging machines, and offshore and onshore oil and gas equipment.

Malaysia, however, continues to be a net importer of machinery and equipment. Imports of machinery and equipment, excluding electrical machinery, amounted to RM33.2 billion from January to November 2005. The bulk of the imports were specialized and process machinery, machine tools, material handling equipment, heavy construction machinery and supporting machinery used in manufacturing. The government offers financial and tax incentives to encourage the development of this industry.

Vessels undergoing repair in MMHE's dry dock in Pasir Gudang, Johor.

Shipbuilding and ship-repairing

The shipbuilding and ship-repairing industry is fragmented. The majority of companies are small shipyards. The principal player in this field is Malaysia Marine and Heavy Engineering Sdn Bhd (MMHE), formerly known as the Malaysia Shipyard and Engineering Sdn Bhd (MSE). MSE was incorporated by the government in 1973 to undertake ship repairs, shipbuilding and offshore and onshore engineering. It was subsequently privatized in 1991. Its core business in 2006 is marine and heavy engineering, deepwater support services for the oil and gas industry, dry docking and heavy engineering.

The demand for boats and ships in Malaysia is based on replacement of ships scrapped due to age or damage, demand for new ships on a jobbing basis, the development of the oil and gas industry, and the requirements of the military and police. From January to November 2005, exports of ships, boats (including hovercraft) and floating structures amounted to RM2.1 billion, while imports totalled RM2.9 billion. Five new projects were approved in 2005, with investments amounting to RM97.6 million. These were locally owned and based in Sabah and Sarawak.

The automotive and motorcycle industry

After Independence, the automotive industry was largely confined to the local assembly of foreign makes. In the 1980s, however, the industry became a key initiative in the country's strategy for developing heavy industries. The project chosen to launch the initiative was the manufacture of a national car, followed thereafter by the national motorcycle.

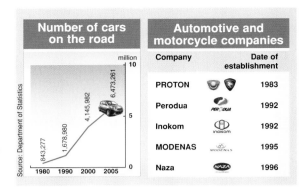

Number of cars on the road	Automotive and motorcycle companies		
	Company		Date of establishment
	PROTON		1983
	Perodua		1992
	Inokom		1992
	MODENAS		1995
	Naza		1996

Trade and Industry Minister Dr Lim Swee Aun (left) at the launch of Malaysia's first car assembly plant, Swedish Motor Assemblies Sdn Bhd, in 1968.

PROTON cars lined up at the company's main manufacturing plant at Tanjung Malim in 2005.

The national car project

The national car project had four objectives. First, to rationalize the local automotive industry. Second, to spearhead the development of a local automotive components industry, and enhance utilization of local components. Third, to raise the level of technology, knowledge of engineering, and technical skills in the country. Fourth, to promote and develop Bumiputera participation in the automotive industry.

The establishment of Perusahaan Otomobil Nasional Berhad (PROTON) in 1983 marked the start of the national car project: the infrastructure was put in place, and the requisite human resources assembled. A partnership with the Japanese car manufacturer Mitsubishi provided the framework for technology transfer to take place. Heavy Industries Corporation of Malaysia (HICOM) held 70 per cent of the equity and Mitsubishi Motors Corporation and Mitsubishi Corporation each held 15 per cent. In 1985, the first PROTON Saga rolled off the production line.

A model for the industry

Through the PROTON car project, Malaysia acquired a vast amount of experience in the technology, management, research and development, and marketing required by such a major industrial venture. It was an achievement which had a tremendous impact on the subsequent development of the automotive and other technology-based industries. This became particularly apparent in the 1990s, which saw the emergence of several new automotive projects, most of them following the model of development set by PROTON, and structured around joint technical assistance ventures with internationally established car manufacturers.

In the early 1990s, Usahasama PROTON-DRB Sdn Bhd (USPD), a joint venture between PROTON and Diversified Resources Berhad (DRB), was set up to develop and market PROTON variants. Between 1994 and 1996, USPD launched a number of models, including the Tiara, the result of a collaboration with Automobiles Citroên.

The PROTON Saga

The first sketches of Malaysia's first national car, the PROTON Saga, were only published in the press in March 1985, but this did not stop over 1000 people from placing their orders in December 1984 and paying the RM500 deposit without having any idea of what the car would look like. Special commemorative car registration numbers—'PROTON 1' to 'PROTON 1001'—were issued exclusively for the first 1001 cars sold.

On 18 April 1985, the first 30 PROTON Sagas rolled off the production lines. Commercial production commenced on 9 July 1985, and on 1 September the same year, the cars went on sale, with sales and marketing operations handled by Edaran Otomobil Nasional (EON).

Dealing in what was essentially considered a luxury commodity, the fledgling automobile industry was badly hit by the recession of the mid-80s. The PROTON Saga managed to capture an 11 per cent share of the domestic market in 1986, but domestic sales alone were insufficient for PROTON to meet its original targets for optimal production. Export to foreign markets was seen as a solution, and export production began, first focussing on countries that required only minor alterations to the car to meet local regulations, and later on countries requiring substantial modifications.

Between 1985 and 2005, PROTON launched ten new models and their variants.

Prime Minister Dato' Seri Dr Mahathir Mohamad (right) buys his PROTON Saga from EON Chairman Tan Sri Jamil Mohammed Jan in September 1985.

PROTON City at Tanjung Malim, Perak is Malaysia's first auto city. Built on a 518-hectare site, the plant is five times larger than PROTON's other plant in Shah Alam and can produce one million cars a year.

Machines at work in PROTON's bodyshop.

In October 1992, Perusahaan Otomobil Kedua Sdn Bhd (PERODUA), a joint venture between several Malaysian companies and Daihatsu of Japan, was established as the second national car company. In July 1994, it launched the Kancil, a model designed to meet popular demand for a compact, and economical car. The third national car company, Inokom Corporation Bhd, is a manufacturer of light commercial vehicles, including vans, Inokom Atos and Inokom Matrix. It is a joint venture with Hyundai of South Korea and Renault (SA) and was incorporated in 1992. In 1995, Malaysia's first sports car was launched; the Bufori, a joint venture with an Australian company, and in 1996, the Delfino, a two-seater sports car designed by a Malaysian, was unveiled in Langkawi. The fourth national car company, Naza, another joint venture with the South Korean company Kia, was established in 1996. Motosikal Dan Enjin Nasional Sdn Bhd (MODENAS), a joint venture with Kawasaki Heavy Industries, produces Malaysia's motorcycle, the Kriss, a 4-stroke, 110cc engine model launched in November 1996.

Apart from the manufacture of passenger cars and motorcycles, the automotive industry produces heavy commercial vehicles, namely, passenger buses, luxury coaches, four-wheel drive vehicles and trucks. Of these, the Malaysian truck, the Perkasa, and Malaysian buses, the Karisma and Dominan, are produced by Malaysian Truck and Bus Sdn Bhd, a joint venture with Isuzu Motors Asia Ltd.

The future

As of 2006, PROTON and PERODUA jointly control about 70 per cent of Malaysia's car market

Heavy traffic in Kuala Lumpur. In 2005, there were 537,900 new cars and 422,255 new motorcycles registered in Malaysia.

but face increasing pressure from Japanese and Korean car makers as the market liberalizes with the full implementation of the Asean Free Trade Area (AFTA) agreement. On 1 January 2005, the AFTA Common Effective Preferential Tariff (CEPT) Agreement went into effect, reducing import duties on completely-built-up cars (CBU) to 20 per cent while completely-knocked-down (CKD) components became duty free.

In 2006, about 70 per cent of cars sold are locally manufactured. The remaining 30 per cent are foreign cars imported through the issuance of Approved Permits (APs), as approved and licensed by the Ministry of International Trade and Industry. In 2006, the government released the National Automotive Policy which aims to make Malaysia a regional automotive manufacturing hub.

Parts and components

An important spin-off of the nation's car projects is the development of a network of local parts and components suppliers. In the 1990s, in order to increase Bumiputera participation and reduce costs, PROTON stepped up its localization and Vendor Development programmes under the Local Material Content Policy.

When PROTON launched its operations in 1985, local vendors including PROTON itself supplied only 228 out of a total of some 5000 parts; the rest were imported from Japan. By 1994, the number of locally produced parts and components had increased to 3444, raising the percentage of local material content in PROTON cars to 80 per cent. During the same period, the number of vendors rose from 17 to 134. Malaysian-made parts and components were also exported. By 2000, exports amounted to RM1042.1 million.

Nevertheless, the net local content in each of the component parts produced remains low; much of the raw materials and sub-components are still imported.

To encourage greater use of local raw materials in industries that support the automotive industry, the government provides incentives such as investment tax allowances and funds to facilitate research and development. In 2006, to support the six automotive manufacturers, nine automotive assemblers, one motorcycle producer, and nine motorcycle assemblers, there were 590 and 170 automotive and motorcycle components and parts manufacturers respectively.

Worker examining spare parts at Honda's automotive factory in Melaka.

Motorcycle market share (2004)

Total units sold: 368,333

- Honda — 40%
- MODENAS — 26%
- Yamaha — 17%
- Suzuki — 13%
- Others — 4%

Source: Motorcycle Association

Involving an investment of RM100 million, the MODENAS plant in Gurun, Kedah was completed in 1996.

Objectives of the National Automotive Policy, 2006

1. Government support and incentives based on sustainable economic contribution.

2. Improve scale via rationalization to enhance competitiveness.

3. Promote strategic linkages with international partners.

4. Becoming a regional hub focusing on niche areas and complementary activities.

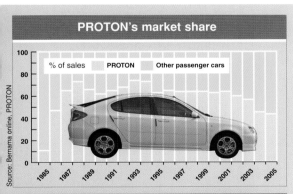
PROTON's market share

% of sales — PROTON — Other passenger cars

Source: Bernama online, PROTON

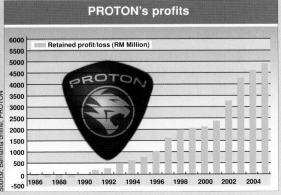
PROTON's profits

Retained profit/loss (RM Million)

Source: Bernama online, PROTON

The construction industry

The construction sector has been a driving force in the Malaysian economy, and in the process has transformed the country's physical landscape. Government support has been strong, not only through the execution of its own construction work, but also through incentives, initiatives and the establishment of a conducive legal framework.

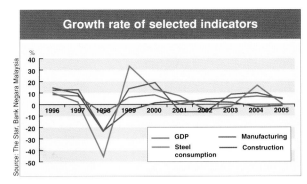

Source: The Star, Bank Negara Malaysia

Growth rate of selected indicators

- GDP
- Steel consumption
- Manufacturing
- Construction

Foreign workers at a construction site in Kuala Lumpur, 2005.

The Electrified Double Track Project between Rawang and Ipoh involves the construction of 179 kilometres of new track and the addition of new stations, bridges and railway technology. It is expected to be completed in 2007.

Nation-building

The physical aspect of nation-building is shaped by the construction and property development sector which links contractors, developers, cement, steel and other building materials suppliers and professionals such as architects and engineers. Other related parties include financial institutions, property buyers and various end-users.

The construction industry has generally mirrored trends in the economy and in society. Population growth led to a demand for residential buildings. The national car project not only required assembly plants, but also led to public transport construction projects when high vehicle usage caused urban congestion. The discovery of petroleum led to downstream activities requiring petrochemical plants. Other factors that have affected the construction industry include global economic trends, fiscal policy and interest rates and government rulings on foreign labour.

Brief history

As the west coast of Peninsular Malaysia had a sizable population, substantial economic activity, abundant natural resources and suitable topography, construction activity was concentrated there in the post-Independence years. Pioneer projects included the Merdeka Stadium (1957), the Klang Gates Dam and water supply scheme (1958) and the first RM125-million Cameron Highlands hydroelectric power scheme.

In the 1960s and 1970s, notable projects were the 18-storey Parliament House (1963), the RM50 million Subang International Airport (1965) and urban renewal projects such as the Komtar building in Penang (1978) which at 65 storeys high was the tallest building in Malaysia at that time. The early 1980s saw phenomenal growth in the construction industry with the influx of foreign contractors. New construction technology and management techniques were introduced, and foreign contractors were invited to implement the construction of the Penang Bridge, the Dayabumi complex, the North–South Expressway, the Petronas Twin Towers and the Kuala Lumpur International Airport.

The 1980s and 1990s saw the completion of those 'mega' projects. Then came the Seventh Malaysia Plan (1996–2000) which aimed to make all government ministries and agencies IT enabled. That spurred the development of the Multimedia Super Corridor (see 'The Multimedia Super Corridor'). The construction sector grew at an average rate of 7.2 per cent during the 1990s, fuelled mainly by the 'mega' projects as well as the development of infrastructure to support the growing economy. A highway linking Bukit Kayu Hitam in Kedah all the way to Johor Bahru was completed, and public transport systems such as the Light Rail Transit (LRT), the Monorail, the Commuter Railway and the Express Rail Link (ERL) were implemented (see 'Roads and railways').

By 2005, the sector's growth trend had abated because of the completion of the 'mega' projects, fewer infrastructure projects and lower government spending on construction projects in general.

Labour and skills

Foreigners comprised 70 per cent of the 769,300 construction workers in 2001. To improve the productivity and quality of local construction workers, the Construction Industry Development Board (CIDB) has made training its biggest single function. With government support, CIDB

Legislation affecting construction

Environmental Quality Act 1974
Environmental Impact Assessment (EIA) reports are required for many construction projects including developments covering an area of 50 hectares or more, airports, airstrip development in state and national parks, dams and man-made lakes of 200 hectares or more, expressways, highways and new townships. Each EIA must reasonably predict environmental impact and propose mitigating measures.

Town and Country Planning Act 1976
By virtue of this Act, Malaysia's 145 local authorities control all land development within their jurisdiction.

Other legislation
The Street, Drainage and Building Act 1971, the Uniform Building By-Laws 1974, the Factories and Machinery Act 1967 and the Occupational Safety and Health Act 1994 ensure that activities meet standards of safety, health and comfort for the public and for workers. Under the Factories and Machinery Act 1967 and the Factories and Machinery (Building Operations and Works of Engineering Construction) (Safety) Regulations 1986, an employer must designate a competent person to supervise work on six specific tasks: concrete works, safety nets, scaffolds, demolition works, piling works and blasting and use of explosives.

Department of Occupational Safety and Health officers inspecting a construction site in Kuala Lumpur.

The Pekeliling flats in Kuala Lumpur, c. 1966. This was the first development to use Industrialized Building Systems. The flats are in the process of being demolished in 2006.

has invested resources to establish six regional training centres called Malaysian Construction Academies (Akademi Binaan Malaysia or ABM).

Globalization and integration

While trade liberalization provides opportunities, local construction companies currently dependent on the local market will have to compete with foreign contractors in delivering products and services that conform to international standards. The global trend of integration of different sectors of the construction industry has led to the popularity of 'design and build and build-operate-transfer' contracts.

Malaysian construction companies have ventured to India and the United Arab Emirates and, likewise, foreign contractors have made inroads into the local scene. The market share of foreign contractors increased from 4.2 per cent in 2001 to 7.6 per cent in 2004, translating to an increase in contract value from RM2.1 billion to RM7.6 billion respectively. This can be partly attributed to the shift to higher value-added construction projects, particularly in the energy and oil and gas industries.

The 2005 Budget encouraged the use of Industrialized Building Systems (IBS) by giving levy exemptions for housing projects with at least 50 per cent IBS usage. IBS, which involves prefabricated products that are transported to construction sites and erected, has been identified as a viable long-term solution to reduce the over-dependence on foreign labour and improve the overall quality of the construction industry.

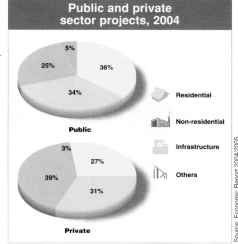

Public and private sector projects, 2004

Public: 36%, 34%, 25%, 5%

Private: 27%, 31%, 39%, 3%

Residential · Non-residential · Infrastructure · Others

Source: Economic Report 2004/2005

Notable construction projects

1. The 13.5-kilometre Penang Bridge, connecting Penang island to the mainland, was completed in 1985.

2. The Petronas Twin Towers, completed in 1996, cost RM1.8 billion and stand at 452 metres. The towers are joined at the 41st and 42nd floors by a 58.4-metre, 750-tonne sky bridge. It was the world's tallest building from 1996 to 2004.

3. The Sepang Formula 1 Circuit is 5.543 kilometres long and the track features 15 turns and eight straights with access speeds of more than 300 kilometres per hour. It was completed in 1999.

4. When completed in 1984, the 35-storey Dayabumi complex was the largest turnkey project and the first steel frame building in Malaysia.

5. The RM4.5-million Klang Gates Dam and water supply scheme was the largest such project when it opened in 1958.

Key organizations

Various ministries, departments, district offices and state and local authorities regulate and promote the construction sector. The government executes its construction work by awarding contracts through government procurement procedures. Contractors are registered and classified according to financial capability, number of professionals and staff employed and ownership of construction plants and equipment.

The Public Works Department (Jabatan Kerja Raya, or JKR), the foremost government department in terms of national infrastructure, has been in existence since 1872.

The Construction Industry Development Board (CIDB), whose function is to act as 'custodian' of the construction industry, was formed in 1994.

The Master Builders Association Malaysia (MBAM) is the umbrella organization representing and promoting the construction industry.

The Building Industry Presidents' Council (BIPC) serves as a platform for trade associations and professional bodies involved in the building and construction industry to deliberate on pertinent issues facing the industry and collectively identify and formulate action for the betterment of the industry. Other bodies include the Malaysian Institute of Architects (Pertubuhan Akitek Malaysia, or PAM) and the Housing Developers' Association (renamed REHDA in 2000) (see 'Housing').

JKR

CIDB MALAYSIA

MBAM celebrated its 50th anniversary in 2004.

Small and medium enterprises

Malaysia adopted the Japanese model of vertical integration that encouraged the formation of small and medium enterprises (SMEs) in order to further the objectives of the New Economic Policy for the benefit of all races. The government has formed various agencies to assist SMEs.

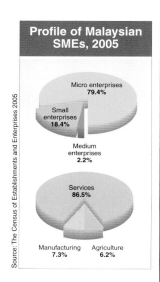

Profile of Malaysian SMEs, 2005

Micro enterprises 79.4%
Small enterprises 18.4%
Medium enterprises 2.2%

Services 86.5%
Manufacturing 7.3%
Agriculture 6.2%

Source: The Census of Establishments and Enterprises 2005

Workers making mooncakes at a factory in Kuala Lumpur. In 2005, there were 33,113 SMEs in the manufacturing sector, accounting for 29 per cent of manufacturing output, 31 per cent of value added and 44 per cent of employment.

Characteristics of SMEs

Small- and medium-scale enterprises (SMEs) or industries, by their very nature, lack the industrial might of larger firms, and can therefore be a vulnerable component in a country's industrial structure. Many SMEs are still run as traditional, family businesses catering to narrow market segments. In terms of business processes, SMEs are often not as advanced as large enterprises; nor do they necessarily enjoy the ease of access to funds, technical expertise or human resources.

However, SMEs, as a result of their size, are able to respond quickly to changing circumstances. As supporting industries, SMEs also play a critical role in a cluster-based industrial strategy as outlined in the Second Industrial Master Plan (see 'Industrial policies and plans'). SMEs are also effective vehicles for achieving policy objectives pertaining to employment, income distribution and regional development.

According to the SME Annual Report 2005, 99.2 per cent (or 518,996) of the business establishments in Malaysia were SMEs. The majority of SMEs were in the services sector, mainly in the retail, restaurant, wholesale, transportation and communication and professional services industries. Although only 7.3 per cent of SMEs were in manufacturing, SMEs comprised 89.3 per cent of the total number of companies in the manufacturing sector in 2005. These SMEs were primarily concentrated in the food and beverage, textiles and apparel and metal and mineral products industries.

Promotion of SMEs

Government promotion of SMEs began after the adoption of the New Economic Policy in 1971, when the Second Malaysia Plan (1971–75) highlighted the potential of SMEs in industrialization. An Advisory Council on Consultancy and Advisory Services for Small Scale Industries and Businesses was established in 1972 to coordinate the services provided by the different agencies. In the early 1980s, a Small Enterprises Division was created in the then Ministry of Trade and Industry. Today, SME development is led by the Small and Medium Scale Industries Development Corporation (SMIDEC). Through the decades, SME initiatives have been

Brochures of two SME conferences held in 2005. The government has identified SMEs as the engine of growth for the economy.

Bank Negara special funds for SMEs, 2005

Fund for Small and Medium Industries
RM4.75 billion

New Entrepreneurs Fund
RM2.35 billion

Fund for Food
RM1.3 billion

Rehabilitation Fund for Small Businesses
RM200 million

Bumiputera Entrepreneurs Project Fund
RM300 million

Source: Bank Negara Annual Report 2005

implemented largely in tandem with the prevailing policy objectives of industrialization. SMEs have thus at various times been developed as a means of achieving greater participation of the Bumiputera Commercial and Industrial Community in the economy (see 'New Economic Policy: 1971–1990').

Following the example of successful industrialized countries in Asia, the government has actively promoted the development of SMEs in order to upgrade and integrate them into the mainstream of the industrial sector. Programmes and institutions have been designed to address the challenges confronting these enterprises.

Global markets require that SMEs be more competitive. In an effort to further strengthen the SMEs, several programmes were implemented, including the Industrial Linkage Programme, Global Supplier Programme, Vendor Development Programme, as well as technology development and acquisition, skills development and upgrading, market development, infrastructure development and financial support.

Financial assistance

The banking system is the major provider of funds to the SMEs, approving RM35.8 billion in new loans to over 85,000 SME accounts in 2005. However, there are other alternative sources of financing for SMEs, including development financial institutions and various special funds established by the government.

Among the development financial institutions are Majlis Amanah Rakyat (MARA), Bank Pembangunan Malaysia Berhad, Bank Kerjasama Rakyat Malaysia, Malaysian Industrial Development Finance (MIDF), Bank Pertanian Malaysia and the Credit Guarantee Corporation. In 2005, the development financial institutions authorized RM2.3 billion in loans to 5,223 SMEs.

Under the Promotion of Investment Act 1986, a variety of incentives were aimed at encouraging SME development. These promote stronger linkages between large-scale industries and SMEs, stimulate research and development, and reward manufacturers of superior products.

The Industrial Technical Assistance Fund (ITAF) was established by the government in 1990 to provide grants to SMEs. It offers matching grants for planning and development, product and process improvement and market development. There are also soft loan schemes for modernization and automation and for quality enhancement.

In 2003, Bank Negara Malaysia established the SME Special Unit to assist viable SMEs in obtaining financing. In 2005, the SME Bank was formed. A wholly-owned subsidiary of Bank Pembangunan Malaysia Berhad, the SME Bank provides both financial and non-financial assistance to SMEs.

Technical assistance, training and marketing and infrastructure

Since the late 1970s, the National Productivity Centre (NPC), MARA, the then Ministry of Culture, Youth and Sports, the Malaysian Entrepreneur Development Centre (MEDEC) and the National Entrepreneur Research Development Association (NERDA) have all conducted training programmes for SMEs.

SME Bank's head office in Kuala Lumpur.

To help SMEs promote their products in export markets in the 1980s, links between SMEs and research agencies, such as Malaysian Agricultural Research and Development Institute (MARDI), were established to provide technical and advisory services and up-to-date market information as well as to ensure product quality and market competitiveness. SMIDEC was formed in 1996 and took over the role of providing technical assistance, training and marketing services.

The government announced in the 2006 Budget that the role of the Export-Import Bank of Malaysia (EXIM) was to be strengthened to encourage SMEs to venture abroad and expand their exports of goods and services.

SMIDEC's Infrastructure Development Programme assists SMEs in purchasing or leasing affordable factories, and facilitates accessibility to state assistance. By 2005, eight SME industrial estates had been developed.

National SME Development Council

SMEs have been significant contributors to the economy and have demonstrated great growth potential. Thus, in 2004, Bank Negara Malaysia initiated the establishment of the National SME Development Council, chaired by the Prime Minister. The Council is the highest policy-making body responsible for charting the direction and strategies for the future development of SMEs. In December 2005, the Council endorsed the National SME Development Blueprint for 2006, a one-year action plan that includes a total of 245 programmes involving a financial commitment of RM3.9 billion to develop SMEs.

Key organizations in SME development

Small and Medium Scale Industries Development Corporation (SMIDEC)

Recognizing the need for a specialized agency to promote the development of SMEs, the government established SMIDEC in 1996. SMIDEC develops SMEs in the manufacturing sector through the provision of advisory services, fiscal and financial assistance, infrastructure, market access and other support programmes.

Projects undertaken to assist SMEs include human resource development, promotional activities, and participation in relevant exhibitions and seminars at home and abroad. As a coordinating agent, SMIDEC promotes cooperation among SMEs by arranging business amalgamations, technical collaboration, the procurement of common equipment, and the establishment of funds. It also acts as a centre for all SME-related information and referrals, and works with other agencies on programmes for the development of SMEs. Recognizing that many SMEs are involved in the services sector, SMIDEC is extending its projects to involve such SMEs.

The variety of financial assistance offered by SMIDEC to SMEs.

Brochures of the PROSPER and SME schemes offered by PUNB.

Perbadanan Usahawan Nasional Berhad (PUNB or National Entrepreneur Corporation)

Wholly-owned by Yayasan Pelaburan Bumiputra (Bumiputra Investment Foundation), PUNB was established in 1991 to increase the number of Bumiputera entrepreneurs in accordance with the government's aim to develop a dynamic, resilient and progressive Bumiputera Commercial and Industrial Community (BCIC).

PUNB focuses on providing integrated support to Bumiputera entrepreneurs. Its SME Entepreneurial Development Package for instance, offers funding, corporate development and monitoring support and entrepreneur development and training.

PROSPER, the acronym for Projek Usahawan Bumiputera dalam Bidang Peruncitan or Project for Bumiputera Entrepreneurs in the Retail Sector is a special scheme introduced in 2000 to increase Bumiputera participation and involvement in the retail sector. Again, financial and non-financial assistance is offered. PUNB has also initiated franchise businesses and concept shop programmes.

Malaysian Industrial Development Finance Berhad (MIDF)

MIDF was incorporated in 1960 to promote the development of the manufacturing industry in Malaysia through the provision of medium and long-term loans. In 1992, MIDF became the first and only development finance institution in the country to be listed on the Kuala Lumpur Stock Exchange.

Malaysian Industrial Estates Limited (MIEL)

A wholly-owned subsidiary of MIDF, MIEL was established in 1964 to develop SMEs by providing comprehensive and integrated industrial estates.

Credit Guarantee Corporation (CGC)

CGC was established in 1972 with Bank Negara Malaysia and all the commercial banks as its shareholders. As SMEs usually lack ready access to affordable institutional finance, CGC steps in and provides guarantees in support of bank loans. In this manner, CGC is deemed a 'credit enhancer' of SMEs. CGC is now classified as a development financial institution.

Visitors at the SME 2003 Expo at the Putra World Trade Centre, Kuala Lumpur.

The Enterprise 50 Awards: Top Glove Sdn Bhd

Winner of SMIDEC's Enterprise 50 award for eight consecutive years since 1998, Top Glove is the archetype of a company that has benefited from SMIDEC's SME assistance programmes. Beginning with just one factory in 1991, in 2005 it had 11 factories, and its gloves are exported to 160 countries worldwide. Since early 2004, it has been the world's largest natural rubber glove manufacturer.

ABOVE: Workers checking gloves for defects prior to packing.

LEFT: The Top Glove headquarters in Klang, Selangor.

Hi-tech industrialization

As Malaysia entered into a new phase of industrial development under the Sixth Malaysia Plan (1991–95), it began to emphasize the growth of export-oriented, high value-added, high-technology industries by utilizing domestic research and development. Several important programmes and policies have been implemented to propel Malaysia to the forefront of modern growth, industrialization, information and communication technology (ICT) and biotechnology.

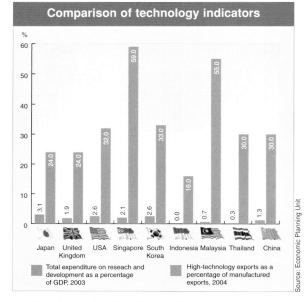

Comparison of technology indicators

	Japan	United Kingdom	USA	Singapore	South Korea	Indonesia	Malaysia	Thailand	China
Total expenditure on research and development as a percentage of GDP, 2003	3.1	1.9	2.6	2.1	2.6	0.0	0.7	0.3	1.3
High-technology exports as a percentage of manufactured exports, 2004	24.0	24.0	32.0	59.0	33.0	16.0	55.0	30.0	30.0

Source: Economic Planning Unit

Top: Workers assembling semiconductors at STATS ChipPAC's facility in Kuala Lumpur.

Above: MIMOS CEO Tengku Mohd Azzman Shariffadeen (left) and Vice President Mohamad Rafee bin Yusoff displaying a wafer and the first locally developed Pesona microchip in 2002.

Hi-tech growth industries

Under the Ninth Malaysia Plan (2006– 10), five industries will be targeted for growth and development:

1. Biotechnology

2. ICT
- Semiconductors and microelectronics
- Internet Protocol version 6, grid computing and language engineering
- Information security

3. Advanced materials

4. Advanced manufacturing

5. Nanotechnology

Building technological capability

Early attempts at industrial promotion did not emphasize the development of domestic technological capability. It was only in 1975, with the introduction of the Industrial Coordination Act, that a framework was established for a more orderly development of industry and, along with it, technological capability. In the same year, the government began formalizing technology transfer agreements through the Technology Transfer Unit, part of the Ministry of Trade and Industry (now the Ministry of International Trade and Industry).

Despite these initiatives, domestic technological capability developed slowly. A major factor was the country's dependence on foreign direct investment, and the fact that multinational corporations obtained many of their technological innovations from abroad. Most local manufacturing firms continued to engage in simple manufacturing activities for the domestic market.

In the early 1980s, the government sought to stimulate the economy through investment in heavy industries with the long-term objective of broadening the industrial base and strengthening indigenous technological capabilities (see 'Heavy industry'). Thus, a more proactive policy was adopted for building up local technological capabilities through tie-ups with foreign firms.

Wafers manufactured by Malaysian Institute of Microelectronic Systems Semiconductor Sdn Bhd (MIMOS).

Aside from heavy industry, however, efforts to build up domestic technological capability continued to face challenges. Well into the 1990s, foreign-owned firms dominated the technology-intensive and scientific manufacturing sub-sectors.

In 1992, the Malaysian Technology Development Corporation (MTDC) was incorporated as a government-industry joint venture. By providing venture capital, it aimed to commercialize research results of universities and research institutions, identify and transfer emerging and strategic technologies for adoption by industries and encourage the growth of technology-based enterprises.

The Academy of Sciences was established in 1995 in Kuala Lumpur to provide advice to the government on matters related to science,

engineering and technology, and assist in upgrading the technological capability and competency of local industries.

In 2004, foreign investment in the electrical and electronics sub-sector amounted to RM6.8 billion (79.1 per cent of the total) while domestic investment totalled RM1.8 billion (20.9 per cent).

Hi-tech industrialization

The tight labour market of the 1990s further highlighted the urgent need for the strengthening of the nation's technological base. It became clear that future growth must come from increased efficiency in the utilization of natural and human resources, higher technology, and an effective combination of resources with technology.

Malaysia's planned evolution towards technological self-sufficiency was based on two approaches: first, improving the competitiveness of all industries through the incorporation of higher levels of technology and research and development in management and production processes; and second, promoting the growth of specific industries directly involved in the design and manufacture of high technology products.

A Malaysia Microelectronic Solutions Sdn Bhd (MY-MS) engineer and wafer specialist at work. In 2005, national gross expenditure on research and development in the science and technology sector amounted to RM4.3 billion.

Technicians at work at a semiconductor plant in Kuala Lumpur.

Advanced electronics

Despite its long presence in Malaysia, and its economic importance in terms of export earnings (see 'Manufacturing'), the electronics industry has been dominated by foreign multinational corporations. As electronics form the base for many high technology processes and products, the domestic electronics industry is striving to be more capital- and technology-intensive, to upgrade its technology and to focus on enhancing its capacity in the areas of microelectronics, wafer fabrication, automated manufacturing and computer-aided design and engineering. According to the United Nations Conference on Trade and Development (UNCTAD), Malaysia was the second largest exporter of semiconductor devices among developing countries in 2004.

Information technology (IT)

The establishment of the National Information Technology Council (NITC) marked the beginning of more systematic planning for IT development at the national level (see 'Towards a knowledge economy'). In formulating the framework for national IT planning and development, the NITC is guided by the following goals: bringing order to national IT planning and management, creating a shared national vision of IT, generating the necessary human resources, accelerating the development of IT infrastructure and initiating and facilitating organizational restructuring.

Biotechnology

Biotechnological processes have long been used in Malaysia. In the cultivation of rubber, oil palm, sago, rattan, bamboo, fruit and vegetables, biotechnology has been, and continues to be, used to increase yields and produce crop strains that are more resistant to pests and diseases. In the pharmaceutical industry, biotechnology is used to develop and improve immunological and medical products. In animal husbandry, cattle that not only produce more milk and meat, but also are more resistant to diseases, have been developed. And in the food and beverage industry, biotechnology is used in industrial fermentation and other processes.

Through the National Biotechnology Programme, the government has implemented projects to upgrade the biotechnological capability of the country. These include projects in molecular biology, genetic engineering, industrial and environmental biotechnology and medical biotechnology. In the early 1990s, the National Biotechnology Centre was established to coordinate all activities relating to biotechnology and to establish various funds devoted to training in this field. The private sector is being encouraged to undertake research and development in biotechnology on a larger scale.

In 2002, three research and development centres were set up: the Institute for Genomics and Molecular Biology, the Institute for Pharmaceuticals and Natraceuticals and the Institute of Agricultural Biotechnology. All three are housed in BioValley, which is part of the Multimedia Super Corridor. In 2005, the National Biotechnology Policy was launched. It stated key measures to facilitate the development of this sector.

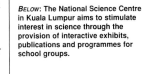

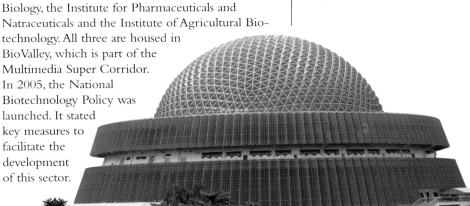

Top: Prime Minister Dato' Seri Dr Mahathir Mohamad (far left) admiring students' biotechnology projects at BioMalaysia 2002.

Above: Researcher at a Kumpulan Guthrie Group laboratory. Agricultural biotechnology holds vast potential for biotechnology applications in Malaysia.

Below: The National Science Centre in Kuala Lumpur aims to stimulate interest in science through the provision of interactive exhibits, publications and programmes for school groups.

Towards technological self-sufficiency

Malaysia has adopted comprehensive technology development plans, such as the Action Plan for Industrial Technology Development, launched in 1990. This plan promoted technological deepening in industries classified as 'strategic'. The following measures were carried out:

- The Human Resource Development Fund (HRDF) was introduced in 1993 to increase and facilitate employer-initiated training and retraining of employees. Firms with 50 or more employees were obliged to contribute a levy amounting to one per cent of their payroll to the fund, but could later reclaim the contributions as approved training expenses for tax relief purposes.
- The Malaysia Industry-Government Group of High Technology (MIGHT) and the Malaysian Technology Development Corporation (MTDC), set up between 1992 and 1993, strengthened government-business relationships and stimulated technological upgrading in private firms.
- The Industry-Government Coordination Councils, originally launched in the mid-1980s, became more active in the formulation of technology-related policies.
- Special vendor-development programmes designed to support small- and medium-scale firms—some of which were funded by the Industrial Technical Assistance Fund (ITAF)—were revamped.
- The Standards and Industrial Research Institute of Malaysia (SIRIM) Berhad successfully introduced and managed the implementation of the ISO 9000 series.
- Major technology-based institutions such as Syarikat Telekom Malaysia Berhad, Tenaga Nasional Berhad, and the Malaysian Institute of Microelectronics System (MIMOS) were corporatized in order to enhance their role in servicing firms and spawning technology.

The National Biotechnology Policy

The National Biotechnology Policy was launched in April 2005. Phase one (2005–10), 'capacity building', will see the establishment of advisory and implementation councils, education and training of knowledge workers, business development and industry creation in agricultural biotech,

healthcare biotech, industrial biotech and bio-informatics.

Phase two (2011–15), 'creating business out of science', involves developing expertise in the discovery and development of new drugs derived from natural resources, while the final phase (2016–20) will focus on taking Malaysian companies global.

The main thrusts of the policy are to provide tax breaks to the biotechnology sector to attract private investment, and setting up Malaysia Biotech Corporation (MBC), a dedicated professional one-stop agency to coordinate biotech initiatives from all relevant government ministries.

Prime Minister Dato' Seri Abdullah Ahmad Badawi (right) and Minister of Science, Technology and Innovation Dato' Dr Jamaluddin bin Dato' Mohd Jarjis at the launch of the National Biotechnology Policy.

1. Suria KLCC forms part of a 40-hectare development located in Kuala Lumpur. It was awarded the International Real Estate Federation (FIABCI) Prix d'Excellence for the retail category in 2004.

2. Architects discussing and designing plans at a firm in Kuala Lumpur. Between 2001–05, the number of registered professionals rose by 24.4 per cent.

3. Doctors in action at the Kuala Lumpur General Hospital.

4. Vegetable seller at the Kota Bharu market in Kelantan. Wholesale and retail trade, along with hotels and restaurants, accounted for 14.7 per cent of GDP in 2005.

5. Commemorative stamp celebrating the career of P. Ramlee, the renowned actor, director, musician and screenwriter who died in 1973.

6. Checkout counter at Tesco. The British chain of hypermarkets opened its first store in Malaysia in 2002.

7. Pangkor Laut Resort, on Pangkor Laut Island, was voted Number one in the World by *Condé Nast Traveller* UK, 2003. Owned by YTL Corporation, there are 148 Malaysian-style luxury villas in the main resort and eight estates in a nearby cove.

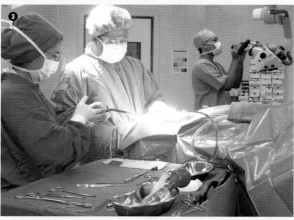

THE SERVICES SECTOR

The services or tertiary sector can be divided into three categories which coordinate the activities of the primary (agriculture and mining) and secondary (manufacturing and construction) sectors. The services sector ensures that goods produced by each of the other sectors reach consumers.

The first category, producer or intermediate services, comprises distribution (transport, storage and communications) and production activities (insurance, real estate, finance, professional and business services). Transport (roads, air, rail and sea) includes traditional services whereas communication (telecommunications, post and information) encompasses newer services.

The second category, public sector services, encapsulates activities such as public administration and utilities. This involves the provision of health, education, defence and security as well as gas, water and electricity.

The third category is final services; this includes hotels, restaurants and the wholesale and retail trade.

Since the late 1960s, the services sector has been the single largest contributor to the country's GDP. In 2005, this sector formed 58.1 per cent of GDP, and 51.0 per cent of the total work force was engaged in the provision of services. Growth of 5.8 per cent was recorded within this sector in 2005, driven by higher consumer spending amidst rising disposable incomes, higher tourist arrivals and increased trade-related activities. Areas of new growth include private education and private healthcare services (see 'Health and education'), Islamic financial services (see 'Islamic financial services'), shared services and outsourcing, and supply chain management, which includes the development of operational headquarters, regional distribution centres, international procurement centres and IT services. In the 2006 Budget, it was announced that a Health Tourism Unit will be established under the Ministry of Health to improve the quality of health services and to attract more foreigners to seek private health services here.

As the services sector contains a varied number of sub-sectors which fall under the purview of various ministries and agencies, the Malaysian Industrial Development Authority (MIDA) has been given the responsibility for coordinating the non-financial services sectors in addition to the manufacturing sectors. There is still great potential to expand the services sector to the level in developed countries where it typically accounts for more than 70 per cent of the GDP.

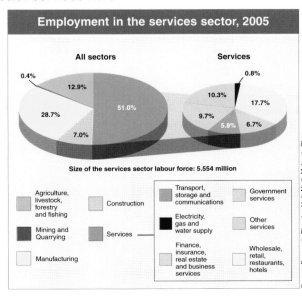

Employment in the services sector, 2005

All sectors

0.4%
12.9%
28.7%
51.0%
7.0%

Services

0.8%
10.3%
17.7%
9.7%
5.8%
6.7%

Size of the services sector labour force: 5.554 million

- Agriculture, livestock, forestry and fishing
- Mining and Quarrying
- Manufacturing
- Construction
- Services
- Transport, storage and communications
- Electricity, gas and water supply
- Finance, insurance, real estate and business services
- Government services
- Other services
- Wholesale, retail, restaurants, hotels

Source: Economic Planning Unit, Ninth Malaysia Plan

Professional services

The professional services sub-sector encompasses occupations which are characterized by technical expertise and specialized knowledge. In 1957, professionals were mainly teachers and nurses; by the 1970s, a far more diverse range of occupations was represented, and since then the number of professionals has increased dramatically. Some of the most highly paid individuals in the economy are professionals. Remuneration for some professions is markedly higher in the private sector than in the public sector.

Attorney General of Malaysia Tan Sri Abdul Gani Patail (centre) greeting Sarawak Attorney General Datuk J.C. Fong before addressing the courthouse to mark the start of the legal year in Sarawak, 2005.

Professional services, 2005	
Occupation	Number registered
Engineers	49,201
Professional engineers	11,523
Accountants	21,589
Professional accountants	15,402
Doctors	15,574
Lawyers	11,750
Architects	3001
Professional architects	1653
Dentists	2608
Surveyors	4920
Professional surveyors	2065
Veterinary surgeons	1339

Source: Ninth Malaysia Plan

Categories of professional services

Government statistical records group all professional services under the single category of 'professional and technical services'. Professional services contribute significantly to the country's pool of human capital and are among the highest-paid occupations in the economy.

Growth

In 1957, out of the 2.1 million economically active persons in Peninsular Malaysia, only 3.1 per cent were professional, technical and related workers; the majority of these individuals were school teachers and nurses.

From 1970 onwards, however, there was a steady rise in the proportion of the workforce who were professionals, reaching 9.4 per cent in 1995. In addition to school teachers and nurses, the size of professions such as doctors and lawyers grew.

This growth of the service establishments within each professional group was a result of market forces and government policies. In 1986, for example, doctors led the field with 1399 establishments. This prevalence of the medical profession was partly attributable to the

government's policy of making professional medical services more accessible to the public in all regions of the country.

In the late 1990s, ICT professionals began playing an increasingly important role in the emerging knowledge economy (see 'Towards a knowledge economy'). As the demand for knowledge workers grows, so will the requirements for the education and training institutions that produce them. Given the high premium placed on being a professional, there is a high demand for places in professional courses at local tertiary institutions.

Over the course of the Second Outline Perspective Plan (1991–2000), the fastest growing occupational category was the professionals, followed by the technical, managerial and administrative categories.

The Third Outline Perspective Plan (2001–10) has projected a requirement of 201,615 engineers, 470,810 engineering assistants, 45,878 medical and health personnel, 147,405 allied health professionals, and 369,756 school teachers by the year 2010.

Stopping the brain drain

On 1 January 2001, the Malaysian government sought to reverse the brain drain by offering highly skilled, expatriate professionals incentives to return. This programme was aimed at filling a shortage of skilled workers, especially in technology and engineering. Thousands of trained Malaysians work in Singapore, United Kingdom, United State, Australia and elsewhere. The programme offers tax exemption for all assets brought into the country, and as of 2006, each applicant or couple is entitled to bring in two cars tax free, without the requirement of prior ownership for the preceding six months. Non-Malaysian spouses and children receive permanent resident status after six months in Malaysia, and the children are allowed to enter international schools upon their return.

The incentives are targeted at Malaysians with doctorates and other higher qualifications. An earlier programme aimed at enticing scientists to return was abandoned as a result of the Asian financial crisis in 1997–98. Applications for this programme are processed by a special committee under the Ministry of Human Resources.

Accountants

The accounting profession in Malaysia is governed by the Malaysian Institute of Accountants (MIA), which was established under the Accountants Act 1967. Under the act, no one can practise as an accountant unless he or she is registered as a member of the MIA.

The profession consists of groups in public practice, commerce and industry, the public sector and academia, and has recorded substantial growth over the past two decades, having increased from 3234 accountants in 1984 to 20,019 in 2004. The majority (69 per cent) of the profession work in commerce and industry, while 25 per cent serve in public practice and six per cent in the public sector.

An accountant at work.

The role of accountants has expanded from that of being mere bean-counters to that of key advisors and decision makers within organizations.

As globalization, trade liberalization and information and communication technology redefine the rules of how business is conducted, there is a need for the profession to evolve further, particularly in light of the forthcoming opening of the market to foreign players. The merger of small practices into larger conglomerates is one such step.

Lawyers

The legal profession is regulated by the Legal Profession Act 1976. In 2005, there were 11,750 lawyers registered with the Malaysian Bar Council. Of these, 38 per cent were Malays, 37 per cent Chinese and 24 per cent Indians. As of 2005, there were nearly 3000 law firms nationally, two-thirds of which have only one or two partners and sometimes a limited number of assistants. Their focus tends to be on general litigation, conveyancing and general corporate work. It was estimated in 2005 that there were only six firms with more than 50 lawyers, and fewer than 20 firms with 40 to 50 lawyers. The largest law firm had more than 100 lawyers. Larger firms offer a full range of legal services and have specialized departments. While litigation, conveyancing and corporate work remain the mainstay of the legal profession, niche practices in intellectual property and ICT have developed in recent years.

Alternative methods of dispute resolution have also gained importance since the 1990s. The Regional Centre for Arbitration Kuala Lumpur (RCAKL) was established in 1978 to promote arbitration and other methods of dispute resolution such as mediation and conciliation. In 1999, the Bar Council established the Malaysian Mediation Centre.

Doctors

A doctor giving patients a free medical check-up in Penang.

In 1957, Malaysia had 763 doctors and a doctor-population ratio of 1:8229. The shift in the administration of healthcare services from the states to the Federal Government in 1958 made the Ministry of Health the main healthcare provider. Healthcare service centres have also expanded from urban centres to rural areas.

The country's first medical school was established in 1961 at Universiti Malaya. As of 2005, there were eight local universities and three medical colleges offering medical studies as well as specialist courses. In 2005, there were 19,779 doctors and 2013 specialists in the country and the doctor-population ratio stood at 1:1321. In 2005, there were 10,943 doctors in the public sector and 8836 doctors in the private sector.

The practice of medicine is governed by the Medical Act 1971 and the professional code of conduct laid down by the Malaysian Medical Council.

Teachers

A teacher utilizing ICT teaching aids.

The teaching profession has been regulated by the Ministry of Education since the implementation of the Education Ordinance 1957. The Ministry is a policy-making, training and developmental body for teachers. In 2004, the Ministry of Higher Education was established to deal with tertiary education.

Teachers are represented by unions. In 2004, the National Union of the Teaching Profession had 135,000 members, representing 70 per cent of unionized teachers and 48 per cent of all teachers in the Peninsula. It is the only teachers' union in the Peninsula; teachers in Sabah and Sarawak are represented by their own teachers' unions.

The contribution of the teaching profession can be seen in the rise of Malaysia's literacy rate to 95.1 per cent in 2004 from 58 per cent in 1970. The number of teachers has also increased over the years, resulting in an improvement in teacher-student ratios for both primary and secondary levels. In 1990, the teacher-student ratio was 1:23.5 in primary schools and 1:20.3 in secondary schools whilst in 2005, the teacher-student ratio stood at 1:17.2 and 1:16.3 respectively (see 'Health and education').

A Public Works Department architect explaining the model of a disabled-friendly complex.

Architects

The Board of Architects Malaysia (Lembaga Arkitek Malaysia, or LAM) is the statutory body that registers and regulates professional architects, architects and building draughtsmen. LAM is also responsible for enforcing the Architects Act 1967.

The Malaysian Institute of Architects (Pertubuhan Akitek Malaysia, or PAM) is a professional body for architects. Originally established as the Institute of Architects Malaya in 1920, it became the Federation of Malaya Society of Architects in 1948. PAM was registered in 1967 as a society to promote the study and practice of architecture.

Architects have been an integral part of the transformation of Malaysia into a modern society. From the post-Independence buildings and monuments of nationhood to recent 'mega' projects, such as Putrajaya and Cyberjaya, architects have sought to create an environment which reflects the country's culture and development.

The Malaysian Architectural Policy, promulgated by PAM in 1999, provides broad guidelines for architects. In 2002, there were 732 architectural firms which employed 8466 individuals and generated RM698.7 million in revenue.

Engineers overseeing the construction of a hotel in Bandar Utama, Petaling Jaya.

Engineers

The Board of Engineers (BEM) is a statutory body formed in 1972 that regulates the registration of engineers in accordance with the Registration of Engineers Act 1967. In 1974, the BEM had registered 2900 engineers. The Institution of Engineers is the professional body for engineers while the Association of Consulting Engineers Malaysia seeks to promote the advancement of the profession of consulting engineering. In 2004, there were 47,875 engineers of whom 11,857 were professional or registered engineers and 36,018 graduate engineers. Civil engineers formed the largest proportion in both categories, followed by mechanical and electrical engineers.

Over the years, projects undertaken by engineers have increased in size and complexity. Efforts have been made to gain international recognition and accreditation of local engineering degrees with the establishment of the ASEAN Engineer Register, the ASEAN Chartered Professional Engineer and the Washington Accord.

Retail

The formal retail sector, once consisting mainly of family-run stores serving local neighbourhoods, now includes such varied forms as the department store, the supermarket, the shopping complex, the franchise, and the direct-selling company. Establishments are run by both local and foreign retailers. The informal sector—including wet markets, farmers' markets, night markets, stalls, provision shops and pavement shops—further expands the range of shopping opportunities.

Carrefour hypermarket in Johor. An international corporation headquartered in France, Carrefour opened its first hypermarket in Malaysia in 1994. In 2005, there were 81 hypermarkets in Malaysia, 84 per cent of which were foreign-owned.

Retailing over the decades

Retailing is the final stage in the movement of merchandise and services through various distri-bution channels from producer to consumer. Any organization or distributor that sells to a consumer is a retailer.

Retailing in Malaysia has retained its traditional forms while also embracing modern concepts. Thus, one continues to find wet markets, night markets, provision shops and Chinese medical halls alongside department stores and hypermarkets.

Up to the early 1950s, retailers in Malaysia were primarily sole proprietorships or family-managed enterprises. Such stores were designed to meet the requirements of the immediate neighbourhood and offered a limited variety of merchandise. Situated at prominent street corners or in downtown shopping areas, retailing was largely dominated by establishments that are today deemed to be part of the informal sector. Consumers then were less sophisticated and did not consider ambience necessary to their shopping experience.

In the 1960s, the growth of urban centres and a middle-class population led to a corresponding growth in retailing. Central business districts such as Jalan Tuanku Abdul Rahman and Petaling Street in Kuala Lumpur became the focal points for retailing activities. Sole proprietorships which originally sold textiles—Globe Silk Store, Mun Loong and Voon Wah—introduced modern retail concepts like fixed pricing, with attention paid to aspects such as store dressing, ambience and comfort of shoppers.

These single-line specialty stores were soon joined by department stores that offered one-stop shopping for general merchandise. One such department store was Emporium Supermarket Holdings which opened stores in the Klang Valley, Penang and other states. Home-grown chain Metrojaya opened its first department store in 1976.

In the food sector, the family-run provision stores evolved into mini-markets and supermarkets which introduced the self-service and self-selection concept in the late 1970s. The 1970s saw tremendous growth in the retail sector. From an estimated turnover of RM350 million in 1974, the sector grew at an average of 28 per cent per annum to reach over RM4 billion in 1984.

The mid-1980s, however, saw a downturn, with the retail industry experiencing negative growth between 1985 and 1987. The period saw major restructuring taking place, with new players emerging to take over struggling establishments. Approximately 25 retail giants collapsed during this period. New

ABOVE: Shophouses in Kuala Lumpur. The Pre-Independence shophouse had space for retail activities on the ground floor, and living quarters for the shopkeeper and his family on the upper floors.

TOP: Jalan Tuanku Abdul Rahman in Kuala Lumpur, a shopper's haven in its heyday, c.1970.

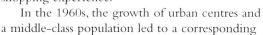

Entrance of Metrojaya, a local department store which carries its own in-house labels as well as international brands, at Mid Valley Megamall in Kuala Lumpur, 2006.

LEFT TO RIGHT: Malay traders at the Pekan Rabu in Alor Star, Kedah, Chinese sundry shops and Indian news vendors compete with modern shopping centres for the consumer dollar. As of 2005, there were 297,000 shop units in Malaysia.

Source: AC Nielsen

Where shoppers spent their money, 2004	
Hypermarkets and large discount stores	45%
Supermarkets	33%
Traditional grocery and mini markets	15%
Traditional grocery	8%
Minimarts	7%
Wet markets/night markets	4%
Others	2%
Chinese medical halls	1%

local entrants included entities such as Parkson Corporation Sdn Bhd (established in 1987), which bought over two ailing chains, Yu Yi and Emporium Holdings.

The 1990s saw new growth in the industry, fuelled by a buoyant economy and the increasing spending power of the population. Foreign retailers like Japan's Isetan and Singapore's CK Tang entered the local market for the first time. This period also saw the emergence of foreign hypermarkets, or very large-scale supermarkets, specializing in bulk selling. These were Makro from Holland, Carrefour from France and Tesco from Britain. The first nationwide Mega Sale Carnival was introduced in 2000 by the Malaysian Retailers Association (MRA) to make shopping an important facet of tourism and to boost the economy. MRA was formed in 1982 with the aim of bringing together all retailers under one umbrella for the advancement of their common interests. To assist local chain retailers in their expansion overseas, the Malaysian Retailer-Chains Association was formed in 1992.

The shopping centre industry

The shopping centre is a major nucleus of economic activity, combining in one physical location businesses such as push-carts, single-line stores, department stores and supermarkets. The management of a shopping centre involves numerous aspects such as space leasing and sales, advertising, promotions and marketing, car park and security management, building maintenance, finance, accounting, administration and public relations.

The first true shopping centre was Ampang Park Shopping Centre in Kuala Lumpur. Built in 1973 at a cost of RM10 million, it had a lettable area of 327,000 sq ft and 242 shoplots.

The first generation shopping centres were located in the city centre and generally had insufficient carparks, a haphazard tenant mix, improper layouts and a lack of shopper amenities. Over the years, shopping centres have improved, and by 2000, there were 160 fourth generation shopping centres with built-up areas of over two million square feet. These shopping centres had multiple anchor tenants and an average of over 400 retailers; they offered a lifestyle concept: shopping, leisure and entertainment under one roof. Location-wise, they were developed as regional suburban centres.

With the proliferation of shopping centres, newer entrants are differentiating themselves by targeting niche markets, such as by specializing in ICT retailers and high fashion. Themed-malls, such as Sunway Pyramid (Egypt), The Mines (Venice) and 1 Utama (rainforest), have been able to tap into the foreign tourist market. The first 'power centre', Ikano Power Centre in Petaling Jaya, where large speciality stores are the anchor tenants, opened in 2004.

By 2010, it is projected that there will be 260 shopping centres with a total gross built up area of 140 million square feet and total value of RM55 billion. Every town with a population in excess of 100,000 will have a shopping centre of 0.5 to 1 million square feet. There will also be a growth of stand alone hypermarket centres with the hypermarket as the main tenant. Hypermarket operators are likely to develop and design buildings for their own use and rent out complementary retail space. This development model is premised on the 'main turnover from retailing, main profit from rental' principle.

Shopping centre indicators, 2005 (Q1)	
Number	200
Total gross built up area	104.5 million sq ft
Value	RM38 billion
Net Lettable Area (NLA)	64.5 million sq ft
Occupancy	80%
Electricity cost per month	RM42.6 million
Water cost per month	RM3.9 million
Manpower cost per month	RM153 million
Total manpower	189,000

Source: Malaysian Association for Shopping and Highrise Complex Management (PPKM)

Programme of the Asian Conference of Shopping Centres 2005 organized by PPKM in Petaling Jaya.

Definition of a shopping centre

According to the Malaysian Association of Shopping Complex and Highrise Management (Persatuan Pengurusan Kompleks Malaysia or PPKM), a shopping centre is a purpose-built commercial development devoted to retailing with supporting facilities.

Key features:
- Total gross retail area exceeds 500,000 sq ft.
- Total number of specialty shop lots exceeds 150.
- Other components may include: residences, offices and commercial space, hospitality, food and beverage outlets, convention or exhibition halls, leisure and entertainment centres.
- A common entrance usually services all the components.
- Urban- or suburban-based.

ABOVE: As of 2006, 1 Utama in Petaling Jaya was the largest shopping centre in Malaysia with a net lettable area of 1.8 million square feet and over 600 retail outlets. It was awarded the 'Shopping Complex of the Year' Platinum Award in the Retail World Excellence Awards 2006–2007.

BELOW LEFT: Mid Valley Megamall in Kuala Lumpur.

BELOW RIGHT: The Venice-themed canal inside the Mines Shopping Centre in Selangor.

Wholesaling and franchising

Traditionally, wholesaling involves the selling of goods in bulk to retailers. Another business concept is franchising, which has become popular in recent years as a system to increase the size of the Bumiputera Commercial and Industrial Community.

Central purchasing or regional procurement offices of non-specialized wholesalers such as Tesco are edging out traditional wholesalers.

Wholesaling, 2004	
	Amount (RM billion)
CONSUMER GOODS:	**54.0**
Non-specialized	
F&B & tobacco	4.5
Household goods	2.4
Others	7.5
Specialized	
F&B & tobacco	18.9
Household goods	20.7
NON-CONSUMER GOODS	**82.8**
TOTAL	**136.8**

Source: Ministry of Domestic Trade and Consumer Affairs

Wholesaling

Wholesaling is a key component of the system that delivers goods from producers to consumers. In particular, the term 'wholesalers' refers to the middlemen between manufacturers and retailers. In Malaysia, wholesalers are generally small family-owned businesses who buy in bulk from importers and local producers. The wholesalers then sell the goods in bulk to retailers. In the late 19th century, most of the wholesalers were Chinese while a small minority were South Indian Muslims (the Moplahs and Marakkayars). These communities continue to dominate the wholesaling business.

The wholesale sector generated sales totalling RM136.8 billion in 2004, of which 40 per cent were consumer goods, and the rest, non-consumer goods. Within the consumer sector, there are two sub-sectors: specialized and non-specialized wholesalers. Non-specialized wholesalers include hypermarkets, supermarkets and mom-and-pop stores, while specialized wholesalers focus on single types of goods like food and beverages, electrical items and textiles.

The distributive trade industry, which is the distribution network of goods to consumers through wholesaling and retailing, is the third-most important component of the economy, contributing 14.9 per cent of the country's GDP in 2004. In the period 1993 to 2001, specialized wholesalers dominated the wholesale sector, both in terms of number of establishments and market share.

The prevalence of wholesaling has decreased over the years. In 2001, some 16,386 wholesale establishments were recorded, 29 per cent fewer than the 22,940 establishments in 1993. Employment in the sector also declined 29 per cent in the same period to 179,540 in 2001. The fall in the number of wholesale establishments is, in part, due to the reduction in the number of smaller retailers. In addition, central purchasing or regional procurement offices at hypermarkets and supermarkets have taken over the role of wholesalers by directly importing fresh fruit, vegetables and meat themselves.

At the same time, wholesaling, which has long been dominated by small companies, has also become an increasingly fragmented business. In 2001, three-quarters of wholesalers had fewer than ten employees. Retailers are also sourcing goods from more wholesalers, with an average of ten wholesalers serving every one retailer in 2001, compared to the seven to one ratio of 1993. Nonetheless, wholesalers continue to play an important role in connecting goods to consumers. Value-added roles in the sector include collection, warehousing, bulk-breaking, product sorting, quality assurance, and delivery.

Government efforts

The distributive industry in Malaysia, including wholesaling, is governed by many regulations that are, in turn, supported by an enforcement framework including price controls, limits on expansion of foreign-owned retailers, trade description and consumer protection.

Although Malaysia has not yet committed to opening up her market to distributive trade, including wholesaling, under the World Trade Organization, foreign operators are allowed to engage in the industry. As of 1994, foreign parties wishing to participate in the local distributive trade need approval from the Distributive Trade Committee of the Ministry of Domestic Trade and Consumer Affairs.

The government, through the Federal Agriculture Marketing Authority (FAMA), is trying to involve more Bumiputera in the wholesaling of fresh fruit and vegetables. FAMA was formed as a marketing agency under the Agriculture Ministry in 1965. Its

Wholesale markets, Selangor

1. Vegetable wholesaler operating his stall, Selayang.

2. Lorries unloading their produce early in the morning in Serdang.

3. Fresh seafood on display, Selayang.

4. A trader examining baskets of imported lychees, Selayang.

5. A fruit and vegetable wholesaler surrounded by his goods, Serdang.

Examples of home-grown franchises

Bonia—handbags, shoes and fashion accessories.

Royal Selangor—pewter gifts and tableware.

Reliance—travel agency.

Secret Recipe—bakery and café.

Marrybrown Fried Chicken—fast food.

Noor Arfa—batik-themed apparel.

1901—hot dogs.

Manhattan Fish Market—Western-style seafood restaurant.

tasks include supervising, coordinating, improving and developing the marketing of agricultural products.

In addition, Malaysia's ambition to become a regional hub for *halal* products, including meat products and consumer products, means the role of wholesalers will become more important. The wholesale industry can provide more value-added services, particularly the sourcing of animals, slaughter methods, processing methods, transportation and storage.

Franchising

Franchising in Malaysia has been in existence since the early 1900s when pioneers such as Singer, Bata, petrol stations and automotive services began establishing outlets all over the country. In the 1970s, franchising was popularized by fast food restaurants. However, it has only been since the 1990s that franchising experienced rapid growth nationwide with the entry of home-grown franchises. As of June 2006, there were 260 registered franchise systems in Malaysia.

The Franchise Act 1998 defines a franchise as a contract or an agreement between two or more persons by which the franchisor grants the franchisee the right to operate a business according to the franchise system as determined by the franchisor. The franchisor has the right to monitor and control the business continually within a stipulated timeframe and provides specified assistance for concept development, advertising and promotion, training, and consultancy services. In return, the franchisee is required to pay royalty and other expenses stated in the franchise agreement to the franchisor.

Government initiatives

Realizing its potential for wealth creation and empowerment of Bumiputera, the government has developed pro-franchising policies aimed at stimulating the growth of franchising, in particular, home-grown franchises. In 1992, the Franchise Development Programme through the Implementation and Coordination Unit of the Prime Minister's Department was established. A key strategy to develop entrepreneurship, this programme aimed to produce a Bumiputera Commercial and Industrial Community in line with the New Economic Policy (see 'New Economic Policy: 1971–1990') and subsequent economic policies.

The Malaysian Franchise Association (MFA) was formed in 1994 to support the government's effort to promote entrepreneurship through franchising. Activities undertaken by the MFA include training programmes, seminars, national and international exhibitions and conferences, trade missions, road shows, research and development, and matching programmes for promotion and marketing purposes.

The enactment of the Franchise Act 1998 in 1999 was a milestone for the industry. Malaysia was the first country worldwide to enact specific franchise laws. The Act ensures the protection of local entrepreneurs and creates a framework of governance. A year later, all franchises were required to register with the Registrar of Franchise under the Ministry of Entrepreneur and Co-operative Development.

In 2004, Perbadanan Nasional Berhad (PERNAS) was appointed as the lead implementative agency to spearhead franchise development by introducing financing and soft loan schemes, training programmes and marketing assistance.

To develop home-grown brands, the Franchise Homegrown Product Development Programme has been established to identify potential local businesses and lend them a hand in transforming into a franchise. Co-branding and conversion strategies are other alternatives to encourage existing businesses to venture into franchising. Since 2000, local franchising has been expanding at an average rate of about 15 per cent per annum. As of 2006, 13 per cent of home-grown franchises have successfully ventured abroad into foreign markets.

Directory produced by the Malaysian Franchise Association.

Distribution of franchise business activities, 2006

Retailing and supermarkets 7.57%
Healthcare 3.98%
IT and communications 3.19%
Furniture and landscaping 1.59%
Others 7.18%
Food business 31.47%
Service and maintenance 18.33%
Apparel and accessories 15.14%
Childcare and pre-school education 11.55%

Source: Ministry of Entrepreneur and Cooperative Development

Director of the Sate King franchise, Datin Rosnaini Karim, with a selection of her products.

Advertising

The Malaysian advertising industry manifests many of the current trends and issues affecting advertising development both in Asia and elsewhere in world. Multi-racial and multi-lingual Malaysia provides an interesting study of consumer diversity and media fragmentation.

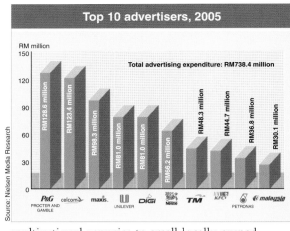

Top 10 advertisers, 2005

Source: Nielsen Media Research

Advertising expenditure by media, 2005

	% shares
Newspaper	60.9%
Television	28.7%
Radio	3.9%
Magazine	3.5%
Outdoor	1.6%
Point of sale	0.8%
Cinema	0.6%

Source: Nielsen Media Research

Adoi is a monthly magazine featuring key movements and developments in the local advertising industry.

Top 10 advertising expenditure by product, 2004

	RM million
Classified ads	599.5
Mobile line services	270.0
Mobile interactive services	201.5
Female facial care	124.4
Hair shampoo and conditioner	120.8
Local government institutions	105.8
Residential estates	102.3
Credit cards	74.9
Cinema advertising	68.7
Fast-food outlets	64.4

Source: Nielsen Media Research

Brief overview

The overall market for advertising has recorded seven years of robust growth since the downturn of 1998. In 2004, Malaysian advertising expenditure (ADEX) recorded an outstanding annual growth of 17 per cent to RM4.42 billion.

Modern advertising

Advertising in Malaysia performs more than the traditional communication and promotion functions and has evolved to encompass turnkey solutions for the creation, development and management of brands. So much so that for many advertisers, the 'creative process' often begins not with advertisements, but rather with the identification and distillation of a brand's true essence.

In terms of the forms which advertising takes, much of the investment here is still channelled into mass media in general, and newspapers in particular. Malaysia's 31 newspapers constituted over 60 per cent of total ADEX in 2004. However, recent diversification activities of key TV and radio brands have resulted in a 30 per cent annual growth for these media in 2004.

Apart from the traditional trinity of newspapers, TV and radio, there is also a growing, and potentially large, market for new forms of advertising that reach out to customers within their natural purchasing environments. These span from customer relationship management (CRM), to branded programming content, to enterprise marketing via mobile phones. Recent upgrades in the public transportation infrastructure in and around Kuala Lumpur have led to the proliferation of new forms of transit advertising on monorails, Light Rail Transits, KLIA Express and buses.

Online advertising, estimated at less than one per cent of total in ADEX in 2004, was also projected to grow with key online companies such as MSN, Yahoo! and Google each establishing a local presence. While online growth was inhibited somewhat by slow broadband expansion, mobile phone ownership in 2004 stood at 53 per cent of the population and climbing, fuelling the entrepreneurial rise of mobile marketing consultancies aimed specifically at helping advertisers target mobile phone users.

Advertising agencies

There are over 400 advertising agencies in Malaysia. These range from full-service multinational agencies to small locally owned shops. Historically, early advertising was shaped by multinational agencies, with these agencies gradually hiring more local talent to develop indigenous concepts. Skill shortages do occur, but the industry does have access to growing pools of new talent from schools specializing in advertising and communication such as the Association of Accredited Advertising Agents (4As)-managed Institute of Advertising Communications Training.

Advertising Malaysian-style

With Malaysia's mix of religions, cultures and languages, advertising has to be customized to reach out to ethnically segmented and language-specific audiences. These include the three major ethnic groups of Malay, Chinese and Indian as well as the many indigenous Bumiputera sub-groups in Sabah and Sarawak. In addition to a multilingual media mix, many marketers also use language- and ethnicity-specific brand names, packaging and promotional channels to reach culturally diverse audiences.

However, despite the push for segmentation and the volume of culturally specific advertising, advertisers have also played a role in helping to bring together the various facets of Malaysian culture. Festive advertising, involving the use of advertising for festive greetings and sometimes for

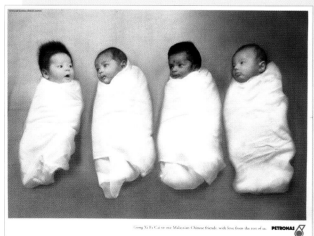

PETRONAS's community service festive advertisements: Chinese New Year 1999, National Day 2001, Gawai and Kaamatan 2004.

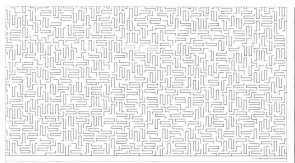

This Sony Playstation 2 advertisement entitled 'Maze' by McCann-Erickson Malaysia won the Golden Kancil Award in 2005.

The Nikon print advertisement by Naga DDB that won Malaysia's first International Design and Art Direction (D&AD) Yellow Pencil in 2005 with the caption 'The widest lens in its class'.

ASSOCIATION OF ACCREDITED
ADVERTISING AGENTS MALAYSIA

Key organizations

The Association of Accredited Advertising Agents (the 4As) was formed in 1964 to promote responsible advertising and the interests of advertising agencies and their clients, the advertisers.

The Malaysian Advertisers' Association represents the views and interests of Malaysian advertisers, both local and multinational, as well as helps keep advertisers abreast of industry trends impacting their business here.

social reflection on the state of the nation, is popular. Many Malaysian corporations, of which PETRONAS is probably the most notable example, have over the years used festive advertising to pioneer an emerging 'Malaysian identity' that cuts across traditional racial lines. Other local conglomerates, including banks as well as government-linked corporations, have developed their own style of festive advertising ranging from Malaysia Airlines' celebration of Malaysian achievements to Perodua's salute to timeless Malaysian values of warmth, courage and humility.

FROM TOP: Print advertising targeted specifically at Malay, Chinese and Indian women.

Creative excellence

There are two major local creative awards that recognize the home-grown creative excellence in Malaysian advertising: the Association of Accredited Advertising Agents' (4As) Awards (commonly referred to as the Kancils) which began in 1978, and the three-year-old Malaysian Creative Circle Awards (known as MC2).

Malaysian agencies excelled creatively in 2004–05. In 2004, J. Walter Thomson Malaysia became the first-ever Malaysian agency to win a Cannes Grand Prix while Naga DDB brought home Malaysia's first Design & Art Direction (D&AD) Yellow Pencil in 2005 for its print work for Nikon. This is in addition to consistently successful showings at other international and regional festivals such as The One Show, the Clios and the Thai-hosted Asian Adfest.

Advertisements on billboards and the KL Monorail at Bukit Bintang, Kuala Lumpur.

Regulating the advertising industry

The advertising industry is governed by the Advertising Code, strict rules and regulations published by the Ministry of Information which are meant to promote ethical practices and positive values. There are guidelines relating to sexual stereotyping and sexism in advertising. Religious insinuations and comparative product advertising are forbidden. Other regulations—such as censorship of violence, sex and horror—set the parameters within which advertisers and agencies can work.

In the late 1970s, Malaysia's advertising industry received a boost from a ruling requiring commercials to be locally produced if viewed locally. This 'Made In Malaysia' policy was formulated to protect Malaysian values and identity, while promoting Malaysian culture, encouraging and nurturing the growth of the local advertising industry and protecting local production houses from external pressure and competition.

In 1993, with the enactment of the Control of Tobacco Product Regulations, Malaysia banned tobacco advertising in print and on television, radio and billboards. These regulations were further tightened in 2004. Measures taken by broadcasters and the government have increased advertising revenue despite the loss of revenue from tobacco advertisers. For example, the relaxation of the Made-in-Malaysia ruling and the removal of restrictions for sanitary products to be advertised on television.

One of the many anti-smoking billboards put up by the Ministry of Health, which spent over RM10 million on advertising in 2004.

Tourism and hospitality

'Truly Asia' is the tag line created by the Ministry of Tourism which emphasizes Malaysia's rich natural, cultural and historical heritage. Efforts since the 1990s to attract a more diverse tourist base have focused on linking tourism with areas such as agriculture, shopping, sports, health and business. Intensive promotion and the development of products and services have led to a steady stream of visitors from all over the globe.

Key indicators, 2005	
Number of tourist arrivals	16,431,055
Total tourism receipts	RM31 billion
Per capita expenditure	RM1890
Hotels (total)	2256
Hotel rooms (total)	170,873
Average length of stay (nights)	7.2
Hotel occupancy rate (%)	63.5
Population employed in tourism	451,000

Source: Economic Planning Unit, Ministry of Tourism

Crowds are a common sight at the Kuala Lumpur International Airport (KLIA) in Sepang.

Events such as the Formula 1 Grand Prix (above) and the Tour de Langkawi (top) are accompanied by a surge in foreign tourist arrivals.

Promoting tourism

Tourism links several major industries, among them transportation (See 'Infrastructure and Transport'), the retail sector (see 'Retail') and the hospitality industry.

Malaysia has actively promoted tourism since 1972, when it hosted the Pacific Area Travel Association (PATA) conference. In the same year, the Tourist Development Corporation (TDC) was formed by statute as an agency under the former Ministry of Trade and Industry. After the establishment of the Ministry of Culture and Tourism in 1987, and the transfer to it of TDC, tourism became an important sector of the economy. Large budget allocations were made for infrastructure, product development and promotional activities. Visit Malaysia Year 1990, the first large-scale campaign to promote tourism, resulted in the annual number of tourist arrivals shooting up to 7.4 million, more than twice the number in 1985.

A National Tourism Policy was formulated for 1991–2000 to provide long-term strategies for an integrated development of the tourism industry.

In 1992, the TDC Act 1972 was repealed and replaced by the Malaysia Tourism Promotion Board (MTPB) Act 1992. With this change, the MTPB, more popularly known as 'Tourism Malaysia', was formally established. By 1994, another Visit Malaysia Year, the tourist industry was the third largest foreign exchange earner, after manufacturing and petroleum.

A National Eco-tourism Plan was formulated by the Ministry of Culture, Arts and Tourism (known as just the Ministry of Tourism in 2006) in 1997. The government strove to promote Malaysia, provide the necessary infrastructure and tax incentives, and maintain the regulatory framework to ensure that tourism development did not adversely affect the country's cultural and environmental heritage. At the regional level, Malaysia works closely with other ASEAN countries to resolve issues on travel and border crossing and to encourage joint-venture tourism projects and campaigns such as 1992's Visit ASEAN

Domestic tourism

Domestic tourism is an important component of the tourism sector. Between 2000 and 2005, the number of domestic hotel guests more than doubled to 29 million. This is in line with rising household incomes. The introduction of budget airline AirAsia in 2001 has accelerated the growth of domestic tourism. The implementation of the five-day work week for the public sector since July 2005 was another factor that has boosted domestic tourism.

Hotel guests by state and Federal Territory, 2004			
Place	Local	Foreign	Total
Kuala Lumpur	47.2%	52.8%	13,771,684
Pahang	63.1%	36.9%	4,814,967
Sabah	55.3%	44.7%	4,473,319
Penang	52.5%	47.5%	4,110,122
Kedah	64.9%	35.1%	3,875,715
Johor	65.9%	34.1%	3,004,819
Sarawak	72.0%	28.0%	2,994,142
Selangor	48.7%	51.3%	2,946,432
Melaka	52.4%	47.6%	2,391,102
Perak	77.1%	22.9%	2,264,035
Negeri Sembilan	77.2%	22.8%	1,331,394
Terengganu	86.0%	14.0%	810,426
Kelantan	88.3%	11.7%	624,750
Labuan	73.8%	26.2%	213,736
Putrajaya	41.5%	58.5%	87,386
Perlis	84.3%	15.7%	84,833
TOTAL	58.1%	41.9%	47,799,061

Tourist expenditure, 2005

TOTAL: RM31.0 BILLION

Accomodation 33.1% | Shopping 24% | Food and beverage 17.4% | Others 25.5%

Source: Tourism Malaysia

MALAYSIA: My Second Home

... enjoy international class facilities, safety, leisure and elegant living at affordable price.

The 'Malaysia My Second Home' programme allows foreigners who fulfil certain criteria to stay in Malaysia on a renewable Social Visit Pass valid for an initial five years. Between 2001 and 2005, this programme attracted 7308 participants.

Year. However, it is the private sector that has taken the lead in developing and providing tourism products and services.

Emphasis has been placed on diversification in order to appeal to a broader spectrum of travellers. Besides marketing the country's many natural, cultural and historical attractions, efforts have been made to promote Malaysia as the regional centre for shopping,

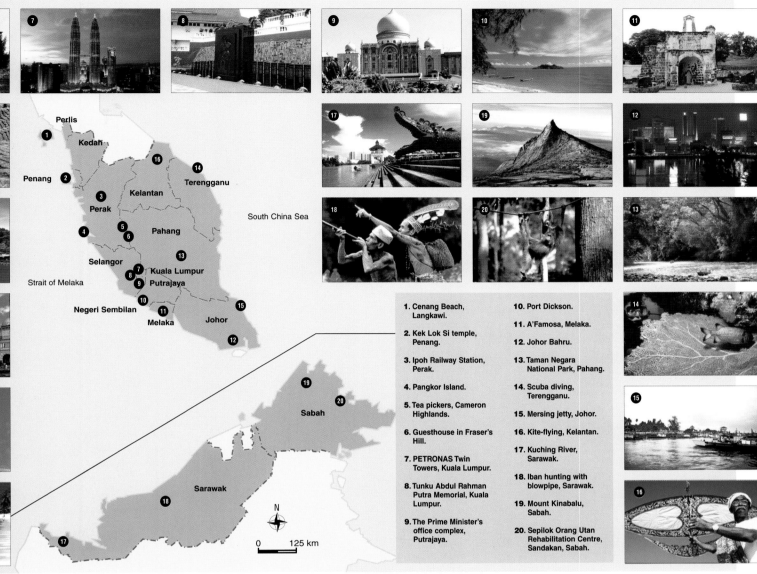

1. Cenang Beach, Langkawi.
2. Kek Lok Si temple, Penang.
3. Ipoh Railway Station, Perak.
4. Pangkor Island.
5. Tea pickers, Cameron Highlands.
6. Guesthouse in Fraser's Hill.
7. PETRONAS Twin Towers, Kuala Lumpur.
8. Tunku Abdul Rahman Putra Memorial, Kuala Lumpur.
9. The Prime Minister's office complex, Putrajaya.
10. Port Dickson.
11. A'Famosa, Melaka.
12. Johor Bahru.
13. Taman Negara National Park, Pahang.
14. Scuba diving, Terengganu.
15. Mersing jetty, Johor.
16. Kite-flying, Kelantan.
17. Kuching River, Sarawak.
18. Iban hunting with blowpipe, Sarawak.
19. Mount Kinabalu, Sabah.
20. Sepilok Orang Utan Rehabilitation Centre, Sandakan, Sabah.

food, sports, business and conventions, cruises, island resorts, and special interest tourism such as eco- and agro-tourism, and health tourism. Promotional activities are due to increase in 2007, which has been designated as another Visit Malaysia Year in conjunction with the celebration of the 50th anniversary of Malaysia's Independence.

Tourism growth areas

Malaysia is also being marketed as an educational tourism destination. In 2005, there were more than 50,380 foreign students studying here. Health and medical tourism is another growth area. In 2004, more than 129,318 foreign patients received medical treatment in the country. Health and medical tourism generated foreign exchange earnings of RM925 million in 2005.

Between 1999 to 2002, the fastest growing group of tourists was from the Middle East. In 2005, a 'Feel At Home' programme was launched which introduced various conveniences and facilities to accommodate West Asian tourists.

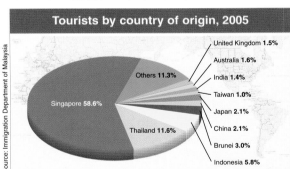

Tourists by country of origin, 2005

Source: Immigration Department of Malaysia

Singapore 58.6%
Others 11.3%
Thailand 11.6%
United Kingdom 1.5%
Australia 1.6%
India 1.4%
Taiwan 1.0%
Japan 2.1%
China 2.1%
Brunei 3.0%
Indonesia 5.8%

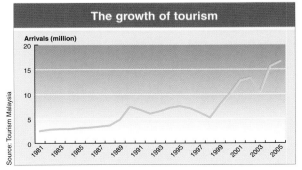

The growth of tourism

Arrivals (million)

Source: Tourism Malaysia

A comprehensive guide on seeking medical treatment, produced by the Penang Medical Tourism Project and Penang State Government.

Film and music industries

The growth of the Malaysian film and music industries has been primarily driven by the private sector. The government, however, has provided support through organizations such as the National Film Development Corporation (FINAS) and the Recording Industry Association of Malaysia (RIM).

Moviegoers waiting outside of the Golden Screen Cinemas at Mid Valley Megamall in Kuala Lumpur, 2006.

Key indicators, 2005

Local films with the highest gross takings

	(RM million)
Gangster	2.9
Pontianak Harum Sundal Malam	2.7
Baik Punya Cilok	2.6
KL Menjerit 1	2.5
Senario XX	2.3

Gross takings of films in local cinemas

Chinese films RM34.51 million (17.4%)
Other films RM22.75 million (7.5%)

RM217.35 million (100%)

Local films RM26.71 million (22%)
English films RM133.38 million (53.1%)

Total admissions for films in local cinemas

Chinese films 4.09 million people (15.8%)
Other films 2.67 million people (10.3%)

25.92 million people (100%)

Local films 3.74 million people (14.4%)
English films 15.42 million people (59.5%)

Source: National Film Development Corporation of Malaysia

The film industry

The first local films to be produced were in the 1930s in Malay. The 1950s and the first half of the 1960s were the 'golden era' of Malay film during which the Shaw Brothers' Malay Film Productions and Loke Wan Tho's Cathay-Keris were regularly releasing a film a month. The Shaws brought with them technical expertise and equipment from China.

The popularity of Malay language films began to wane in the second half of the 1960s. Production costs began to rise while audiences declined. Further, the Indonesian market was closed to Malay films as a result of Indonesia's confrontation with Malaysia. By the mid-1960s, almost all films produced in the United States were in colour, and this development was adopted by the industries in Hong Kong and Indonesia. However, in Malaysia, black and white films remained the norm as colour film was unaffordable. The Shaw Brothers' Malay Film Productions studio eventually closed in 1967, and the Cathay-Keris studio suffered a similar fate in 1972. The increasing popularity of television due

Sepet won several awards including the Best Film-Gold Award at France's Creteil Film Festival, 2005. It was produced at a cost of RM1 million. *The Red Kebaya* was released in 2006. Its production cost totalled RM2.5 million.

Cinemas

From the 1950s to the 1970s, cinemas such as the Odeon, Rex, Federal, Pavilion and Cathay were developed as freestanding buildings around Kuala Lumpur. However, the advent of videotapes, then LDs, VCDs, DVDs and movie piracy led to the demise of these freestanding cinemas by the late 1980s.

Since the late 1990s, multiplexes have sprouted up in shopping centres. As of 2006, Golden Screen Cinemas Sdn Bhd operates the largest cinema network with a total of 108 screens in 18 locations. A merger of Golden Communications (M) Sdn Bhd and Cathay Cinemas Sdn Bhd, it is the biggest entity in the Malaysian cinema entertainment business and the largest local distributor of independent English films. TGV Cinemas Sdn Bhd is another major operator with 48 cinemas and six multiplexes nationwide.

Brochure of the 3D IMAX Theatre in Berjaya Times Square, Kuala Lumpur.

Filming a scene from *Puteri Gunung Ledang*. Released in 2004, it was the first Malaysian film to be distributed internationally. It was also Malaysia's first entry at the Academy Awards and the Venice Film Festival.

to improvements in the quality of locally produced television programmes and the extension of broadcast hours also impaired the growth of Malaysian cinema in the late 1960s and early 1970s.

The local film industry languished until Deddy Borhan set up Sabah Films in 1975. He was the first truly independent Bumiputera film-maker.

In 1981, the National Film Development Corporation (Perbadanan Kemajuan Filem Nasional Malaysia, or FINAS) was established to advance and expand the local film industry. That year, 25 Malaysian films were produced. The industry, however, suffered a major set-back during the Asian financial crisis (see 'Malaysia's innovative response to the financial crisis') with only four films being released in 1999.

In 2005, the National Film Policy, introduced by the Ministry of Culture, Arts and Heritage considered the production, marketing, equipment, infrastructure, finance and human resources development, and clearly stated the advantages of technology for film-making. Pursuant to this, the government expended RM7.1 million on FINAS under the Eighth Malaysia Plan (2001–05) and allocated RM3 million under the Ninth Malaysia Plan (2006–10) to upgrade the capability and quality of local film post-production work. FINAS is equipped with high definition (HD) cameras and kine transfer facilities to process digital format films into celluloid films. The move was a part of the government's strategy to put the local film industry on a par with the international film industry. There were over 300 film companies registered with FINAS in 2005.

With the progress of film-shooting technology, the use of 35-mm and 16-mm celluloid films has been superseded by HD digital technology. This new technology helps save costs in film making, facilitates the production of special effects and images which are of better quality compared with those using celluloid films. In 2005, 90 per cent of short and documentary films were produced in digital format.

The music industry

The first local recording company, Life Records, also known as Hup Hup Sdn Bhd, was incorporated in 1949. In the late 1960s, it was the first Asian company to be appointed as a licensee for foreign labels, including CBS and MCA. It had a firm foothold in Malaysia, Singapore and Hong Kong between the late 1960s and early 1970s, and is still in business today. The first multinational record company to set up a subsidiary in Malaysia was EMI in 1996.

The industry grew steadily until 1996 when it began to be stifled by increasing piracy. From an industry that was worth over RM80 million in 1996, its value declined to RM20 million by 1999. The worst hit sector was that of the locally produced albums. As a result, many small local production houses closed down. In 2003, the number of locally produced albums fell to 57 from 70 the previous year. Music piracy has been the primary cause of this continued decline. In 1988, Public Performance Malaysia was established. A licensing body under the Copyright Act 1987, it gives record companies legal rights to control and grant licences for the public performance, playing or showing of their sound recordings and music videos. It is a non-profit subsidiary of the Recording Industry Association of Malaysia (RIM).

In terms of sales of both foreign and domestically produced music, EMI Malaysia was the market leader from 2002 to 2004, with a 22 per cent market share. EMI's business is built on catalogues (established artistes and music already under the label) and current assets (new music and acts). Catalogues are used to create compilations, which are very popular in the local market.

Music accessed from the internet and mobile phones is becoming increasingly popular in Malaysia. With legal download sites spreading internationally, more users are buying songs in digital format and record companies are achieving their first significant revenues from online sales.

P. Ramlee was the most celebrated and prolific local artiste of the 1950s and 1960s with 359 songs, 66 films, two stage plays and three radio and television dramas to his credit.

1. Sudirman Haji Arshad performing in front of fans in 1988.

2. The Alleycats at a performance in 2001.

3. Siti Nurhaliza signing autographs for fans in London.

4. Tan Sri S.M. Salim (left) and Ibrahim Din performing at a concert, c. 1970.

5. Local Malaysian artistes performing at the Force of Nature concert in 2005.

6. Life Records' early releases include an album by Frances Yip.

7. Jaclyn Victor, winner of the first Malaysian Idol competition, performing at a concert in Kuala Lumpur, 2005.

The Recording Industry Association of Malaysia (RIM)

Since its founding in 1978, RIM (initially known as the Malaysian Association of Phonogram and Videogram Producers and Distributors, or MAPV) has worked to protect the intellectual property rights of recording companies and to address issues in the music industry. As of 2006, RIM represented over 112 locally incorporated recording companies, from subsidiaries of international record companies (BMG, EMI, Warner Music and Sony) to local record companies (NSR, Life Records, KRU Records and Positive Tone) to production houses and manufacturers (CD plants and cassette factories), all of which encompass over 95 per cent of the total music market.

RIM

PERSATUAN
INDUSTRI
RAKAMAN
MALAYSIA

The media

In addition to being industries in their own right, Malaysia's press and broadcasting media provide the economy with knowledge in the form of news, data and analysis. Technological innovations have resulted in new media forms, with satellite television and online media being significant new sources of timely and accurate information.

Average daily newspaper sales (1 July–31 Dec 2005)

Newspaper	Average net sales
Sin Chew Daily	323,238
The Star	309,029
Harian Metro	241,860
Berita Harian	205,555
Utusan Malaysia	212,255
New Straits Times	138,896
China Press[1]	133,380
Borneo Post (Sarawak)	50,180
Daily Express (Sabah)	29,610

[1] - 1 July 2004–30 June 2005.

TOP: Government printing press in Sabah, 1967.

ABOVE: Loading newspapers at *The Star*'s printing plant in Selangor.

The press

Malaysian newspapers cater to readers of each of the nation's four most widely spoken languages: Malay, Chinese, Tamil and English.

From a single newspaper, *The Prince of Wales Island Gazette*, first published in 1806, the newspaper industry grew to include 81 daily and weekly newspapers in 2003. Of the dailies, 17 were in Malay, 14 in English, 22 in Chinese, three in Tamil and one in Punjabi. In 2004, newspapers garnered 60.4 per cent of all advertising expenditure amounting to RM2.67 billion (see 'Advertising').

The first romanized Malay newspaper to be published after World War II was *Berita Harian* in 1957. *Utusan Malaysia* appeared in 1967. Its Sunday edition, *Mingguan Malaysia*, had the largest circulation of any Malaysian newspaper in 2003.

Chinese newspapers outnumber dailies in other languages, but most have a significantly smaller circulation. Many are published only in Sabah and Sarawak. The most widely circulated Chinese dailies are *Sin Chew Daily*, *China Press* and *Nanyang Siang Pau*.

The largely Tamil Indian community is served by the *Tamil Nesan* and *Malaysia Nanban* newspapers. Both newspapers, apart from carrying local and national news, carry a two-page news section from India, mainly from Tamil Nadu.

Of the English language newspapers, *The Star*, first published in 1971, had the largest circulation in 2005. The *New Straits Times* merged with its sister newspaper, *Business Times*, in 2002, in an effort to improve its circulation and cut costs. Another English-language daily, *The Sun*, introduced in 1991, has been distributed free of charge since 2002.

In Sarawak and Sabah, the national newspapers are available in Kuching and Kota Kinabalu, and certain other locations. In addition, Sarawak has two local English dailies, while Sabah has three. Newspapers published in Sarawak include *The Borneo Post, Eastern Times, Utusan Sarawak* and the *See Hua Daily News*, all published by the See Hua Company. In Sabah, the *Daily Express, New Sabah Times* and *Borneo Post* are locally established dailies. Sabah is unique because many of the English dailies carry Malay and Kadazandusun pull-out sections.

Radio

From amateur beginnings in the 1920s, radio broadcasting rapidly developed after World War II, especially after Independence. The Department of

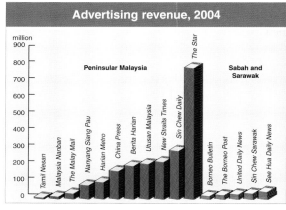

Advertising revenue, 2004

million

Peninsular Malaysia: Tamil Nesan, Malaysia Nanban, The Malay Mail, Nanyang Siang Pau, Harian Metro, China Press, Berita Harian, Utusan Malaysia, New Straits Times, Sin Chew Daily, The Star

Sabah and Sarawak: Borneo Bulletin, The Borneo Post, United Daily News, Sin Chew Sarawak, See Hua Daily News

A deejay broadcasting in an IKIM.fm studio. IKIM.fm, part of the Institute of Islamic Understanding, was Malaysia's first Islamic digital radio station and was launched in 2001.

Broadcasting was established in 1946 in Singapore, and it moved to Kuala Lumpur in the early 1950s. From 1956, following the Department's move to Federal House in Kuala Lumpur, broadcasting began to flourish with stations opening across the country, including in Sabah and Sarawak. Commercials were first aired in 1960, providing a new source of revenue for the government.

Radio Malaysia's national network began a 24-hour service in 1972, and FM Stereo broadcasts started in 1975.

Bernama: Malaysia's national news agency

Malaysia is served by a national news agency called Bernama (Pertubuhan Berita Nasional Malaysia). A statutory body established in 1968, the agency is a joint-venture between the Government and newspaper organizations in Malaysia. Newspapers and broadcasting stations in Malaysia subscribe to Bernama for national and local news. Bernama also provides foreign news sourced from the Organisation of Asia-Pacific News Agencies (OANA) and Smart News Network International (SNNi). Bernama news is also available online.

Launch of Bernama news services by the Minister of Information and Transmission, Senu bin Abdul Rahman, in 1968.

The country's first private radio station, Johor's Best 104, was launched in Johor in 1989. By 2004 there were seven national radio stations, 14 privately owned stations and several state stations broadcasting in a variety of languages. A 2004 study found that in the Peninsula, radio reaches 90 per cent of people aged 12 years old and above, and listeners tuned in an average of 3.7 hours a day.

Television

The first television broadcast in Malaysia was made on 28 December 1963, airing for 24 hours a week from temporary studios in Jalan Ampang, Kuala Lumpur. In 1969, Television Malaysia began transmission from the Angkasapuri Broadcasting Complex in Kuala Lumpur. In November 1969, Television Malaysia's second channel was launched, and Radio Malaysia and Television Malaysia integrated into a single Department of Broadcasting under the Ministry of Information.

Colour television transmissions began over what was then known as Network 1 (now TV1) on 28 December 1978, followed by Network 2 (now TV2) in May 1979. In 1982, Network 2's broadcast range was expanded to Sabah and Sarawak.

Private television licences were first granted, as part of the government's privatization policy, in 1983 (see 'Public sector, private sector'). The first licence was issued to Sistem Televisyen Malaysia Berhad, the operators of TV3, which began its pilot transmission in the Klang Valley. Licences were also issued to operators of Metrovision, launched in 1994, and NTV7, launched in 1998. Metrovision suspended broadcasting in November 1999 because of poor advertising revenue, but was subsequently brought back as 8TV in 2004. TV9 was a privately owned station which started broadcasting in 2003, went off the air in 2005, and was renamed and launched as Channel 9 in April 2006 after being acquired by Media Prima Berhad.

Cableview Services Sdn Bhd, a subsidiary of TV3, pioneered pay-television in June 1995 with an eight-channel service, MegaTV. It claimed a subscriber base of 130,000, but this dwindled to 10,000. The station finally shut down in 2001 as a result of competition from satellite pay-television

Terrestrial television advertising revenue, 2005

tv9 1%

43%

Total: RM1,309,859,748

ntv7 25%

12%

TV 16%

3%

Source: Nielsen Media Research

Covering the economy

In 1957, the average businessman most likely obtained economic and business news from newspapers. In 1976, the New Straits Times Group became the first publisher to set up a separate publication, *Business Times*, which focused exclusively on business news. However, it was subsequently merged with the *New Straits Times* in 2002 due to declining circulation. Other business publications include *The Edge*, a weekly newspaper, and the magazine *Malaysian Business*.

Radio provides another source of business intelligence, as does television. Domestically produced programmes, such as TV3's 'Money Matters' which first aired in 1990, provide analysis and coverage of the economy. In addition, ASTRO offers viewers access to international networks such as CNN, BBC and Bloomberg.

Malaysian Business is published by the Berita Publishing Group.

operator, Astro All Asia Networks plc (ASTRO), which by 2006 claimed a subscriber base of 1.9 million. ASTRO offers 56 channels as well as two movie-on-demand channels. Small satellite dishes are installed on roofs or balconies of subscribers for reception. Unlike the satellite technology used by ASTRO, another pay-television operator MiTV Corporation Sdn Bhd (MiTV), entered the market in September 2005, offering 50 channels at a flat monthly rate. MiTV uses a locally developed wireless technology called Internet protocol (IP) over ultra-high frequency (UHF) for its broadcast. MiTV combines an enhanced television viewing experience with interactive and internet features. A third pay-television operator, FINE TV, started operations in 2006.

Television and print journalists interviewing Minister of Foreign Affairs Dato' Seri Syed Hamid Albar at the 11th ASEAN Summit in Kuala Lumpur, 2005.

Online media

In 1987, the Malaysian Institute of Microelectronic Systems (MIMOS) introduced the Malaysia Computer Network, on which connections were primarily dial-up. It ran on Telekom Malaysia's X.25-based Maypac service. In 1992, JARING, the country's first internet service provider, was launched by MIMOS. This marked the beginning of the internet in Malaysia.

The World Wide Web was then still a closed project, and was only opened to the public in 1993. In 1999, JARING launched its 2.5 gigabits per second (Gbps) SuperJaring network which at the time was considered the longest and fastest IP-over-fibre network in the world. Two years later, JARING established a multiprotocol label switching system, and in 2004, it offered wireless broadband service to home and business users.

In 2004, the government launched the National Broadband Plan in order to expand and develop internet services in Malaysia. In terms of the market share of subscribers, the largest internet service providers in 2005 were TM Net (56.5 per cent), JARING (25.5 per cent) and TIMENet (16.5 per cent).

The Star was the first newspaper in Malaysia to go online, on 23 June 1995. Other newspapers available online include *Sin Chew Daily* and *Utusan Melayu*.

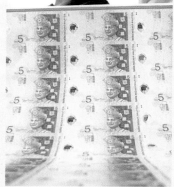

Assets of the financial system, year end 2005

Merchant banks 2.4%

Islamic banks 2.3%

Discount houses 1.4%

Development financial institutions 5.2%

Finance companies 1.4%

Other financial intermediaries 5.5%

Other provident and pension funds 3.0%

Life insurance funds 4.4%

Total assets: RM1908.5 billion

Provident, pension and insurance funds 22.2%

Commercial banks 44.1%

Bank Negara Malaysia 15.5%

Employees' Provident Fund 13.8%

General insurance funds 1.0%

Source: Bank Negara Malaysia Annual Report 2005

1. Bank Negara Malaysia Governor Tan Sri Dr Zeti Akhtar Aziz handing the first copy of the Financial Sector Master Plan to Finance Minister Tun Daim Zainuddin in 2001.

2. Stock market investors watching the rise of the Kuala Lumpur Composite Index when it broke the 1000 point level for the first time on 10 February 2000.

3. Banking hall inside the Kuala Lumpur branch of the Hongkong Bank (now known as HSBC) in 1957.

4. A Bank Islam Malaysia Berhad officer attending to customers at the the bank's headquarters in Kuala Lumpur, 2006.

5. Bank Negara Malaysia staff with a sheet of uncut polymer RM5 notes which were introduced in 2005. The RM5 polymer notes are more durable and longer lasting than paper notes and also have added security features.

6. Advertisement from Malaysia National Insurance Berhad (MNI), the largest composite insurer in 2005.

7. Menara Maybank in Kuala Lumpur, the headquarters of Malaysia's largest bank.

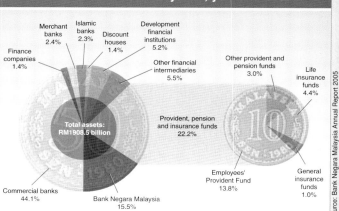

Only one world class insurer stands behind the nation's greatest achievements.

And only one is focused on taking you to new heights.

- Member of Permodalan Nasional Berhad (PNB) Group of Companies • Over RM8 Billion in Assets • Over RM1 Billion in Shareholders' Equity • Over 30 years in the industry • 26 branches across Malaysia and Brunei

Malaysia National Insurance Berhad (9557 T)
Level 26, Tower 1, MNI Twins, 11, Jalan Pinang, 50450 Kuala Lumpur.
Tel: 603-2178 9000 Fax: 603-2178 9090
www.mni.com.my

MNI⊕Insurance

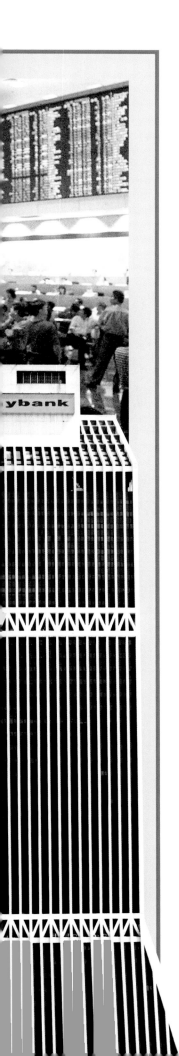

THE FINANCIAL SECTOR

After Independence, the development of the financial system was complicated by the separation of Singapore from Malaysia in 1965 and resulting issues related to the currencies and the stock markets of the two countries. By 1970, however, the foundations of the three major systems that define the current Malaysian financial landscape were in place: the banking system, non-bank financial intermediaries and the capital markets.

Local institution building, including the establishment of key regulatory bodies such as Bank Negara Malaysia (the Central Bank of Malaysia) led to the decline in the number of financial institutions. Rationalization of the banking industry has seen the merger of finance companies and commercial banks. In 2006, the merger of merchant banks, stockbroking companies and discount houses to form investment banks is underway.

Capital markets such as the stock market and the private debt securities market play the role of matching investors with companies seeking funds. Starting with four stockbrokers in 1960, the capital market has evolved and matured significantly. Key developments arose in response to market needs: the Kuala Lumpur Stock Exchange (KLSE) Second Board was established to cater to smaller companies seeking funds; the Malaysian Exchange of Securities Dealing and Automated Quotation (MESDAQ) was created as a market in which technology companies could source for funds; and derivatives market trading tools were introduced to provide investors with the capacity to manage the risks inherent in capital market transactions. The capital market was instrumental in the privatization exercises of the 1980s.

Malaysia pioneered Islamic banking in 1983, which led to the emergence of two parallel financial systems, with Islamic financial products based on the principle of profit-sharing offered as an alternative to conventional, interest-based products. Following the success of Islamic banking, Islamic insurance and Islamic money markets and capital markets were established. Efforts to position Malaysia as an international Islamic financial hub are underway.

The Asian financial crisis of 1997–98 occurred when the actions of currency speculators set off a series of interrelated events in Asia that very quickly led to a period of immense economic and social hardship. At the heart of the crisis lay the financial sector, faced with the problem of a depreciating currency, non-performing loans, collapsing share and property prices, and corporations going bankrupt. The government reacted by creating a stable environment through pegging the Ringgit at 3.80 to the US dollar, and establishing the National Economic Action Council to formulate recovery measures, aided by institutions such as Danamodal Nasional Berhad, Pengurusan Danaharta Nasional Berhad and the Corporate Debt Restructuring Committee. With the subsequent strengthening of the economy, a shift in the exchange rate regime to a managed float was adopted in July 2005.

In 2005, Malaysia was the first country worldwide to complete the migration to high-security, chip-based credit cards using the Europay-MasterCard-Visa (EMV) technology. By 2006, the incidence of fraud had been reduced by 96 per cent.

The financial services sector is a driving force in the economy. Growing at an average rate of 8.1 per cent per annum, it increased its share of GDP from 12.7 per cent in 2000 to 15.1 per cent in 2005.

Banking and insurance

The early foreign dominance of the financial sector has been offset by the growth of local banks and the establishment of key regulatory institutions. The introduction of Islamic banking in 1983 and the Labuan International Offshore Financial Centre in 1990 added further depth and diversity to the industry. The 1990s and 2000s, however, presented major challenges, among them the Asian financial crisis and the liberalization of the financial sector within the context of World Trade Organization agreements.

In 1984, the Kuala Lumpur Automated Clearing House commenced operations to expedite the clearing of the rising volume of cheques.

Customers have access to both conventional and Islamic financial services at Maybank.

Financial institutions

Financial intermediaries, comprising the banking system and the non-banking financial intermediaries, channel funds from lenders to borrowers. As of the end of 2005, licensed banking institutions included 23 commercial banks, six Islamic banks, three finance companies and ten merchant banks. Non-bank financial intermediaries include Malaysian Industrial Development Finance Ltd (MIDF), the Employees Provident Fund (EPF) and insurance companies.

Financial intermediaries provide vital services which include basic facilities for individuals, such as savings accounts, cheques, hire-purchase financing, and sophisticated financial instruments used by companies. Since 1983, the Malaysian banking system has featured both Islamic banking (See 'Islamic financial services') as well as conventional banking.

The insurance sector has fostered economic development in that it has effectively mobilized long-term savings and has provided a wide spectrum of insurance products, offering financial security for the insured.

The insurance sector

Domination of the insurance sector by branches of foreign firms came to an end with the enactment of the Insurance Act 1963 which increased participation of domestic insurers and local incorporation of foreign branches. The number of Malaysian-incorporated insurance companies rose from six in 1963 to 49 in 2004.

In 1979, domestic insurers outnumbered foreign insurers for the first time, and the introduction of the Insurance Act 1996 substantially strengthened the regulatory regime. There were only two foreign-incorporated insurers in the direct insurance market in Malaysia in 2004.

Bank Negara Malaysia's (BNM) supervision of the insurance industry since 1988 has strengthened the sector. In 1993, BNM approved the first Malaysian bancassurance collaboration to distribute insurance products to bank customers. Initiatives under the first phase of the Financial Sector Master Plan (2001–10) were directed towards enhancing the capacity and capabilities of domestic insurers to compete more effectively and improving the regulatory and supervisory framework to promote greater efficiency and stability within the sector.

The industry has experienced robust growth, especially in the life sector. Total premium income (general and life business) increased from RM3.17 billion in 1990 (2.9 per cent of GNP) to RM23.6 billion in 2005 (five per cent of GNP). Combined assets of insurance funds expanded from RM9.5 billion (8.6 per cent of GNP and 2.9 per cent of total assets of the financial system) in 1990 to RM96.7 billion (23 per cent of GNP and five per cent of total assets of the financial system) in 2005.

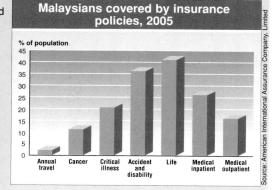

Malaysians covered by insurance policies, 2005

% of population

Source: American International Assurance Company, Limited

(Bar chart categories: Annual travel, Cancer, Critical illness, Accident and disability, Life, Medical inpatient, Medical outpatient)

Malayan Banking Berhad (Maybank)

Maybank officer and customers at the retail banking division of the bank's headquarters in Kuala Lumpur.

The country's largest financial services group, Maybank was incorporated in May 1960 and commenced operations in September 1960. It started with an authorized capital of RM20 million and an issued and paid-up share capital of RM7.5 million. Maybank's mission was to finance new industries under the government's development programmes and to extend banking facilities to rural areas. Over the years, Maybank has expanded its operations throughout the country as well as regionally and in major financial centres of the world. In 2005, it had total assets of RM209 billion and operated over 440 branches in Malaysia.

Foreign banks in Malaysia

In 2006, there were 14 foreign banks in Malaysia and they accounted for almost 30 per cent of the total assets of the banking industry. Foreign banks began operations in Penang in the late 19th century to service European traders and the British government. In the years preceding Independence, these banks were mainly involved in the provision of credit to the primary industries and the establishment of trade financing facilities. Post-Independence, foreign banks catered to the financial needs of foreign multinationals, acting as custodian banks for international fund managers and stockbrokers.

Citibank has headquarters for its Malaysian operations in Kuala Lumpur.

In 1957, foreign banks controlled over 90 per cent of the banking market. By 1998, however, their market share was only 18 per cent. This decline was the result of deliberate government policy to develop the domestic banking sector. Since 1971, foreign banks have been prohibited from opening new branches and the last banking licence to a foreign institution was granted in 1973. The incorporation of local branches of all foreign-owned banks occured in 1994. In May 2003, a change in policy viewed foreign banks as catalysts for change and three new licences were granted to foreign Islamic banks.

Banking and Financial Institutions Act 1989 (BAFIA)

In 1986, several deposit-taking cooperatives (DTCs) collapsed in a mire of fraud and mismanagement. This crisis led to the formulation of BAFIA, which was promulgated to provide supervision of the Malaysian financial system and the regulation of scheduled and non-scheduled business institutions.

BANGKING AND FINANCIAL INSTITUTIONS ACT 1989 (ACT 372), REGULATIONS & SELECTED ORDERS

(AS AT 5TH JULY 2004)

ILBS International Law Book Services

The cover of BAFIA, which set forth new laws for the licensing and regulation of banking institutions.

The Overseas Union Bank Ltd branch in Kuching, Sarawak in 1964.

Chronology

1957 At Independence, there were 26 banks in operation.

1959 Central Bank of Malaya established (renamed Bank Negara Malaysia in 1963) (see 'Monetary Policy and Bank Negara Malaysia').

First finance company, Tai Cheng Finance Berhad, incorporated.

1960 Malaysian Industrial Development Finance Berhad (MIDF), set up as a bank to provide medium- and long-term financing (see 'Small and medium enterprises').

Malayan Banking Berhad (Maybank) established. In 2006, it was the largest bank in terms of assets and branches.

1963 First discount house, Short Deposits (Malaysia) Berhad, incorporated.

1970 First merchant bank, Chartered Merchant Bankers Malaysia Berhad, incorporated.

1972 Credit Guarantee Corporation (CGC) established to guarantee loans to small-scale enterprises (see 'Small and medium enterprises').

1974 National Savings Bank (Bank Simpanan Negara) established to aid public savings and investments.

1978 Commercial banks allowed to determine their own deposit and lending rates (previously set by BNM).

Merchant banks brought under umbrella of the Banking Act 1973.

Bankers acceptances (loans secured by trade bills) and negotiable certificates of deposit (fixed deposits) introduced to increase savings.

1981 First Automated Teller Machines (ATMs) introduced.

1983 Islamic banking introduced with establishment of Bank Islam Malaysia Berhad (see 'Islamic financial services')

All loans anchored to a bank's base lending rate (BLR), with the exception of loans to priority sectors, which carried a fixed lending rate.

1989 The Banking and Financial Institutions Act (BAFIA) 1989 introduced.

1990 International offshore financial centre set up in Labuan.

1994 BNM instituted two-tier system for commercial banks to prepare for liberalization of the banking sector.

1999 BNM announced a consolidation programme for domestic banking sector.

2000 Internet banking introduced. Nationwide Payment and Clearing System Project started.

2001 Financial Sector Master Plan and Capital Market Master Plan launched to foster the growth of the banking system and capital market over ten years.

2004 Amendment to BAFIA 1989 created a new banking entity—a banking and finance company (BAFIN).

BNM introduced a new interest rate framework. Banks able to determine BLR based on their own cost structure and lending strategies.

2005 SME Bank established (see 'Small and medium enterprises').

The early banks

Local and foreign banks operated in two largely separate contexts. The foreign banks, primarily British-owned, served the colonial administration and private enterprises in tin mining, plantations and trading. The local banks, mainly Chinese-owned, financed the business activities of the Chinese community.

Early institution building

After Independence, the government pursued a programme of institution-building to offset foreign dominance and to add sophistication and depth to the financial structure. Three wholly-owned local banks were set up between 1960 and 1965: Malayan Banking Berhad, Bank Bumiputra Malaysia Berhad and Public Bank Berhad. Key institutions included the Central Bank of Malaysia

Opening ceremony of the first rural branch of Bank Bumiputra in Sabak Bernam, Selangor in 1968.

(see 'Monetary policy and Bank Negara Malaysia'), and the Employees Provident Fund (EPF) (see 'Protection through the law'). Other financial intermediaries introduced in the post-Independence period included finance companies and merchant banks.

By 1970, the building blocks of the major systems that define the current Malaysian financial landscape (the banking system, the non-financial intermediaries, and the various financial markets) were in place.

Labuan International Offshore Financial Centre

In October 1990, an international offshore financial centre was set up in Labuan. Financial institutions operating in Labuan offered offshore services including banking, insurance, corporate funding, investment and trust management. A major incentive was the imposition of low or no tax on income, profits, dividends, and interest earned from offshore activities.
In 1996, the Labuan Offshore Financial Services Authority was established.

Liberalization in the 1990s

For many years, foreign banks were not allowed to open new branches or to relocate existing branches. However, pressure exerted by developed countries in the second half of the 1990s through the General Agreement on Trade in Services (GATS) made liberalization inevitable, not only in banking but also in insurance and stockbroking. To prepare local banks for the challenges of liberalization, BNM took two major steps.

First, between 1994–96 it instituted a two-tier system (TTRS) for commercial banks. By imposing higher requirements on Tier 1 financial institutions (banks with a larger pool of assets) on the one hand, and granting them greater privileges on the other, BNM created a core of highly capitalized and well-managed financial institutions. TTRS was extended to finance companies and merchant banks in 1996. Second, local banks were encouraged to merge. Beginning in 1996, several mergers took place, mainly among government-linked banks such as between Bank Bumiputra Malaysia Berhad and Bank of Commerce Berhad to form Bank Bumiputra Commerce Berhad in 1999.

Consolidation programme

The Asian financial crisis of 1997–98 (see 'Malaysia's innovative response to the financial crisis') provided the impetus for the consolidation of the banking industry. BNM embarked on a programme of strengthening the banking sector for long-term survival and growth. There was a need to organically increase the size of the various participants in the financial sector.

The effect of this consolidation exercise was to increase the financial base of each entity. Efficiency could be achieved through better management of a smaller number of institutions. Consolidation merged the 'smaller' financial institutions with the 'bigger' ones. Between 1999 and 2002, 71 banking institutions were merged into ten 'anchor' institutions.

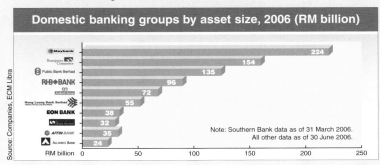

Domestic banking groups by asset size, 2006 (RM billion)

Source: Companies, ECM Libra

Maybank	224
Bumiputra Commerce	154
Public Bank Berhad	135
RHB BANK	96
	72
Hong Leong Bank Berhad	55
EON BANK	38
	32
AFFIN BANK	35
Alliance Bank	24

Note: Southern Bank data as of 31 March 2006. All other data as of 30 June 2006.

RM billion: 0, 50, 100, 150, 200, 250

Financial markets

Financial markets play a vital role in mobilizing and allocating funds. An efficient and competitive capital market is an important precondition for the mobilization of financial resources. The government's Capital Market Master Plan covering the period 2000–10 continues to provide the framework for shaping the future development of the country's capital market.

The Securities Commission in Bukit Kiara, Kuala Lumpur.

Capital supply and demand

The capital market plays a pivotal role in development—it matches companies seeking to raise capital with investors in search of investment opportunities. Investors comprise individuals, large institutional investors such as the Employees Provident Fund and other pension funds (see 'Protection through the law'), unit trust schemes managed by PNB (see 'New Economic Policy: 1971–1990') and insurance companies.

The capital market refers to markets for medium- to long-term financial assets, and encompasses corporate stocks as well as public and private debt securities. Up to the 1980s, the government's financial needs dominated fund-raising in the capital market. Privatization in the late 1980s and 1990s resulted in increased financing needs in the private sector and the capital market expanded to meet this demand. At the end of 2005, stock market capitalization reached RM695 billion with 1021 companies listed on the Main and Second Boards and MESDAQ market. Services which support these markets—investment management funds, stockbrokerages and advisory services—have also expanded.

With the increased importance of the capital markets comes disintermediation: a shift from bank lending to direct financing through capital markets.

Selected indicators of unit trust funds, 2005

Number of management companies	36
Number of approved funds	340
Units in circulation (billion)	139.4
Net Asset Value (NAV) of funds (RM billion)	98.49
NAV to Bursa market capitalization (%)	14.17

The private debt securities (PDS) market

PDS are the main source of financial market funding for the private sector, with the equity market also providing a sizeable portion through rights issues and initial public offerings. One of the earliest bond issuers was Cagamas Berhad, the national mortgage corporation, established in 1986 to improve the availability and affordability of housing loans, particularly for the lower income group. The proceeds of Cagamas bonds finance the purchase of housing loans from financial institutions, selected corporations and the government. These bonds are traded through an increasingly active secondary market.

Logo of Cagamas Berhad.

Bond issues played a significant role in financing long-term infrastructure projects including the North–South Expressway and Kuala Lumpur International Airport.

Another catalyst for the PDS market was the setting up of the Rating Agency of Malaysia (RAM) in November 1990. The first of its kind in the ASEAN region, RAM's primary function is to rate corporate bonds, providing potential investors with a guide to a bond issuer's creditworthiness.

The Securities Commission (SC)

The government has taken various measures aimed at maintaining the integrity of the securities industry and safeguarding the interest of investors.

In 1988, it established a task force to propose measures for streamlining the various regulatory bodies that had been overseeing the Malaysian capital market. The outcome was the establishment of the SC on 1 March 1993 under the Securities Commission Act 1993 as a one-stop agency overseeing and regulating the development of the capital market.

The SC is a self-funding statutory body with investigative and enforcement powers. It reports to the Minister of Finance and its accounts are tabled in Parliament annually.

Suruhanjaya Sekuriti
Securities Commission

An important component in the SC is the Issues and Investment Division, which regulates the issuing of securities by public limited companies, corporate take-overs and mergers, and matters relating to unit trusts and other collective investment schemes.

In 2000, the SC released its policy framework for the consolidation of the stockbroking industry. In 2001, the ten-year Capital Market Master Plan to chart the strategic positioning and future direction of the Malaysian capital market was released.

Broad objectives of the Capital Market Master Plan:
- to develop the capital market as the preferred fund-raising centre for Malaysian companies
- to promote an efficient investment management industry and create a more conducive environment for investors
- to enhance the competitive position and efficiency of market institutions
- to develop a stronger and more facilitating regulatory regime
- to establish Malaysia as an international Islamic capital market centre

The derivatives market

Derivatives such as options and futures are instruments which are created out of conventional direct dealings in securities, currencies and commodities. They are useful instruments in managing risk, such as the risk that is related to price fluctuations.

The Kuala Lumpur Commodities Exchange (KLCE) was launched in 1980, with the subsequent introduction of trading in crude palm oil, tin, cocoa and RBD palm olein futures. In 1992, the Futures Industry Act was introduced. Then in 1996, the Malaysian Monetary Exchange (MME) was established to provide derivatives such as the 3-month Kuala Lumpur Interbank Offered Rate (KLIBOR) futures. In 1998, the KLCE merged with the MME to form the Commodity and Monetary Exchange of Malaysia (COMMEX).

The Kuala Lumpur Options and Financial Futures Exchange (KLOFFE) began operations in December 1995. In 2001, COMMEX and KLOFFE merged to form the Malaysia Derivatives Exchange Berhad (MDEX) or Bursa Malaysia Derivatives (BMD). In the same year, BMD ended open outcry floor trading and became fully electronic.

The old COMMEX trading floor in 1998 where derivatives such as palm oil futures were traded.

The stock market

Bronze sculptures of the bear and bull in front of Bursa Malaysia in Kuala Lumpur.

Starting points

Formally organized trading of stocks and shares began in May 1960 when four stockbrokers met daily to determine share prices. Some months later, these four stockbrokers formed the Malayan Stock Exchange. Business links between Malaya and Singapore were so closely intertwined that in 1961 the board system was introduced whereby the two trading rooms, linked by direct telephone lines, listed the same stocks and shares at the same prices on their boards. In 1964, the Malayan Stock Exchange was renamed the Stock Exchange of Malaysia, which in turn was renamed the Stock Exchange of Malaysia and Singapore in 1965 when Singapore separated from Malaysia. In 1973, the common stock exchange split into the Kuala Lumpur Stock Exchange (KLSE) and the Stock Exchange of Singapore (SES). However, Malaysian-incorporated companies continued to be listed on the SES and vice versa until the end of 1990, when there was a mutual delisting of companies registered in one country from the stock exchange of the other. In 2004, the KLSE became a demutualized exchange and was renamed Bursa Malaysia.

The Kuala Lumpur Stock Exchange in the 1980s.

Bursa Malaysia Berhad (Bursa)

BURSA MALAYSIA

Investors, stockbroking companies, financial institutions and listed companies participate in the country's capital market through Bursa. Bursa governs the conduct of its members (stockbroking firms) in securities dealings. It enforces the observance of the listing, disclosure and standards requirements imposed on companies listed on its boards.

Bursa's Securities Exchange consists of the Main Board, Second Board and the Malaysian Exchange of Securities Dealing and Automated Quotation (MESDAQ). Counters on the Main Board are listed under categories such as industry, plantation, property and construction. Typically the category with the highest representation has been industry. The formation of the Second Board in 1988 allowed smaller capitalized companies to tap into funds directly from the market. In addition, rules were liberalized to encourage the participation of Bumiputera and infrastructure companies in Initial Public Offerings.

Since 1986, the Kuala Lumpur Composite Index (KLCI) has been used as the barometer of local market performance. The KLCI has comprised 100 component companies since 1995. There were 14 major indices calculated by the Bursa in 2005, including the Exchange Main Board All Share (EMAS) Index introduced in 1991, the Syariah Index created in 1999 and the Technology Index established in 2000.

Bursa retained the exchange function of KLSE after demutualization and the securities exchange business was transferred to Bursa Securities. At the end of 2005, Bursa Malaysia had 1021 listed companies categorized into 15 different sectors representing a diversity of over 50 different economic activities.

Top ten companies by market capitalization, 2006

	Company	Market cap
Maybank	Malayan Banking	RM42.57 billion
TENAGA NASIONAL	Tenaga Nasional	RM40.99 billion
MISC	MISC	RM32.18 billion
TM	Telekom Malaysia	RM30.72 billion
	Public Bank	RM23.63 billion
maxis	Maxis Communications	RM21.96 billion
Bumiputra Commerce	Bumiputra-Commerce Holdings	RM20.20 billion
IOI GROUP	IOI Corporation	RM19.56 billion
PETRONAS	Petronas Gas	RM17.31 billion
	Genting	RM16.44 billion

Note: As of 20 September 2006

Source: Bursa Malaysia

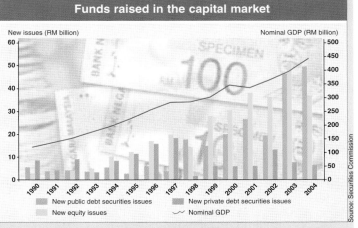

Funds raised in the capital market

New issues (RM billion) / Nominal GDP (RM billion)

- New public debt securities issues
- New private debt securities issues
- New equity issues
- Nominal GDP

(years 1990–2004)

Source: Securities Commission

The technology of the stock market

A fully automated on-line trading system for stockbrokers was made available when the System on Computerized Order Routing and Execution (SCORE) was implemented in 1992. In November 1992, the clearance and settlement process underwent similar upgrading when the Central Depository System (CDS) was introduced, rendering the physical scrip delivery system obsolete by the end of 1996. With the implementation of the Broker Front End System (WinSCORE) in 1994, the order-entry process and real-time market information was made available. The upgrading of these systems boosted trading volume and increased the global competitiveness of the capital market.

Prime Minister Dato' Seri Abdullah Ahmad Badawi (fifth from left) launching Bursa's listing on the Main Board in March 2005.

The Malaysian Exchange of Securities Dealing and Automated Quotation (MESDAQ) market

A separate stock exchange, the MESDAQ, commenced trading in April 1999 and merged with the KLSE in 2002. It caters to technology and high-growth companies that, despite having no earnings record, have viable business models and high-growth potential. The consolidation of the two equity exchanges was a significant step towards the creation of a single Malaysian exchange as recommended in the Capital Market Master Plan, and towards the development of a more efficient financing base for emerging high-growth issuers in Malaysia.

The MESDAQ listing requirements set out 12 Technology Priority Areas.

Islamic financial services

Islamic banking was introduced in 1983. Based on the principle of profit-sharing instead of interest, Malaysia was the first country to have an Islamic banking system operating side by side with a conventional banking system. Islamic insurance, Islamic money and capital markets are all aspects of Islamic financial services.

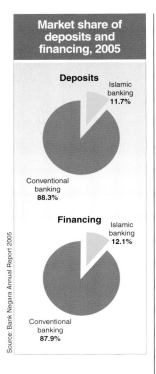

Market share of deposits and financing, 2005

Deposits
Islamic banking **11.7%**
Conventional banking **88.3%**

Financing
Islamic banking **12.1%**
Conventional banking **87.9%**

Source: Bank Negara Annual Report 2005

The development of Islamic banking

The first Islamic bank, Bank Islam Malaysia Berhad (BIMB), was established under the Islamic Banking Act 1983 with a paid-up capital of RM79.9 million. The activities of the bank are based on *syariah* principles.

The Government Investment Act 1983 was enacted shortly thereafter to empower the government to issue Government Investment Issues, which are government securities based on *syariah* principles.

In 1993, Islamic banking became a full-fledged banking system with the launch of the Interest-Free Banking Scheme (IFBS). Islamic banking services were provided by all conventional commercial banks, merchant banks and finance companies via their network of branches. The parent bank, however, must have already established an interest-free banking unit and fund. By mid-1996, IFBS was offered by 46 financial institutions through 1663 branches, and public confidence in the concept of Islamic *mudharabah* (profit sharing) was proven with the popularity of *mudharabah* investment accounts.

The National Syariah Advisory Council on Islamic Banking and Takaful (NSAC) was set up by Bank Negara Malaysia in 1997 as the highest *syariah* authority on Islamic banking and *takaful*.

Malaysia's second Islamic bank, Bank Muamalat Malaysia Berhad (BMMB), commenced operations in 1999 and RHB Islamic Bank Bhd became the nation's third Islamic bank in 2005. The liberalization of Islamic banking in 2005 also saw the opening of the first foreign Islamic bank, Kuwait Finance House (Malaysia) Berhad.

Islamic banking has flourished, with total assets of RM111.8 billion in 2005. The introduction of innovative financing products was a key factor in mobilizing surplus funds. Only 55 per cent of Islamic deposits were used in financing as opposed to 84 per cent of deposits in the conventional banking sector.

Bank Islam headquarters in Kuala Lumpur. Bank Islam was Malaysia's first full-fledged Islamic bank.

The US$600-million Malaysia global *sukuk* (trust certificates) issued in 2002 was the world's first Islamic global bond issue. Listed on both the Labuan International Financial Exchange and the Luxembourg Stock Exchange, the global *sukuk* is a floating rate note maturing in 2007 and is backed by an *ijarah* (lease) on government property.

The Islamic Interbank Money Market

In 1994, the government introduced the Islamic Interbank Money Market (IIMM) to support the Islamic banking system. The IIMM facilitates Islamic interbank cheque clearing, interbank trading of Islamic papers, interbank investments and short-term funding among Islamic banks and IFBS participants. Only Islamic banks, commercial banks, merchant banks and eligible finance companies and discount houses are allowed to participate in the IIMM. The IIMM is dominated by Government Investment Certificates, which represent loans to the government under the concept of *qardhul hassan* (benevolent loan).

The Islamic capital market

With the increase in Islamic funds requiring placement, an Islamic capital market became a priority in the 1990s. A fully Islamic securities firm, BIMB Securities Sdn Bhd, was established in

ABOVE: A handshake signifies the completion of payment of *zakat* at a collection booth located in Pertama Complex, Kuala Lumpur.

RIGHT: The *halal* mark used by the Department of Islamic Development (JAKIM) to certify *halal* products and services.

Islam in the modern economy

Examples of Islamic economic practices include the collection and distribution of *zakat* (tithe), the Islamic tax on wealth, and the development of *waqf* (endowment) properties by the State Religious Councils. Where bequests are concerned, Malaysian Muslims are governed by Islamic regulations, and are not permitted to write wills which conflict with these regulations.

Halal certification for food products has been practised since 1982. In 2003, the *Halal Pages* was introduced to offer *halal* products and services as an alternative to conventionally advertised ones.

Muslims are also forbidden from engaging in certain forms of economic activity, such as those linked to the gaming industries.

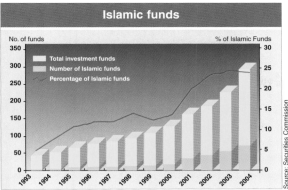

Islamic funds

A Takaful Nasional booth in Seremban during the 2005 Malaysian Trust Fund Week.

Islamic insurance

Islamic insurance is premised on the concept of *takaful* (joint guarantee) whereby participants mutually agree amongst themselves to guarantee each other against defined losses or damage by contributing to *takaful* funds. Syarikat Takaful Malaysia Berhad (STMB) was set up as a subsidiary of Bank Islam under the Takaful Act 1984. In 1996, STMB was converted into a public listed company on the Main Board of the then Kuala Lumpur Stock Exchange.

The *takaful* business is broadly divided into family (Islamic life insurance) and general *takaful* business (Islamic general insurance). In 1995, the ASEAN Takaful Group was formed to facilitate the exchange of business among *takaful* operators in ASEAN. Then in 1997, ASEAN Retakaful International (L) Ltd was set up in Labuan. As of 2006, other registered *takaful* operators are Takaful Nasional Sdn Bhd (established in 1993), Mayban Takaful Berhad (2001), Takaful Ikhlas Sdn Bhd (2003) and Commerce Takaful Berhad (2006). In 2004, family and general *takaful* net contribution grew by 10.8 per cent to RM1.1 billion.

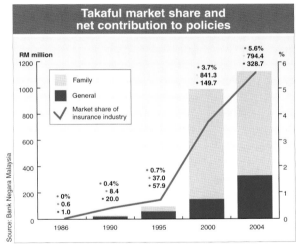

1995, an index of Islamic stocks was created in 1999, and two firms provided Islamic stockbroking services at that time. As of October 2005, 857 (85 per cent of counters listed on the Bursa Malaysia) were declared *syariah*-compliant by the National Syariah Advisory Council. At the end of 2005, there were 77 Islamic unit trust funds with a net asset value of RM6.8 million (eight per cent of that of the total unit trust industry).

Islamic private debt securities are a potential growth area based on the Islamic concept of *bai al-dayn* (debt trading). The first primary issue of such securities was in 1990, in the form of *shahadah al-dayn* certificates (promissory notes) issued by Shell MDS Sdn Bhd Malaysia. This facility is particularly suitable for financing large development projects and was used to fund the construction of the Kuala Lumpur International Airport. In 1994, the issue of *mudharabah* (mortgage) bonds, gave further diversity and depth to the market.

Lembaga Tabung Haji (Pilgrims' Management and Fund Board)

Established in 1962, Lembaga Tabung Haji (LTH) was the first modern Islamic financial institution in Malaya. LTH provides a systematic and efficient savings facility for Muslims wishing to perform the *hajj* (pilgrimage). At the same time, it enables Muslims through their savings to participate in investments approved by Islam. While not a major player in the country's financial sector, it was nevertheless of seminal importance to the later development of Islamic banking. In 1963, LTH had 1281 depositors and RM46,600 in deposits. At the end of 2003, it paid a bonus rate of four per cent to its 4.7 million depositors, and its total assets stood at RM11.6 billion. The breakdown of funds stood at 32 per cent in equity, 16 per cent in real estate, 29 per cent in conventional and Islamic financial investments and the remaining 23 per cent in group and subsidiary companies.

The Tabung Haji building in Kuala Lumpur was completed in 1984.

The Kuala Lumpur Stock Exchange (KLSE) Syariah Index
Introduced in 1999, the KLSE Syariah Index comprises securities of Main Board companies whose activities are not contrary to *syariah* principles. Securities are excluded from the list based on these criteria:
• operations based on *riba* (interest) such as commercial banks and merchant banks
• operations involving gambling
• activities involving the manufacture and/or sale of *haram* (forbidden) products such as liquor and pork
• operations containing the element of *gharar* (uncertainty) such as conventional insurance.
As of October 2004 the KLSE Syariah Index was comprised of 479 companies.

A brochure on the KLSE Syariah Index.

Some Islamic financial products
Islam proscribes the giving and taking of *riba* (interest). Islamic financial institutions therefore offer alternative forms of financial services based on profit-sharing. Some Islamic banking facilities are counterparts of products offered by conventional interest-based banks, while others are products not offered outside the Islamic banking system.

Products in the Islamic banking system that are also available in the conventional banking system include current and savings accounts (*wadiah* and *mudharabah* concepts) and certain financing contracts like higher education financing (*bai' bithaman ajil*, *bai' inah* and *murabahah* concepts).

Products which are only available in the Islamic banking system include pawnbroking services (*ar-rahnu*) and benevolent loans (*qardhul hassan*).

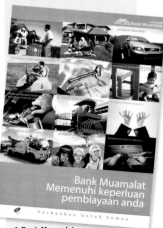

A Bank Muamalat advertisement shows the range of financial products offered.

Malaysia's innovative response to the financial crisis

In 1997, the actions of currency speculators triggered a series of inter-related events in Asia that very quickly changed the prevailing scenario from one of rapid expansion to one of immense economic and social hardship. Malaysia's response, which departed from the prescribed measures of the International Monetary Fund (IMF), ultimately proved successful in minimizing the effects of the crisis.

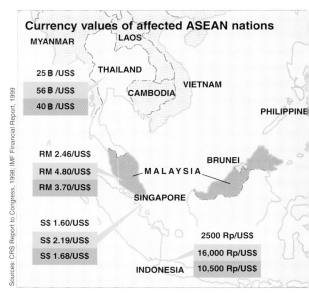

Currency values of affected ASEAN nations

Sources: CRS Report to Congress, 1998; IMF Financial Report, 1999

ABOVE TOP TO BOTTOM: Some of the major infrastructure projects delayed by the financial crisis include the Bakun Dam (to be completed in 2008), the Express Rail Link to the Kuala Lumpur International Airport (completed in 2002), and the Kuala Lumpur monorail (completed in 2003).

Setting the scene

From 1987 to 1996, Malaysia's economy grew remarkably, averaging 8.8 per cent per year. In 1996, however, Malaysia and other ASEAN countries, including Thailand, Indonesia and the Philippines, experienced a slowdown in growth, a substantial rise in current account deficits, weaker exports due to currency appreciation, and large external debts.

During the 1990s, these countries had accelerated financial liberalization by relaxing capital and exchange controls. This resulted in significant inflows of foreign capital in the mid-1990s, in the form of foreign direct investment, portfolio investments in local share markets and loans to local banks and companies. The long-term foreign capital inflows were an important source of financing for the development of infrastructure, and key sectors such as manufacturing and services.

At the same time, currency trading flourished. Some of this involved foreign exchange transactions associated with the international trade of goods and services, but a significant portion of transactions was for speculative purposes. These short-term capital flows were more volatile, and had greater potential for destabilizing economies in the event of sudden reversals in economic trends.

The integration of the region with the global financial system, the high speed of computerized financial transactions and the development of large institutional investors (such as investment banks and hedge and pension funds) meant that large amounts of short-term capital could, for speculative purposes, be moved across borders very quickly with potentially destabilizing consequences.

The currency crisis hits

In May 1997, currency speculators sold vast amounts of Thai baht, forcing the Thai government to spend billions of dollars of foreign reserves buying baht to defend its value. It is believed that speculators borrowed baht, then sold it for dollars, so that when the baht fell, they could then buy it back for fewer dollars. On 2 July 1997, unable to defend the baht, the Thai government was forced to float the baht, causing currency devaluation of more than ten per cent.

Similar events occurred in Malaysia, with Bank Negara Malaysia intervening on 8 July 1997 to defend the Ringgit against speculators. In the following months, the Philippine peso and Indonesian rupiah also underwent significant devaluation. These developments fuelled panic-selling as funds began to flow out of the region.

Property and stock market collapse

In Malaysia, the Ringgit's depreciation led to other problems. The burden of servicing foreign loans in

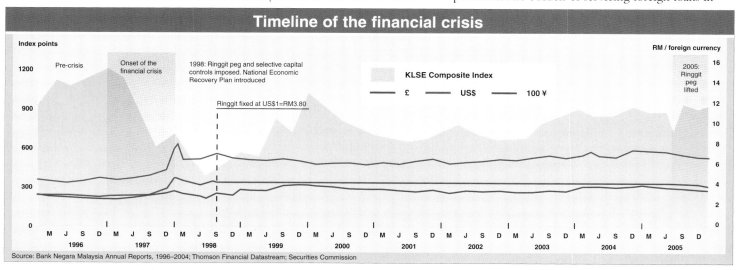

Timeline of the financial crisis

Source: Bank Negara Malaysia Annual Reports, 1996–2004; Thomson Financial Datastream; Securities Commission

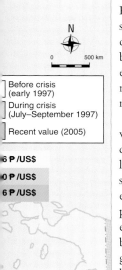

Before crisis
(early 1997)

During crisis
(July–September 1997)

Recent value (2005)

6 P /US$

0 P /US$

6 P /US$

Ringgit terms suddenly became substantially greater. This was compounded by the fact that businesses in the emerging Asian economies relied on bank loans rather than bond or equity markets for funds.

The crisis exposed weaknesses in accounting, disclosure, supervisory and legal frameworks of the banking system. The excessive credit extended to the equity and property markets during the expansion years led to a boom but, as the crisis unfolded, fears grew that foreign funds would be withdrawn. The Kuala Lumpur Stock Exchange Composite Index (KLCI) declined sharply as foreign fund managers liquidated their investments, which further exacerbated the fall of the Ringgit's value. The fall in the value of shares and property, which had been pledged as collateral

for loans, led to even more problems for borrowers. The number of non-performing loans (NPL) grew, and banks weakened.

The impact of the crisis

Malaysia's impressive growth of 1987 to 1996 ended with the onset of the crisis. Real GDP growth fell from 8.6 per cent in 1996 to -7.4 per cent in 1998. The purchasing power of Malaysians was significantly reduced; real income per capita fell from US$3417 in 1996 to US$2220 in 1998. Private real consumption and gross private investment registered negative growth whilst unemployment rose.

The depreciation of the Ringgit made imports costlier, resulting in higher inflation. Among the sectors adversely affected was the tourism industry, heavily reliant on tourists from the Asian region.

The events in Southeast Asia eventually threatened to precipitate a global recession, with the number of countries affected growing to include South Korea, China, Hong Kong, Brazil and Russia. Drops in stock market indices and closures of banks and brokerage firms occurred even in the United States and Japan.

The National Economic Recovery Plan, released by the NEAC in July 1998, promulgated policy measures to stabilize and strengthen the financial system.

Prime Minister Dato' Seri Dr Mahathir Mohamad carrying the 1999 Budget Speech which outlined selective capital and exchange controls.

Malaysia's response

International Monetary Fund (IMF)-prescribed solutions
Governments in Asia were forced to adopt drastic measures to stabilize their economies. Thailand, Indonesia and South Korea (later known as the IMF-3) sought IMF assistance via emergency loan packages. The IMF's insistence on austere measures as a condition of the loans generated efficacy debates. The IMF's stance or the 'Washington Consensus' was unacceptable to Malaysia.

An independent response from Malaysia
As the initial IMF-prescribed policies proved ineffective, Malaysia refused financial assistance from the IMF and adopted an independent stance by practising her own strategies to overcome the crisis.

In January 1998, the government established the National Economic Action Council (NEAC) to find solutions to economic recovery and recession prevention. The six key strategies of NEAC's National Economic Recovery Plan were to stabilize the value of the Ringgit, restore market confidence, maintain financial market stability, strengthen economic fundamentals, continue the nation's equity and socio-economic programmes and revitalize the affected sectors of the economy.

New institutions
On the NEAC's recommendation, the government established three agencies to institute reforms and resolve the liquidity problems of the banking and corporate sectors:
- Pengurusan Danaharta Nasional Berhad (Danaharta), the national asset management company, was set up in June 1998 to reduce the financial sector's non-performing loans (NPLs) by restructuring the NPLs and strengthening the credit evaluation of banks. Danaharta wound up its operations on 31 December 2005 after meeting its lifetime recovery target of RM30.35 billion. Its final loan recovery rate was 58 per cent.

- Danamodal Nasional Berhad (Danamodal) was set up in August 1998 to raise funds to recapitalize, strengthen and promote a healthy and competitive banking system. In October 2003, Danamodal redeemed its entire RM11 billion (nominal value) five-year zero-coupon Unsecured Redeemable Bonds issued in 1998 to fund its recapitalization of affected banking institutions. A total of RM7.59 billion was injected into ten banking institutions. Danamodal ceased operations in February 2004.
- The Corporate Debt Restructuring Committee (CDRC) facilitated corporate debt restructuring with financial institutions, ensuring continued financing of viable businesses. In August 2002, CDRC completed its duties upon achieving a sufficient level of debt restructuring, having resolved 48 cases involving debts of RM52.6 billion.

Selective capital and exchange controls
In September 1998, Malaysia imposed the following measures to create a stable environment and to curb short-term flows, speculation and internationalization of the Ringgit:
- Selective capital controls restricted asset movements and controlled capital outflows. Foreigners could only convert proceeds

Roles of the key agencies

Banks → sells NPLs → DANAHARTA (Malaysia's National Asset Management Company) → M F (Ministry of Finance Incorporated)

Banks → injects capital → DM DANAMODAL NASIONAL BERHAD

Borrowers → restructure debts → Corporate Debt Restructuring Committee (CDRC) → Bank Negara Malaysia

derived from Malaysian securities into foreign currencies after waiting for a year.
- The exchange rate was fixed at RM3.80 to one US dollar to stabilize the Ringgit and to discourage speculative activities. Limits were set on the use of the Ringgit abroad, especially when the spread between the offshore and domestic rates for Ringgit deposits was too high. In addition, temporary controls on foreign exchange prevented currency traders from influencing domestic economic policy by forcing interest rates to exorbitant levels.

Fiscal and monetary policies
Selective capital and exchange controls enabled the government to institute the following policies to engender economic revitalization without having to worry about destabilizing events:
- On the monetary side, Bank Negara Malaysia (see 'Monetary Policy and Bank Negara') enhanced liquidity in the economy by reducing the statutory reserve ratio from 13.5 per cent in 1997 to four per cent in 1998 to increase credit creation and lower interest rates to spur economic activity.
- On the fiscal side, the government increased gross development expenditure by 23 per cent to RM19.4 million in 1998 (see 'Federal Government revenue and expenditure') to fund social programmes to lighten the burden on the lower income groups.

Malaysia managed to come out of the crisis faster than the IMF-assisted nations without having to submit to foreign intervention in her financial and corporate sectors. The above responses restored confidence in the Malaysian economy and resulted in a reduction of NPLs, the rationalization of financial institutions and the stabilization of the Ringgit and the stock market.

Malaysia's Ringgit peg to the dollar was removed on 21 July 2005 and the Ringgit now trades within a managed float system against a basket of currencies.

1. The Seri Saujana bridge in Putrajaya has two three-lane carriageways. The bridge has an overall single span of 300 metres and a total width of 32 metres.

2. A postman at work. In 2005, 60 per cent of Pos Malaysia's users were businesses. In 2004, 1.2 billion mail items were processed.

3. Planes docked at a terminal of Kuala Lumpur International Airport (KLIA). KLIA is equipped with 75 ramp stands and is capable of handling 100 aircraft movements at any given time.

4. The Kuala Lumpur–Ampang highway. Peninsular Malaysia's 63,445-kilometre network of roads (as of 2005) links all parts of the country and is the backbone of the transport system.

5. View of YTL Corporation Berhad's Paka Power Plant in Terengganu. The company was awarded the first Independent Power Producer licence in 1993.

Expenditure on infrastructure under the five-year plans

Share of transport expenditure (%)

Second Malaysia Plan 1961–1965	First Malaysia Plan 1966–1970	Second Malaysia Plan 1971–1975	Third Malaysia Plan 1976–1980	Fourth Malaysia Plan 1981–1985	Fifth Malaysia Plan 1986–1990	Sixth Malaysia Plan 1991–1995	Seventh Malaysia Plan 1996–2000	Eighth Malaysia Plan 2001–2005	Ninth Malaysia Plan 2006–2010*

1961 1966 1971 1976 1981 1986 1991 1996 2001 2006

Airports Ports Railways Roads * Allocation

Source: various Malaysia Plans

INFRASTRUCTURE AND TRANSPORT

Malaysia has a good network of roads and railways, telecommunications, electricity, water supply and sewerage. Within the Peninsula itself, the west coast has a more developed infrastructure than the east coast.

Modern modes of transport are featured on the back of the ten-Ringgit note as a tribute to their importance to the economy.

In line with the National Vision Policy (2001–10) of building a resilient and competitive nation, the emphasis of the Ninth Malaysia Plan (2006–10) is on increasing infrastructure and accessibility in less developed areas, while the focus in urban areas is to improve public transportation.

While the government traditionally shouldered the responsibility of providing the nation's infrastructure, since the early 1980s this burden has been progressively handed over to the private sector.

Elements of Malaysia's transport network that have been privatized include the North–South Expressway, the Kuala Lumpur Light Rail Transit (LRT) system and the monorail. Of Malaysia's federal and state ports, seven are privatized. The country's 39 civilian airports are operated by Malaysia Airports Berhad, which was corporatized in 1992. Keretapi Tanah Melayu Berhad (KTM) was also corporatized in 1992 under the Railways Act 1991. The Kuala Lumpur International Airport (KLIA) is at the centre of a major infrastructure development programme which aims to make it the aviation hub of the Asia Pacific region. The airport is designed to handle a maximum of 60 million passengers per annum and cargo traffic of three million tonnes per annum by the year 2020.

Most utilities have been privatized, but the government still concerns itself with making sure that the public is served with safe, reliable and affordable supplies of electricity and piped water. The Federal Government administers the water supply, but the treatment of sewage from residential areas in Peninsular Malaysia has been privatized. Power production and supply used to be the sole monopoly of the National Electricity Board (NEB) in Peninsular Malaysia, the Sabah Electricity Sdn Bhd (SESB) and the Sarawak Electricity Supply Corporation. The NEB was privatized in May 1992 and renamed Tenaga Nasional Berhad (TNB). Although TNB retains its monopoly over transmission and distribution services, several Independent Power Producers (IPPs) have been granted licences to build and operate power plants for the generation and sale of electricity to TNB and large industrial consumers.

A modern telecommunications system is integral to the growth of the industrial and services sectors. TM (formerly Telekom Malaysia) Berhad is the main supplier of telecommunications services. In terms of postal services, Pos Malaysia Berhad, since its privatization, has acted with market-driven and profit-focused goals, while continuing to fulfil its social obligations.

Roads and railways

Early rail and road networks linked ports with towns and resource-rich areas such as mines. These road and rail systems played an integral role in the economic and social development of the country. Extensive government-financed road construction occurred in the 1960s and 1970s, and in the 1980s privatized toll expressways were introduced.

In 2004, toll collected on PLUS's 966.5-kilometre expressway network amounted to almost RM1.5 billion. The North–South Expressway accounted for 83 per cent of this.

Jalan Universiti in Petaling Jaya, c. 1961. It was the country's first dual carriageway.

The East–West highway crosses Temenggor Lake in Perak. Between 2000 and 2005, RM18.5 billion was spent on road development projects by the government.

National road development

Early roads were limited; they merely connected villages and ports, and provided access to tin mining areas in Perak and Selangor. The 20th century saw 'metalled' roads being constructed, with limestone and laterite replacing earth and gravel. Tar or macadamized bitumen roads were later introduced to accommodate motor vehicles.

By the 1950s, the government began to establish a basic road network, and development accelerated with greater vehicle usage. The Peninsula's west coast progressed faster than the east. Before Independence, there was no continuous link from Kuala Lumpur to Kuantan and Kota Bharu due to the numerous river crossings and floods. After Independence, roads assumed a pivotal economic and social role by increasing access to rural and new growth areas and improving inter-urban linkages.

To meet growing demand, the General Transportation Study (1967–68) outlined plans for both existing and new projects. Projects of the late 1960s included the Tanjung Malim–Slim River Bypass and the Pekan–Batu Balik Road. In the 1970s, new projects included the East–West Highway, the Kuantan–Segamat Highway, the Kuala Lumpur–Karak Highway and the Kuala Lumpur–Seremban Expressway. The new highways resulted

North–South Toll Expressway

Completed in 1994, this 848-kilometre expressway, constructed mainly of asphalt-based pavement, is the backbone of the Peninsula, stretching from Bukit Kayu Hitam, Kedah, to Johor Bahru, Johor, linking large industrial areas, urban centres, ports and airports in the western corridor. It comprises a dual two-lane carriageway, widened to three lanes in urban areas. From end to end, the journey takes less than ten hours. The Malaysian Highway Authority constructed 334 kilometres, with the balance being completed by Projek Lebuhraya Utara-Selatan Berhad (PLUS) under a privatization programme in 1988 which awarded PLUS the right to collect predetermined tolls over a designated time period to recover their financial outlay and maintain the facility over the period.

In 2006, PLUS is the largest toll road operator, managing seven toll networks which account for 60 per cent of all toll roads in the country.

in savings of time and vehicle operating costs. New townships and industrial estates sprouted along the highways.

Road development up to 2010 has been guided by the Highway Network Development Plan (1993), which identified several new inter-urban highways including the East Coast Expressway and the West Coast Expressway.

Toll highways

Road construction and maintenance have primarily been the responsibility of the Public Works Department (Jabatan Kerja Raya, or JKR) and, to a lesser extent, the local authorities. A significant

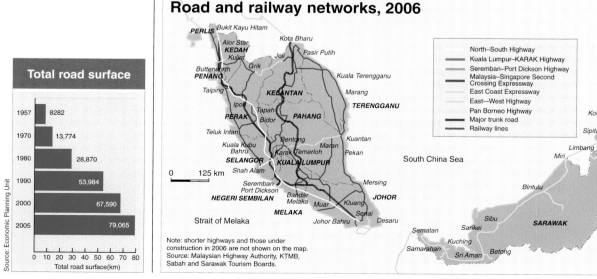

Road and railway networks, 2006

Total road surface

Year	Total road surface (km)
1957	8282
1970	13,774
1980	28,870
1990	53,984
2000	67,590
2005	79,065

Source: Economic Planning Unit

Legend:
- North–South Highway
- Kuala Lumpur–KARAK Highway
- Seremban–Port Dickson Highway
- Malaysia–Singapore Second Crossing Expressway
- East Coast Expressway
- East–West Highway
- Pan Borneo Highway
- Major trunk road
- Railway lines

0 125 km

0 150 km

South China Sea

Strait of Melaka

Note: shorter highways and those under construction in 2006 are not shown on the map.
Source: Malaysian Highway Authority, KTMB, Sabah and Sarawak Tourism Boards.

development was the establishment of the Malaysian Highway Authority (MHA) in 1980. The MHA has been entrusted with the supervision and construction of inter-urban toll highways. These were initially funded by the Federal Government, but in 1984, private companies were allowed to collect tolls in return for funding construction and maintenance of highways.

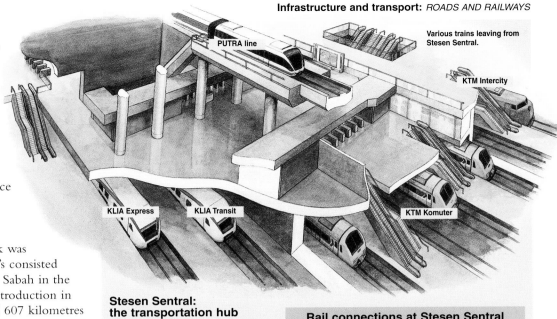

PUTRA line

Various trains leaving from Stesen Sentral.

KTM Intercity

KLIA Express   KLIA Transit   KTM Komuter

Sabah and Sarawak roads

In the 1950s, Sarawak's road network was practically non-existent while Sabah's consisted of basic tracks. Tar roads appeared in Sabah in the 1950s, some forty years after their introduction in the Peninsula. By 1963, Sarawak had 607 kilometres of road, concentrated mainly in the town centres of Kuching, Sri Aman, Sibu and Miri. Sabah had 2409 kilometres of roads.

The First Trunk Road stretched across Sarawak and, with the completion of the Ulu Batang–Mukah/Bintulu section in 1982, motorists could drive from Kuching to Miri and on to Brunei and Sabah on the Pan-Borneo Highway. The hinterland of Sabah today is also accessible from Sarawak by road. In 2005, Sarawak had some 6471 kilometres of roads while Sabah had 16,091 kilometres.

Railway development

Rail services began in 1885 in Perak with a 12.8-kilometre link between the tin mining town of Taiping and Port Weld to facilitate the export of tin ore. Rail networks subsequently became a major means of modernization and social development.

At Independence, a peninsular rail network was already in place, connecting Padang Besar, Prai, Kuala Lumpur, Singapore and Tumpat. In 1958, steam locomotives were replaced with more efficient diesel trains in the first phase of a massive modernization plan. Later years saw improvements to track and signalling systems, as well as the laying of long welded rails.

Rail services today complement other transport systems, and enhance trade and tourism. Since Independence, Keretapi Tanah Melayu Berhad (KTM) has focused on providing safe and efficient integrated rail services for people and goods. KTM's network strategically links the industrial growth centres in the hinterland to major ports. It is also the backbone for the 'landbridge' services, comprising cross-border freight movements between Singapore, Malaysia and Thailand. The KTM Komuter, introduced in 1995, was the pioneer electric train service, operating on electrified double tracks.

The Sabah State Railway, a single 134-kilometre line used to carry both passengers and freight, is operated by the Sabah State Railway Department.

Stesen Sentral: the transportation hub

Stesen Sentral is the country's rail transport nucleus within Kuala Lumpur. Construction began in 1997, funded by Malaysian Resources Corporation Berhad, Keretapi Tanah Melayu Berhad (KTM) and Pembinaan Redzai Sdn Bhd. Operational since April 2001, it is also home to the Kuala Lumpur City Air Terminal, an extension of Kuala Lumpur International Airport (KLIA) in the heart of the city. In 2004, 14 million passengers passed through Stesen Sentral.

Rail connections at Stesen Sentral

KTM Intercity
Main railway line that links major towns along the west coast from Singapore to Bangkok.

PUTRA line
An intracity Light Rail Transit (LRT) system that connects major parts of Kuala Lumpur. Provides access to another LRT network, the STAR LRT.

KL Monorail
Connects Kuala Lumpur's major areas and attractions.

KLIA Transit
Links Stesen Sentral with the KLIA, stopping at three satellite towns—Bandar Tasik Selatan, Putrajaya/Cyberjaya and Salak Tinggi—en route. Travel time is 36 minutes.

KTM Komuter
Links Kuala Lumpur and satellite towns to the north, west and south.

KLIA Express
Goes directly to KLIA in 28 minutes.

Keretapi Tanah Melayu Berhad (KTM)

The Federated Malay States Railway (FMSR), which had existed since 1901, was replaced in 1948 by the Malayan Railway Administration. In 1992, it was corporatized, and renamed KTM.

In the past, KTM's (and before it, FMSR's) involvement in transport extended beyond rail services, to cover services such as bus links connecting train stations with nearby towns, lorry services, and ferry services between Prai and Georgetown. KTM was heavily involved in the development of Port Swettenham (now Port Klang), which began as a small rail port. During the Emergency (1948–60), KTM also managed the five-aircraft Federation Air Service.

Diesel trains were introduced in 1958. In 1995, KTM introduced the Komuter service, Malaysia's first electrified rail system for Kuala Lumpur and surrounding suburban areas.

As of December 2005, KTM had 4665 employees. With its service covering the length and breadth of the Peninsular Malaysia, KTM runs its trains on a metre gauge, over a track length of 2262 kilometres.

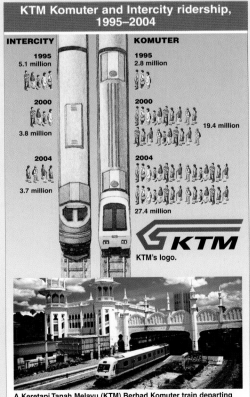

KTM Komuter and Intercity ridership, 1995–2004

INTERCITY	KOMUTER
1995 5.1 million	**1995** 2.8 million
2000 3.8 million	**2000** 19.4 million
2004 3.7 million	**2004** 27.4 million

KTM's logo.

A Keretapi Tanah Melayu (KTM) Berhad Komuter train departing the old railway station in Kuala Lumpur.

Source: KTMB

Ports and shipping

An efficient and competitive port and shipping sector is vital to Malaysia, almost 95 per cent of whose trade is seaborne. Starting with just two major ports and a limited number of minor ones in 1957, Malaysia currently has seven federal ports and numerous state and minor ports, the result of a supply-driven approach and the privatization policy. The nation's shipping fleet size has also expanded markedly over the years.

Early port development

During the first 25 years following Independence, port development was limited and mainly demand-driven, with capacity lagging behind demand. As late as 1970, Malaysia had only two major port facilities, Penang Port and Port Klang.

Several ports were developed in the 1970s and 1980s to meet growing demand and to serve local hinterlands, for instance, the Johor and Kuantan ports, which commenced full operations in 1977 and 1984 respectively. Niche ports were also built, such as that in Bintulu which is dedicated to handling Malaysian liquefied natural gas, and Kemaman, which is designed as a petroleum supply base. These two ports began operating in 1983 and 1982, respectively.

In 1964, the Port Klang Authority commenced commercial operations with the completion of four new berths.

Privatization and development

In the late 1980s, Malaysia adopted a port privatization policy that transferred activities and functions from the government to the private sector. Privatization started with the container operations of the Port Klang Authority which became Klang Container Terminal Bhd in 1986. Subsequently, the Port (Privatization) Act 1990 and Privatization Master Plan (1991) were drawn up to facilitate the privatization of all federal ports.

Rapid trade growth and a perceived over-dependence on Singapore's port subsequently led to the adoption by the government of a pro-active port development strategy. Beginning with the Sixth Malaysia Plan (1991–5), Malaysia adopted a supply-driven approach that focused on increasing infrastructure capacity and enhancing competitiveness. The supply-driven approach was based on the

MISC Fleet Size

Source: MISC

Number of ships: 140, 120, 100, 80, 60, 40, 20, 0

1969 1971 1975 1980 1985 1990 1995 2000 2005

Malaysian International Shipping Corporation (MISC)

The leading Malaysian shipping line, MISC is listed on the Bursa Malaysia Main Board. National oil giant PETRONAS is the majority shareholder. In 2003, MISC further boosted its drive to become the leading global energy transport provider with the acquisition of American Eagle Tankers.

ABOVE LEFT: The Very Large Crude Carrier Bunga Kasturi 2, at 300,500 dwt, is the largest Malaysian-flagged vessel as of 2005.

ABOVE RIGHT: The purchase of Puteri Mutiara 1 in 2005 affirms MISC's standing as the world's single largest owner and handler of liquefied natural gas (LNG) tankers, with 19 tankers having a combined deadweight tonnage of 1,147,574.

The shipping industry

As with ports, the government has played a key role in the industry: the nation's first international shipping line, MISC, was formed in 1968 with a government equity of 30 per cent.

In the 1970s, despite an increase in size of the Malaysian fleet, foreign vessels continued to dominate shipping. In 1979, about 60 per cent of domestic shipping tonnage was carried by foreign vessels. As a result, the Cabotage Act 1980 was introduced. The shipment of goods and carriage of passengers from any port or place in Malaysia to another port or place in Malaysia including the exclusive economic zone had to be by Malaysian registered vessels with valid Domestic Shipping Licences. The number of licences issued to Malaysian registered vessels rose from 164 in 1980 to 340 in 1988. The Cabotage policy has subsequently been relaxed.

The Merchant Shipping Act (Amendment) 1998 also expanded the definition of 'domestic shipping' to include other service-oriented activities, namely dredging, cable and pipe laying, and hydrographic surveys. Ships employed in such activities are therefore subjected to licensing.

Another significant measure by the government was the establishment of the RM800-million Shipping Finance Fund in 1992 for ship financing and venture capital. This amount was increased to RM1.1 billion in 1996, and a further RM1 billion was allocated in 2001, together with an extension of the fund's scope to include shipyard financing. The fund was channelled to and managed by Bank Industri and Teknologi Malaysia Bhd, which also provided financing and financing-related assistance to the maritime industry at concessionary rates.

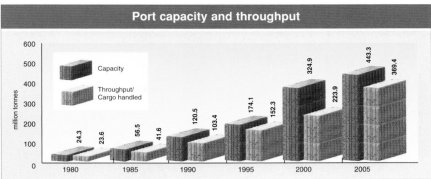

Port capacity and throughput

Source: Economic Planning Unit and Malaysia Plans

ABOVE: Aerial view of the Port of Tanjung Pelepas (PTP) in Johor, the newest local port. As of 2005, PTP had eight berths of 360 metres each, totalling 2.88 kilometres of linear wharf. Directly behind the berths is the port's container yard which has a storage capacity of approximately 110,000 TEUs.

FAR LEFT: The container yard at Westports at Port Klang. Westports' container handling capacity is six million TEUs per year as of 2006.

LEFT: Northport, also at Port Klang, is Malaysia's largest multi-purpose port operator.

idea that an adequate supply of quality infrastructure and services ahead of demand would attract ships and cargoes to Malaysian ports.

Modern port development

In 1998, Klang Container Terminal and Klang Port Management merged to form Northport, which also operates Southpoint. Formerly known as Port Swettenham, Port Klang contains two main ports: Northport and Westports.

Container throughput at Port Klang reached 5.6 million TEUs (20-foot equivalent units) in 2005, with Westports handling 52 per cent, and Northport accounting for the balance. Transhipment traffic (cargo not originating from or destined for Malaysia) constituted 53 per cent of the total containerized cargo handled by Port Klang, while local laden containers (indigenous cargo) accounted for the remaining amount. Southpoint is the centre for coastal trade, particularly between the Peninsula and Sabah and Sarawak. Conventional cargoes brought in from the neighbouring ports are consolidated at Southpoint, then transferred horizontally in containers to Northport to catch mother vessels calling at global ports.

Port Klang was designated by the government in 1993 as the national load centre, regional hub port and transhipment centre under the National Load Centre Policy. This involved the establishment of a free commercial zone (see 'Industrial areas'), the improvement of road and rail connections to facilitate intermodal transport, the adoption of innovative managerial practices, the formulation of promotional strategies, improvements to data and ICT, and the implementation of berth appropriation schemes, an

advanced immigration clearance system (AICS) and pre-customs clearance for containers. An electronic data interchange (EDI) system was introduced in 1994 to improve the logistical interface. The Port Klang Free Zone is expected to be Malaysia's first fully integrated free commercial and industrial area.

The Port of Tanjung Pelepas (PTP), completed in 1999, was developed when Seaport Terminal (Johore) Sdn Bhd entered into a privatization agreement with the government and Johor Port Authority. Complemented by a free zone, PTP has served as a catalyst for the development of southern Johor as an international logistics hub.

Maritime cooperation

Strategic alliances, joint ventures, partnerships and other forms of cooperation between maritime players intensified during the 1990s. Alliances with established port operators and shipping lines included those with Hutchinson International Port Holdings of Hong Kong (which owns 30 per cent of Westports), Maersk-Sealand (which owns 30 per cent of PTP) and Taiwan's Evergreen Marine Corporation, which moved its operations from Singapore to PTP in 2002.

TOP: Aerial view of Southpoint's berths. Southpoint, located at Port Klang, serves as the centre for coastal trade.

ABOVE: Built in 1860, the Tanjung Tuan lighthouse on Cape Rachado, Port Dickson, was the first lighthouse in Malaysia. It continues to be used as a navigational aid for vessels.

Malaysian ports

In Malaysia, there are federal, state and minor ports. The seven federal ports are under the jurisdiction of the Ministry of Transport and regulated by respective port authorities. State ports are governed by state authorities, while an estimated 80 minor ports or jetties are regulated by the Marine Department of the Ministry of Transport. Ports in Sabah and Sarawak are regulated by port authorities under the respective state governments.

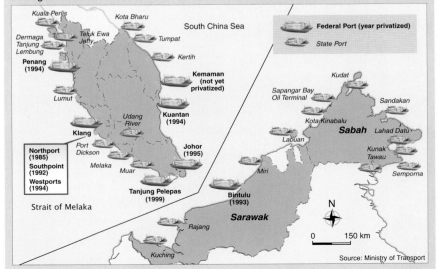

Airports and airlines

Airlines and airports play a critical role in tourism, trade and travel. Air links also help unify the nation and, particularly in Sabah and Sarawak, provide access to remote areas. Malaysian Airline System (MAS) is now a major global carrier, co-existing with several domestic airlines. Kuala Lumpur International Airport, the largest of Malaysia's 39 airports, is one of the world's most advanced.

Traffic at Malaysian airports, 2005

Passengers	
Domestic	25,639,000
International	17,189,000
Total	42,828,000
Cargo (tonnes)	
Domestic	197,783
International	809,031
Total	1,006,814
Commercial aircraft movements (number)	
Domestic	344,630
International	137,378
Total	482,008

KLIA control tower.

The Sultan Abdul Aziz Shah Airport (formerly known as Subang International Airport) in Subang was Malaysia's aviation hub from 1965 to 1998.

Economic impact

In 2005, airlines provided employment to more than 30,000 staff in Malaysia. Pilots, engineers and other aviation-related skilled workers have been an important part of the professional and knowledge-based labour force. Furthermore, MAS's revenue was RM10.9 billion in 2005; this constituted 2.3 per cent of GDP. Air transport has also helped to reduce the balance of payments deficit in services, primarily through tourism- and freight-generated inflows.

As a major trading nation (see 'International Trade'), Malaysia is heavily dependent on air links. Efficient air transport expedites the movement of goods in the logistics chain, improves the competitiveness of exports, and makes new markets accessible. It also promotes investment, both foreign and local, in aerospace, engine overhaul, production of composite materials for aircraft, and travel and tourism. Indeed, transport is an important factor why corporations choose Malaysia as their international or regional headquarters.

Airlines are increasingly involved in developing tourism, working closely with the Malaysia Tourism Promotion Board and international agencies.

Social impact

The aviation industry today is a critical factor in unifying Malaysia's 329,000 square kilometres and encouraging social and cultural interaction among its population. It facilitates national integration between Peninsular Malaysia and Sabah and Sarawak, and provides access to remote areas, thereby enabling health services and other development initiatives to reach all Malaysians (the Rural Air Services serve 15 destinations in Sabah and Sarawak). By supporting tourism, air transport helps sustain social, cultural and artistic traditions. Internationally, airlines complement the government's diplomatic initiatives, including expanding Malaysia's network of trading partners by establishing air links.

Transmile, established in 1993, enjoys a niche position in the intra-Asia Pacific air freight business. Transmile was designated National Cargo Carrier by the Ministry of Transport in 1996.

Air freight

While 95 percent of trade was seaborne in 2005, Malaysia's ability to export and import perishable and other time-sensitive freight was highly dependent on efficient air transport, provided through the extensive air cargo networks of MASkargo and Transmile Air Service. In 1998, MASkargo's Advanced Cargo Centre was launched in KLIA. It is a 43.7-hectare complex built to house the most advanced cargo handling equipment. Together with air-sea links between MASkargo and the national ports, the deployment of freight services between Malaysia and foreign countries continues to spur the development of KLIA as a premier regional and transshipment hub. A 2004 cargo traffic survey by the Airports Council International ranked KLIA 29th worldwide for handling 664,237 metric tonnes of cargo.

Malaysia's airports

In 2006, Malaysia had five international airports, 16 domestic airports and 19 short take-off and landing (STOL) ports which are airports designed for STOL aircraft. STOLports serve communities in less accessible areas of Malaysia.

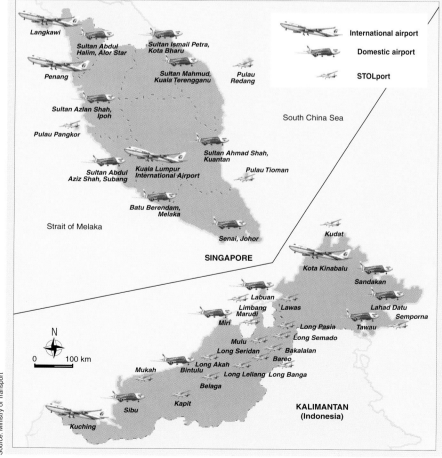

International airport

Domestic airport

STOLport

Langkawi
Sultan Abdul Halim, Alor Star
Sultan Ismail Petra, Kota Bharu
Penang
Sultan Mahmud, Kuala Terengganu
Pulau Redang
Sultan Azlan Shah, Ipoh
Pulau Pangkor
South China Sea
Sultan Ahmad Shah, Kuantan
Kuala Lumpur International Airport
Sultan Abdul Aziz Shah, Subang
Pulau Tioman
Batu Berendam, Melaka
Strait of Melaka
Senai, Johor
Kudat
SINGAPORE
Kota Kinabalu
Sandakan
Labuan
Limbang
Marudi
Lawas
Lahad Datu
Miri
Semporna
Long Pasia
Tawau
Mulu
Long Semado
Long Seridan
Bakalalan
Bareo
Mukah
Long Akah
Bintulu
Long Lellang Long Banga
Belaga
Kapit
KALIMANTAN (Indonesia)
Sibu
Kuching

N

0   100 km

Kuala Lumpur International Airport (KLIA)

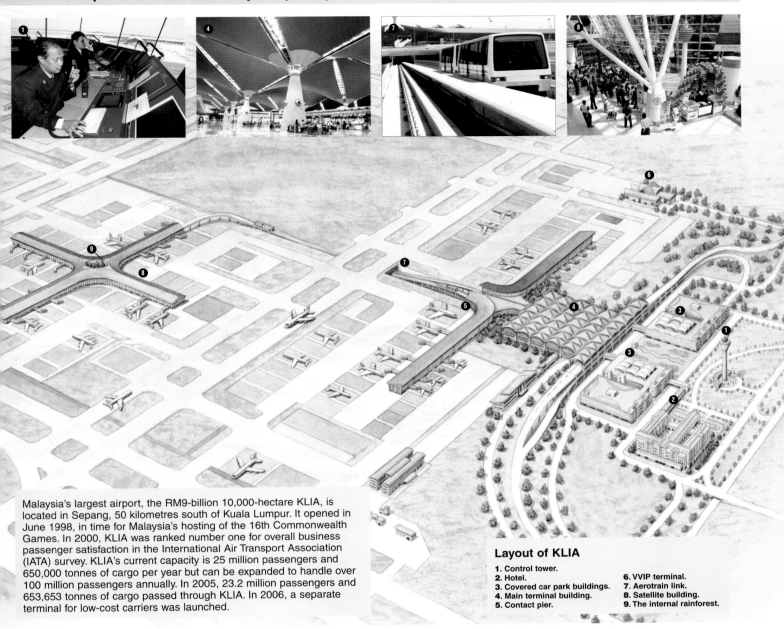

Malaysia's largest airport, the RM9-billion 10,000-hectare KLIA, is located in Sepang, 50 kilometres south of Kuala Lumpur. It opened in June 1998, in time for Malaysia's hosting of the 16th Commonwealth Games. In 2000, KLIA was ranked number one for overall business passenger satisfaction in the International Air Transport Association (IATA) survey. KLIA's current capacity is 25 million passengers and 650,000 tonnes of cargo per year but can be expanded to handle over 100 million passengers annually. In 2005, 23.2 million passengers and 653,653 tonnes of cargo passed through KLIA. In 2006, a separate terminal for low-cost carriers was launched.

Layout of KLIA

1. Control tower.
2. Hotel.
3. Covered car park buildings.
4. Main terminal building.
5. Contact pier.
6. VVIP terminal.
7. Aerotrain link.
8. Satellite building.
9. The internal rainforest.

Airlines

In 2005, MAS had 111 aircraft in its fleet.

The national carrier

Malaysia's first airline, Malaysian Airline System (MAS), was incorporated in 1971 and the inaugural MAS flight to Singapore took off on 1 October 1972. Between 2004 and 2005, MAS carried 17.5 million passengers and 2.7 billion tonne kilometres of cargo.

Other airlines

Sabah Air and Hornbill Skyways have been operating charter helicopter and light aircraft services in Sabah and Sarawak respectively since the 1970s.

In 1987, Malaysia Airline Charter, a small carrier operating charter services, was acquired by MAS and renamed Pelangi Air. Pelangi Air ceased operations in 1999. In the early 1980s, MAS also took over offshore helicopter operations from UK-based Bristow Helicopter, and formed Malaysia Helicopter Services.

In 1989, Berjaya Air, formerly known as Pacific Charter, was formed to meet increasing demand for flights to destinations with STOLports such as the Tioman, Pangkor and Redang Islands. As of 2006, Berjaya Air operates from the Sultan Abdul Aziz Shah Airport in Subang.

In 2001, the first low-cost carrier, AirAsia, commenced operations. In 2002, AirAsia introduced online ticketing through its website. Bookings via SMS were allowed in 2003. This was a first worldwide. With the tagline 'now everyone can fly', 4.8 million people flew with AirAsia in 2005.

Sightseeing with a Sabah Air helicopter.

AirAsia CEO Dato' Tony Fernandes (second from left) and crew members at Kuala Lumpur International Airport in Sepang.

Utilities

Malaysia has succeeded in providing safe and adequate utilities to its people and industries. The management of water, electricity and sewerage was initially the responsibility of the government, but has been gradually corporatized and privatized over the years.

Electrical transmission towers at sunset. In mid-2005, there were 6 million electricity consumers in Peninsular Malaysia, 335,800 in Sabah and 400,348 in Sarawak.

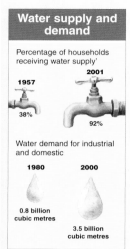

Water supply and demand

Percentage of households receiving water supply'

1957
38%

2001
92%

Water demand for industrial and domestic

1980
0.8 billion cubic metres

2000
3.5 billion cubic metres

Water tank at a golf club in Kuala Lumpur. The typical water supply system is the gravity-fed distribution system in which water moves from a high-level service-reservoir to households and industries.

The Bukit Nanas water treatment plant in Kuala Lumpur, completed in 1959. Together with the Klang Gates Dam, it formed part of the Malay Peninsula's first prominent water supply scheme.

Water

The first formal water supply was established in 1804 in Penang, which then had a population of approximately 10,000. By 1950, more than 100 water treatment plants produced about 195 million litres per day to reach a Malayan population of 1.15 million.

During the First Malaysia Plan (1966–70), the Government emphasized the provision of an adequate and safe water supply, including increasing services to rural areas. In the mid-1980s, the country embarked on a programme of industrialization and there was a high demand for water from a new sector: industry. Demand increased greatly over the next 20 years.

To ensure the provision of water sufficient to the nation's needs, budgets for water supply development have increased with each Five Year Plan. Under the Ninth Malaysia Plan (2006–10), the Federal Government allocated RM8204 million for water supply projects. As of 2006, the country has about 463 treatment plants in operation with a production capacity of 11,900 million litres per day. These channel fully treated water, meeting World Health Organization standards for drinking water, through over 86,890 kilometres of water mains.

Under the Federal Constitution, water supply was, until 2005, the responsibility of the individual states. In that year it was transferred to the Federal Government. In the early years after Independence, the Public Works Department assisted the state governments in developing and operating public water supplies. Later, many states formed their own respective water supply departments or water boards to achieve a more expedient water supply administrative system. This was followed in the late 1980s by the corporatization and privatization of state water supply entities in line with the government's policy of turning over the running of public utilities to the private sector (see 'Public sector, private sector'). Syarikat Bekalan Air Selangor Sdn Bhd (SYABAS) is the privatized entity which oversees water supply in Selangor, Kuala Lumpur and Putrajaya, while SAJ Holdings Sdn Bhd is responsible for Johor. Corporatized entities include Perbadanan Bekalan Air Pulau Pinang Sdn Bhd, Air Kelantan Sdn Bhd and Syarikat Air Terengganu Sdn Bhd.

Electricity

The earliest power generation in Malaysia was in 1894 in what was then a small mining town, Rawang, Selangor. The Peninsula's first public electric lighting was installed at the Kuala Lumpur Railway Station in 1896. The first power station was constructed on the banks of the Sempam River near Raub, Pahang, in 1900.

Penang was the first state to provide a supply of public electricity to consumers in 1904. In 1905, a hydroelectric station was commissioned at Ulu Gombak to supply electricity to Loke Mansion, which became the first residence in Kuala Lumpur to be electrified. In Sarawak, the Public Works Department erected the first power station to supply electricity to Kuching in 1921, and in British North Borneo (Sabah), electricity was first supplied to Sandakan, in 1922.

The Central Electricity Board (CEB) of the Federation of Malaya, with 34 power stations and a generation capacity of 39.88 megawatts came into being in September 1949. The CEB also became the owner of the transmission and distribution systems in Peninsular Malaya. On 22 June 1965, the CEB was

A National Electricity Board advertisement from 1967.

Energy policy and regulation

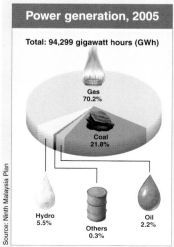

Power generation, 2005

Total: 94,299 gigawatt hours (GWh)

Gas 70.2%
Coal 21.8%
Hydro 5.5%
Others 0.3%
Oil 2.2%

Source: Ninth Malaysia Plan

National Energy Policy
A National Energy Policy was formulated in 1979 to ensure an efficient, secure and environmentally sustainable supply of energy in the future. The Four Fuel Diversification Policy was introduced in 1981, aimed at ensuring reliability and security of supply. The policy was designed to prevent over-dependence on oil as a main energy source. The strategy aims for a supply mix of oil, gas, hydro-power and coal. In 1999, renewable energy has been included as an additional fifth fuel in the Fifth Fuel Diversification Policy. Renewable energy programmes include utilizing the mini hydro, landfill mass and other biomass resources such as wood waste and rice husks.

The national grid

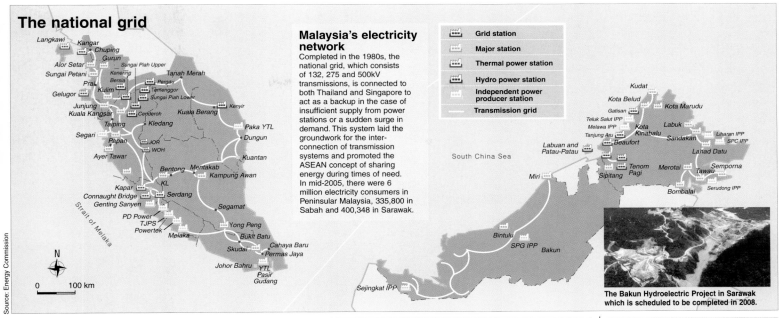

Malaysia's electricity network

Completed in the 1980s, the national grid, which consists of 132, 275 and 500kV transmissions, is connected to both Thailand and Singapore to act as a backup in the case of insufficient supply from power stations or a sudden surge in demand. This system laid the groundwork for the inter-connection of transmission systems and promoted the ASEAN concept of sharing energy during times of need. In mid-2005, there were 6 million electricity consumers in Peninsular Malaysia, 335,800 in Sabah and 400,348 in Sarawak.

	Grid station
	Major station
	Thermal power station
	Hydro power station
	Independent power producer station
	Transmission grid

South China Sea

The Bakun Hydroelectric Project in Sarawak which is scheduled to be completed in 2008.

Source: Energy Commission

renamed the National Electricity Board of the States of Malaya (NEB) to meet national aspirations.

In line with the government's privatization policy, NEB was corporatized in 1990 and privatized in 1992, with Tenaga Nasional Berhad (TNB) becoming the principal provider of electricity in Peninsular Malaysia. Sabah Electricity Sdn Bhd (SESB) and Sarawak Electricity Supply Corporation supply electricity in those two states.

Until the Bakun Dam in Sarawak is completed, Kenyir Dam in Terengganu remains the country's hydro-electric dam.

Sewerage and waste

Sewage management has been the responsibility of local councils and state governments. Indeed, many municipalities were born as sanitary boards to manage sewerage and other common needs—Kuala Lumpur Sanitary Board was the first of these, in 1890. Since 1972, it has been known as Kuala Lumpur City Hall.

Local authorities' responsibility for the provision of sewerage services was transferred to the Federal

Alam Flora Sdn Bhd was formed by the DRB-HICOM consortium for the privatization of solid waste management for the central and eastern regions of the Peninsula. Its services include waste collection; cleaning of roads, highways, drains and beaches; cutting grass; and waste storage and disposal management.

Government in 1993 as a result of the Sewerage Services Act 1993. In 1994, the Federal Government awarded Indah Water Konsortium Sdn Bhd, a company wholly owned by the Minister of Finance Incorporated, the concession for nationwide sewerage services, except in Johor Bahru and the states of Kelantan, Sabah and Sarawak.

Waste collection services were formerly provided by the district and municipal councils in each state. Pursuant to the government's privatization plan, Alam Flora Sdn Bhd was awarded the concession to manage solid waste in the central and eastern regions. Northern Waste Industries Sdn Bhd is responsible for the northern region; Southern Waste Management Sdn Bhd for the southern region; and Eastern Waste Management Sdn Bhd for Sabah and Sarawak.

Sewerage systems

Systems used to include communal septic tanks and Imhoff tanks built in the 1960s. In the 1970s, oxidation ponds were introduced in new housing estates. In the 1980s, when land development accelerated and land became scarce in urban areas, aerated lagoons were introduced in order to serve a larger population with a smaller land area requirement. Mechanical sewage treatment works including activated sludge and trickling filters were introduced in the 1990s. The National Sewerage Project was implemented in 2004 to provide more efficient sewerage services.

Indah Water Konsortium workers clearing the blockage of a public sewer in Taman Melawati, Kuala Lumpur.

Electricity regulation

The electricity industry in Peninsular Malaysia and Sabah is regulated by the Energy Commission (EC), established in 2001, which oversees the technical, service, performance, safety and economic aspects of the industry. The EC took over from the Department of Electricity and Gas Supply, initially formed as the Department of Electricity Supply in 1990, which itself assumed the role of the Electricity Inspectorate Department. In Sarawak, the State Electricity Ordinance 1962 remains in force, and provides the State Electrical Inspectorate with the legal power to continue with its regulatory functions.

TNB launched PD1 in Port Dickson, Negeri Sembilan in 2005. Operating the latest gas turbine combined cycle, it powers the entire southern region and the Klang Valley.

Telecommunications and post

Telecommunications and postal services were seen as important aspects of nation-building in the decades after Independence. Initially developed as government-run services, both were subsequently privatized in the 1980s and 1990s, and were then liberalized in the 1990s.

Smart Digital Communications Berhad provides wideband satellite and internet services and cellular infrastructure.

History

The history of telecommunications in Malaysia began in 1870 with the introduction of a Morse Code Telegraph System linking Penang, Melaka and Singapore. A telephone service was introduced in the office of the British Resident of Perak in 1874. Infrastructure expanded rapidly where Britain's main interests lay: a telephone exchange was set up in Singapore in 1881, and submarine cables laid between Perak and Penang.

In 1894, submarine cables were laid connecting Singapore, Labuan and Hong Kong. Wireless stations were installed in Kuching and Penang in 1917 and 1930 respectively. By 1946, Malaya had formed a Department of Telecommunications.

TOP: Stamps showing how the methods of postal delivery have evolved over the years.

ABOVE: Postmen at the Sabah Central Post Office, c. 1968.

Post-Independence

Between 1960 and 1980, great emphasis was placed on modernizing telecommunications infrastructure to expand the coverage and range of services.

The telecommunications sector experienced steady growth between 1970 and 1980. During this period, the number of subscribers grew from 104,000 to 395,000. The increasing importance of telecommunications was reflected in development expenditure allocations under each five-year Malaysia Plan.

The telecommunications departments of Peninsular Malaysia, Sarawak and Sabah merged to form Jabatan Telekom Malaysia in 1968.

Modernization and integrated services

Remarkable progress was made in the period between 1980 and 1998. Fibre optics and digital-based infrastructure such as Synchronous Digital Hierarchy, Asynchronous Transfer Mode and Integrated Service Digital Networks enabled many services, including Managed Leased Circuit Networks as well as cellular, datel, telefax and international maritime services, to be offered for the first time.

Deregulation and privatization of the telecommunications industry began in 1984. Between 1984 and 1987, the Department of Telecommunications transferred all operations to Syarikat Telekom Malaysia Berhad, a privatized government department. Other companies were awarded cellular, fixed line, international gateway and satellite licences in 1993 to 1994.

Telecommunications had impressive average growth rates after privatization with digitalization and equipment upgrades, improving the capacity and quality of services.

Convergence

Digital technology advancements in the late 1990s increased the usage of computers in broadcasting and telecommunications which led to a

Telecommunications timeline

1957–1979

1960 Introduction of International Radio Telephone services between Sarawak and Malaya.

1962 Introduction of first Subscriber Trunk Dialling (STD) facility between Kuala Lumpur and Singapore.

1970 Commissioning of the first international-standard Satellite Earth Station in Kuantan.

1975 Replacement of the manual Telex Exchange with an automatic system.

1976 Establishment of the Ministry of Energy, Communications and Post.

1979 Introduction of International Direct Dialling facilities.

1980–1989

1980 First fully electronic exchange commission set up in Pelangi, Johor.

Commissioning of the submarine cable project linking Kuantan and Kuching.

1981 Commissioning of second Standard Satellite Earth Station in Lendu, Melaka.

1985 Introduction of the first cellular service (ATUR).

1987 Operations of the Telecommunications Department transferred to Syarikat Telekom Malaysia Berhad.

TOP LEFT: A 1962 telephone directory.

LEFT: A Siemens 1700 teleprinter introduced in the late 1960s.

RIGHT: MEASAT-1 and 2, Malaysia's satellites, provide high quality C-band coverage across Southeast Asia, Greater China, South Asia, Australia and the United States.

1990–1999

1990 Syarikat Telekom Malaysia Berhad listed on the Kuala Lumpur Stock Exchange.

1994 Introduction of competition in the telecommunications sector.

1996 Implementation of the MSC initiative (see 'Multimedia Super Corridor').

Malaysia's first satellites, MEASAT-1 and 2, launched.

1997 Market liberalization. Foreign equity participation in local telecommunications companies allowed.

1998 Introduction of the Communications And Multimedia Act 1998.

Establishment of the Malaysian Communications and Multimedia Commission.

Logo of the Malaysian Communications and Multimedia Commission.

2000–2005

2000 Liberalization of tariffs for cellular services.

2001 Rebalancing of fixed-line tariffs.

2005 Introduction of cellular 3G services.

The TM headquarters in Kuala Lumpur. Syarikat Telekom Malaysia Berhad was rebranded as TM in 2005. The building stands at 310 metres and has 55 floors.

Pos Malaysia

Postal services were first set up in the Straits Settlements in the early 1800s, and the first Postal Department, with its headquarters in Penang, was established in 1826. Adhesive Indian postage stamps without over-printing, were first introduced in 1854.

A postman at a delivery depot in Georgetown, Penang sorting out letters for his beat before delivering them.

The Postal Services Department was corporatized in 1992, to become Pos Malaysia Berhad, as part of the government's policy towards privatization.

The range of services offered has expanded over the years. For example, post offices began to handle payments of electricity bills as early as 1946, and the sale of television licences in 1964. Pos Malaysia collects payments on behalf of a large number of government agencies and private companies. In 1991, the Poslaju courier service was launched.

As of 2005, Pos Malaysia had 651 post offices, 4466 street post boxes, 408 delivery branches, 34 processing centres and 8000 postmen.

Couriers

The first international courier company in Malaysia was established by DHL Worldwide Express in 1975. Other courier companies include TNT Express Worldwide, City-Link Express, Nationwide Express Courier Services, PosLaju, United Parcel Services, Federal Express Services and GDex.

While in the past the main business function of courier companies was the delivery of documents, the advent of the digital age has led to a decline in this aspect of the business, which has been matched by an increase in the use of couriers for the

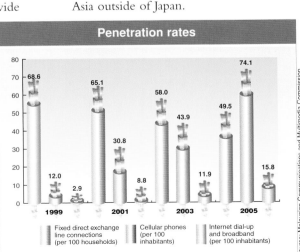

GD Express Sdn Bhd's Central Clearing Hub where documents and parcels collected from customers are sorted then redirected to the appropriate branches in their network for eventual delivery to intended recipients.

distribution of manufactured goods. Indeed, courier companies today are viewed by their clients as a form of business process outsourcing, relieving companies of the need for in-house distribution networks.

The handful of premium express carriers are supplemented by over 100 smaller local courier companies, many of which provide services only within localized areas such as the Klang Valley. Courier companies are licensed by the Malaysian Communications and Multimedia Commission on an annual basis.

convergence of the information technology, broadcasting and telecommunications industries. These industries collectively became the main focus of the government's efforts to transform the economy into a knowledge-based economy (see 'Towards a knowledge-based economy').

The Communications and Multimedia Act 1998 liberalized these sectors by providing for easier licensing, a less regulated environment, greater foreign participation and greater focus on consumers. Competition was introduced in many telecommunications markets, including equipment, paging, long distance services, cellular services, payphones and international services. The Malaysian Communications and Multimedia Commission (MCMC) became the regulator for the converging communications and multimedia industry.

Established in 2004, the Ministry of Water, Energy and Communications formulates policies governing telecommunications infrastructure and postal services. As of 2006, there are five private companies licensed by the Ministry to provide telecommunication services, which cover fixed lines and mobile solutions.

The cellular services market saw an increase in its subscriber base after tariff regulations were abolished in 2000. Similarly, reduced regulation for internet service provision saw a significant increase in internet usage (see 'The media'). In 2005, the number of internet dial-up users was 11.02 million. Sabah registered the lowest internet dial-up penetration rate among all states, while the Federal Territory had the highest. For broadband users, the MCMC recorded an estimated 490,630 subscriptions in 2005, which represented

almost 100 per cent growth from the previous year. However, the penetration rate for broadband technology was still low at 1.86 subscriptions per 100 people in 2005 compared with the dial-up penetration rate of 13.9 users per 100 people.

The ASTRO experience

Satellite broadcasting began with the launching of Malaysia's first satellite, MEASAT-1, in 1996. In the same year, Astro All Asia Networks plc (ASTRO), a Malaysian-based multimedia group involved in TV and radio broadcasting, multimedia and internet services, was established. Utilizing high-powered KU-band transponders on MEASAT-1 to transmit across Malaysia and Brunei, ASTRO reached over 1.9 million homes in mid-2006, making it the largest multi-channel TV business in Asia outside of Japan.

A member of ASTRO's technical crew behind the scenes in their broadcast truck.

Cellular phone companies

Analogue cellular service licences were issued to Syarikat Telekom Malaysia Berhad and Technology Resources Industries Berhad in 1989. This was followed in 1993–94 by the awarding of licences for Global System for Mobile communication, Personal Communications Network and analogue/digital Advanced Mobile Phone Service to seven operators to build and operate their own networks. In late 2002, the government called for cellular phone operators to merge in order to be more cost-effective by avoiding duplication of costly infrastructure, which wastes valuable resources and under-utilizes capacity. As a result, TM Cellular merged with Celcom, and Maxis with TimeCel and as of 2005, there are only three cellular phone operators: Maxis, Celcom and DiGi.

Maxis and Celcom print advertisements.

Penetration rates

Source: Malaysian Communications and Multimedia Commission

	1999	2001	2003	2005
Fixed direct exchange line connections (per 100 households)	68.6	65.1	58.0	74.1
Cellular phones (per 100 inhabitants)	12.0	30.8	43.9	49.5
Internet dial-up and broadband (per 100 inhabitants)	2.9	8.8	11.9	15.8

The Multimedia Super Corridor

To spearhead the development of the multimedia and information and communication technology (ICT) industries, the Multimedia Super Corridor (MSC) was formed as a 'multimedia utopia' in which to implement the National Information Technology Agenda. The MSC serves as a crucial foundation for knowledge-driven growth in the Information Age.

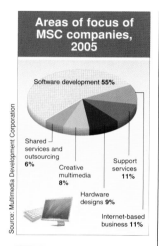

Areas of focus of MSC companies, 2005

Software development 55%
Shared services and outsourcing 6%
Creative multimedia 8%
Support services 11%
Hardware designs 9%
Internet-based business 11%

Source: Multimedia Development Corporation

MSC company ownership, 2006

Nationality of majority shareholder	Percentage of MSC companies
Malaysia	74%
Japan	1%
Australia	1%
India	3%
Singapore	4%
North America	3%
Europe	7%
Others	7%

Note: Total MSC companies = 1552.
Data as of 31 July 2006.

Source: Multimedia Development Corporation

Members of the International Advisory Panel at the opening of Cyberjaya in 1999. Set amidst oil palm plantations, Cyberjaya is a 728.5-hectare intelligent ICT city designed for a population of 240,000. Tax breaks and other financial incentives are offered to companies which relocate there.

A strategic initiative

Established in 1996, the MSC covers a geographical area of approximately 15 by 50 kilometres, from the Kuala Lumpur City Centre and the Kuala Lumpur Tower to the Kuala Lumpur International Airport (KLIA) in Sepang. The MSC was planned to create a 'multimedia utopia' for the conceptualization, design, testing, production and distribution of advanced ICT applications. It is equipped with world-class physical infrastructure—the 'hard' infrastructure, along with 'soft' infrastructure such as incentives, and a sufficiently strong legal and regulatory environment in order to attract top international companies to use the MSC as their hub. By interacting with these companies and by becoming their partners and suppliers, Malaysian companies will over time be able to achieve world-class status.

This aspiration reflected one of the key objectives of the MSC: to lay the groundwork for Malaysia to become a regional and global leader in ICT development and applications. More broadly, the MSC was undertaken to harness the potential of ICT and channel it towards long-term national development. The benefits of the MSC's flagship applications and programmes have spilled over to the rest of the country, thereby diffusing ICT to the wider population. The MSC has also served as Malaysia's link to global centres of excellence and the global web of activities in multimedia development. Finally, partnerships with world-class players have provided a competitive edge for Malaysian companies, while multinationals have also gained access to new ideas, opportunities and regional markets.

Organization and institutions

The MSC's many initiatives are managed under seven flagship applications. The MSC serves as the test-bed for these applications, and enables ICT and multimedia companies to try out their own creative ideas.

Strategic guidance during the establishment of the MSC was provided by the MSC International Advisory Panel (IAP), comprised of experts and corporate leaders from

Developed infrastructure

Hard infrastructure

The MSC is bounded by the Petronas Towers, KL Tower and Technology Park Malaysia in the north, and the Air Traffic Control tower of Kuala Lumpur International Airport in the south. The key components of MSC's hard infrastructure are the twin cities of Putrajaya and Cyberjaya. Putrajaya is a purpose-built intelligent city and the new administrative centre for the Federal Government. Cyberjaya has been built to accommodate ICT companies and businesses, and is poised to become a centre of excellence for the development of ICT products and services to serve the domestic, regional and global markets. It incorporates state-of-the-art intelligent buildings and urban systems. There is also a residential zone. Further, the development of the entire corridor as a garden city with a green environment provides an excellent location in which to live and work.

Criss-crossing the MSC is a growing network of advanced transportation infrastructure, including expressways, light rail and express rail links. This network makes the MSC a multi-modal transportation hub for the country and the region.

Telecommunications infrastructure includes high-speed links with other information technology centres around the world. A broadband backbone running at 2.5 gigabits per second, expandable to 10 gigabits per second, connects the MSC to the entire globe, with a tariff structure among the cheapest in the world.

Soft infrastructure

In addition to being a major infrastructure project in the physical sense, the MSC has been the catalyst for many pioneer efforts in soft infrastructure. Malaysia's first cyberlaws were specially enacted to encourage the growth of the MSC industries. In mid-1997, four such laws were passed by Parliament: the Digital Signature Act, the Copyright Act (Amendment), the Computer Crimes Act and the Telemedicine Act. A Bill of Guarantees was also issued, by which the government is committed to a ten-point undertaking to promote and protect the status of MSC-status companies.

Other policies and regulations have been modified to support MSC companies. The government allows MSC companies to employ foreign knowledge workers without restriction. A Multimedia University was established in 1996 with the aim of training more Malaysians in multimedia skills and technologies. Other incentives for MSC-status companies include tax exemptions, research and development grants and duty-free importation of multimedia equipment.

Malaysia and the global community. The IAP continues to meet regularly to monitor the progress of the MSC.

The Multimedia Development Corporation (MDC) was established in 1996 as an implementing and monitoring agency for all MSC programmes. It processes applications by local and international companies to locate or relocate to the MSC, and markets the MSC locally and globally. It also advises the government on MSC-specific laws and policies. Through its subsidiary, MSC Venture One, it provides venture capital within the MSC.

Kuala Lumpur City Centre (KLCC)

Technology Park Malaysia

Cyberjaya

Putrajaya

Express Rail Link

KLIA

The seven flagship applications

The MSC's many initiatives are managed under seven 'flagship applications':

1. smart schools
2. multipurpose smart card (MyKad)
3. research and development clusters
4. electronic government
5. a worldwide manufacturing web
6. a borderless marketing centre
7. telehealth

MyKad, the multi-application national identification card.

The Universiti Kebangsaan Malaysia–Malaysian Technology Development Council Smart Technology Centre occupies 2.43 hectares in Bangi.

Students at a Smart School in Precinct 9, Putrajaya.

Government offices in Putrajaya, where an e-government programme which seeks to improve the efficiency of government services is in place.

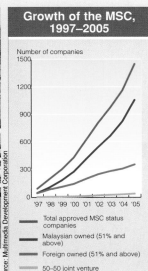

Growth of the MSC, 1997–2005

Number of companies

Source: Multimedia Development Corporation

'97 '98 '99 '00 '01 '02 '03 '04 '05

— Total approved MSC status companies
— Malaysian owned (51% and above)
— Foreign owned (51% and above)
— 50–50 joint venture

1. Residences in Cyberjaya.

2. In 2004, 2872 foreign knowledge workers were employed in MSC-status companies. The majority of them were from India.

3. University Putra Malaysia–Malaysian Technology Development Council server farm complex.

4. The Cyberjaya campus of the Multimedia University. The university aims to be a world-class standard institution in ICT and multimedia. In 2005, 8525 students were enrolled in this campus.

5. Shell's Cyberjaya centre is the largest of its three global information technology (IT) centres and provides Shell companies with comprehensive IT infrastructure services.

State of the MSC

When MSC's Phase 1 ended in 2003, the target of creating the MSC hub had been realized. The MSC will be in Phase 2 until 2010, with the goal of becoming a global ICT hub before finally transforming Malaysia into a knowledge society by the end of Phase 3 in 2020.

By 2002, two flagship applications, the smart card and smart schools, had been exported to Myanmar, China, the United States and countries in the Middle East. In 2005, the MSC created some 27,288 new job opportunities. Total investment in the MSC in 2005 amounted to RM5.11 billion

and export sales accounted for RM1.57 billion.

As of August 2003, MSC Venture Corporation Sdn Bhd, a subsidiary of the MDC, had approved 17 venture capital applications amounting to RM75.4 million from the RM120 million allocated by the government (see 'Towards a knowledge economy').

The MSC vision

1996 → 2003 → 2010 → 2020

Phase 1
Successfully create the Multimedia Super Corridor

Phase 2
Grow MSC into a global ICT hub

Phase 3
Transform Malaysia into a knowledge society

Leapfrog into leadership in the Knowledge Economy

Source: Multimedia Development Corporation

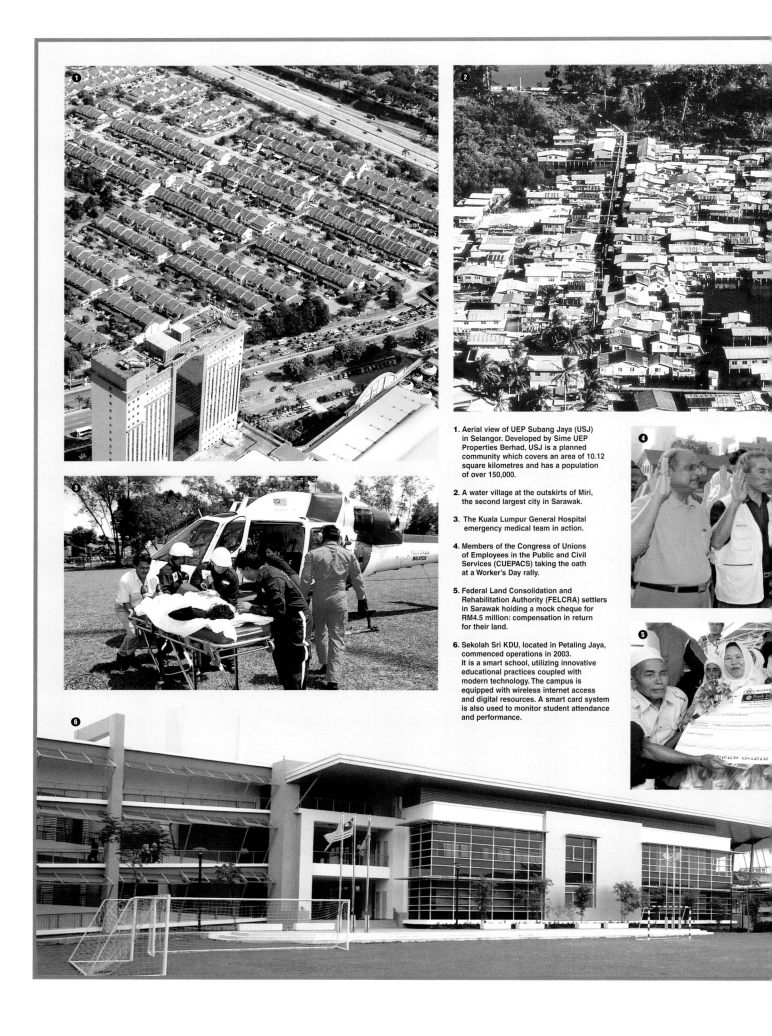

1. Aerial view of UEP Subang Jaya (USJ) in Selangor. Developed by Sime UEP Properties Berhad, USJ is a planned community which covers an area of 10.12 square kilometres and has a population of over 150,000.

2. A water village at the outskirts of Miri, the second largest city in Sarawak.

3. The Kuala Lumpur General Hospital emergency medical team in action.

4. Members of the Congress of Unions of Employees in the Public and Civil Services (CUEPACS) taking the oath at a Worker's Day rally.

5. Federal Land Consolidation and Rehabilitation Authority (FELCRA) settlers in Sarawak holding a mock cheque for RM4.5 million: compensation in return for their land.

6. Sekolah Sri KDU, located in Petaling Jaya, commenced operations in 2003. It is a smart school, utilizing innovative educational practices coupled with modern technology. The campus is equipped with wireless internet access and digital resources. A smart card system is also used to monitor student attendance and performance.

THE SOCIAL FRAMEWORK

Social services are an integral component of economic development as they help create a physically healthy and educated workforce which in turn facilitates increased productivity and adaptation to technology. The Federal Government has raised its development expenditure on social services over the years, from 11.0 per cent in 1970 to 27.6 per cent in 2005. In 2002, social services actually formed 50.2 per cent of the Federal Government development expenditure. The focus of this spending has changed from agriculture and rural development in the 1970s, to transportation in the 1980s and 1990s and to education in the 2000s.

Education, apart from developing the country's human capital, has also been a tool for social restructuring. The initiatives implemented by the Ministry of Education have reflected and responded to changing societal and economic needs. Malay was instituted as the medium of instruction on all levels in order to foster national solidarity, but English later began to be utilized in science and mathematics classrooms to prepare graduates to participate in the global economy. A quota system introduced in tertiary institutions increased Bumiputera enrolment in higher education.

Healthwise, the infant mortality rate, one of the most significant indicators of the overall health and nutritional status of the nation, has, in 2005, fallen to 0.08 per cent of what it was in 1957. Rural and public health programmes such as immunization, maternal and child health, nutrition, sanitation and health education contributed to this improvement.

After Independence, a key objective of the government was to ensure that more Malaysians had access to decent homes through the provision of low-cost housing. Key issues in 2005 were bridging the affordability gap and balancing development with environmental protection and preservation.

Rural migration has led to the emergence of satellite towns at the fringes of urban centres and the development of planned cities such as Putrajaya and Cyberjaya. While factors such as income and infrastructure add to the constant pull of the city, new social problems have emerged as a result. The government has earmarked potential growth areas to absorb the migrant population and has set up agencies to offer advisory and financing services.

The legal framework of the social system protects the rights of employees and employers, consumers, companies, investors and inventors of intellectual property.

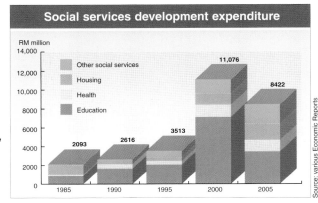

Social services development expenditure

RM million

Other social services
Housing
Health
Education

1985: 2093
1990: 2616
1995: 3513
2000: 11,076
2005: 8422

Source: various Economic Reports

Population and income distribution

Malaysia had a population of 26.7 million in 2005, of which nearly 11 million made up the labour force. Economic disparities exist between ethnic groups and geographical regions. Poverty eradication initiatives in the 1970s and 1980s focused on rural poverty, while efforts under the National Development and National Vision Policies focused on hardcore and relative poverty. The goal of the government is to eradicate hardcore poverty by 2010.

Participants at the 2004 National Day celebrations in Kuantan. In 2004, the average age of Malaysians was 24 years.

Logos of the Ministry of Women, Family and Community Development (left) and the National Population and Family Development Board

Population policies
The National Family Planning Act 1966 was passed and the National Family Planning Board (NFPB) established to implement the National Family Planning Programme which aimed to lower the population growth rate from three per cent in 1966 to two per cent by 1985.

In 1984, a new population policy was introduced. The National Population and Family Development Board (NPFDB) assumed the role of the NPFB. Recognizing that continued population growth did not necessarily have a negative effect on development, the target was to a achieve a population size of 70 million by the year 2100.

A reassessment of the previous policy in 1992 showed that due to rapid industrialization, fertility rates were falling faster than expected.

Under Vision 2020 (1991– 2020), the objective of the previous population policy has had to be recast in line with the new policy of sustained population growth taking into account available resources, human capital and the pace of development.

Population
In 2005, Malaysia had a population of 26.7 million, having grown from 6.3 million in 1957. The growth rate in 2005 was two per cent per annum.

Since the 1980s, the population growth rate has declined. This is attributable to higher education levels, increasing urbanization, late marriages and higher living standards. It is estimated that Malaysia's population will increase to 28.9 million by the year 2010.

Age structure
The age structure of the population largely depends on changing trends in fertility, mortality and migration. In a developing country, a large proportion of the population is typically below 15 years of age while a smaller proportion is aged 65 years and over. The economically active population comprises those in the 15–64 age group.

From 2005–10, the proportion of those in the age group below 15 years is expected to decline from 32.7 per cent to 29.7 per cent, reflecting the decline in the total fertility rate during the period. The aged will increase both in terms of absolute numbers as well as growth rates. This is due to the increase in life expectancy as a result of overall improvement in the quality of life of the population. Recognizing the imminent increase in the number of elderly people, the government has

given greater consideration to the needs of this group in the planning of health, welfare and social security services.

Of particular economic significance is the fact that the proportion of those in the economically active group has increased from 58.8 per cent in 1990 to 63.1 per cent in 2004 and is projected to rise to 65.7 per cent in 2010. This growth can help reduce the extent of labour shortages. Since the economically active population is expected to expand more rapidly than those below 15 and those above 65 years old, the overall dependency burden (the ratio of dependents to every 100 persons of working age) has improved from 61.4 per cent in 2000 to 58.6 per cent in 2005, and is expected to improve still further to 52.2 per cent by 2010.

Income distribution
Income distribution was one of the key issues in the early 1970s, leading to the formulation of the New Economic Policy (NEP) (see 'New Economic Policy: 1971–1990'). The significant achievements of the NEP notwithstanding, income gaps and socioeconomic imbalances still exist in terms of both ethnic groups and geographical regions.

In 2004, the bottom 40 per cent of households had a 13.5 per cent share of income, compared to the top 20 per cent of households, which had a 51.2 per cent share of income. In terms of actual income differences, this equated to a mean

Population statistics

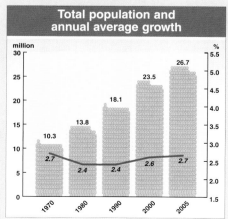
Total population and annual average growth

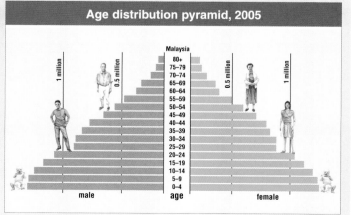
Age distribution pyramid, 2005

Source: Economic Planning Unit

Population of ethnic groups and incidence of poverty by state, 2004

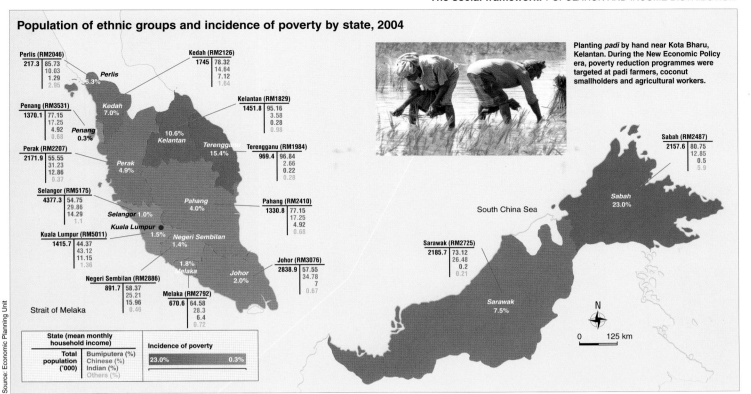

Source: Economic Planning Unit

Perlis (RM2046)
217.3 | 85.73
10.03
1.29
2.95

Perlis
6.3%

Penang (RM3531)
1370.1 | 77.15
17.25
4.92
0.68

Penang
0.3%

Kedah (RM2126)
1745 | 78.32
14.64
7.12
1.64

Kedah
7.0%

Kelantan (RM1829)
1451.8 | 95.16
3.58
0.28
0.98

10.6%
Kelantan

15.4%
Terengganu

Terengganu (RM1984)
969.4 | 96.84
2.66
0.22
0.28

Perak (RM2207)
2171.9 | 55.55
31.23
12.86
0.37

Perak
4.9%

Selangor (RM5175)
4377.3 | 54.75
29.86
14.29
1.1

Selangor 1.0%

Kuala Lumpur (RM5011)
1415.7 | 44.37
43.12
11.15
1.36

Kuala Lumpur

1.5%
Negeri Sembilan
1.4%

Pahang
4.0%

Pahang (RM2410)
1330.8 | 77.15
17.25
4.92
0.68

Negeri Sembilan (RM2886)
891.7 | 58.37
25.21
15.96
0.46

1.8%
Melaka

Melaka (RM2792)
670.6 | 64.58
28.3
6.4
0.72

Johor
2.0%

Johor (RM3076)
2838.9 | 57.55
34.78
7
0.67

Strait of Melaka

Sabah (RM2487)
2157.6 | 80.75
12.85
0.5
5.9

Sabah
23.0%

South China Sea

Sarawak (RM2725)
2185.7 | 73.12
26.48
0.2
0.21

Sarawak
7.5%

N

0   125 km

Planting *padi* by hand near Kota Bharu, Kelantan. During the New Economic Policy era, poverty reduction programmes were targeted at padi farmers, coconut smallholders and agricultural workers.

State (mean monthly household income)		Incidence of poverty	
Total population ('000)	Bumiputera (%) Chinese (%) Indian (%) Others (%)	23.0%	0.3%

---

monthly household income of RM1101 for the bottom 40 per cent, compared to RM8337 for the top 20 per cent.

In ethnic terms, although the overall ratio of Bumiputera to Chinese mean monthly household income has improved from about 44 per cent in 1970 to around 61 per cent in 2004, the inter-ethnic income disparity remains high in certain sectors and occupations. In the manufacturing sector, for example, the mean household income figures for Bumiputera and non-Bumiputera in 2004 were RM2905 and RM4250 respectively.

Intra-ethnic income disparities are still significant, with inequality among the Bumiputera being higher relative to that of the non-Bumiputera, as measured by the Gini coefficient. As such, in 2004, the mean household income of the top 20 per cent of Chinese households was about 6.9 times that of the bottom 40 per cent. The corresponding figure for Bumiputera households was 7.2 times.

Although rural–urban income differentials have narrowed, the average rural income in Peninsular Malaysia in 2004 represented an estimated 48.5 per cent of the urban income. In Sabah and Sarawak, the corresponding figures were 48.9 per cent and 43.6 per cent, respectively.

Improvements in income distribution in the last three decades have not occurred evenly for all three major ethnic groups. This may be due to differences in human skills and educational attainment, and disparities in value of assets and access to capital.

Poverty

The overall incidence of poverty declined from 49.3 per cent in 1970 to 6.1 per cent in 1997. The country suffered a temporary setback during the 1997–98 financial crisis when the incidence of poverty increased to 7.6 per cent and hardcore poverty rose from 1.4 per cent to 1.5 per cent. In 2004, the incidence of poverty was 5.7 per cent while hardcore poverty stood at one per cent. The monthly poverty line income (PLI) stood at RM691. In 2005, the government announced its aim of reducing hardcore poverty to 0.5 per cent by 2009.

The New Economic Policy (NEP) introduced in 1971 targeted a reduction of poverty to 16.7 per cent by 1990. By the end of the NEP period, the number of poor households had fallen not only as a percentage of total households, but also in terms of absolute numbers. Inequalities of income between urban and rural regions, as well as between Bumiputera and non-Bumiputera, were reduced. Nevertheless, pockets of poverty continued to exist, and were highly concentrated in the primary sector

Measuring the incidence of poverty and hardcore poverty in 2005

Definitions of poverty and hardcore poverty are based on the poverty line income (PLI) which comprises the food and non-food PLIs: incomes sufficient to purchase a minimum basket of food and basic needs such as clothing, housing and transport. PLI is defined separately for each household according to its size, demographics and location. A household is poor if its income is less than its PLI and it lacks the resources to meet the basic needs of its members. Hardcore poverty occurs when the income of a household is less than the food PLI.

and rural areas, both predominantly populated by Bumiputera.

The country's rapid industrialization and urbanization, resulting in rural–urban migration, have caused urban poverty to become a more serious issue. In 2005, there were concerns that rising graduate unemployment due to a

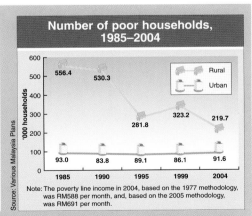

Number of poor households, 1985–2004

Rural
Urban

556.4
530.3
323.2
281.8
219.7

93.0   83.8   89.1   86.1   91.6

1985   1990   1995   1999   2004

'000 households

Source: Various Malaysia Plans

Note: The poverty line income in 2004, based on the 1977 methodology, was RM588 per month, and, based on the 2005 methodology, was RM691 per month.

mismatch between supply and demand could exacerbate urban poverty.

New forms of poverty are emerging in the following groups: single-parent households, the elderly, the handicapped, unskilled workers, the Orang Asli community and families of low-skilled foreign workers.

Human resources

Since Independence, the labour market has experienced dramatic changes in both supply and demand. On the supply side, the quality of labour has risen and the participation of women in the labour force has grown significantly. On the demand side, there has been a clear shift of labour, beginning in the 1970s, from agriculture to manufacturing and services. Since the 1990s, there has been increasing demand for science and technology-based knowledge workers. Where demand has outstripped supply, the economy has had to rely on foreign labour.

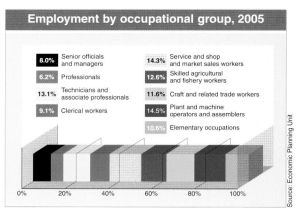

Employment by occupational group, 2005

8.0% Senior officials and managers	14.3% Service and shop and market sales workers
6.2% Professionals	12.6% Skilled agricultural and fishery workers
13.1% Technicians and associate professionals	11.6% Craft and related trade workers
9.1% Clerical workers	14.5% Plant and machine operators and assemblers
	10.6% Elementary occupations

Source: Economic Planning Unit

ABOVE: Young men lining up in front of a workers registration centre in Sabah, 1961.

TOP: Prospective job applicants queuing up when Malaysia Airlines advertised for staff in 1972.

Applicants searching for job opportunities during the Multimedia Super Corridor (MSC) exhibition in Kuala Lumpur, 2004.

Key labour force statistics, 2005

Labour force	11,290,500
Local labour (%)	84.3
Foreign labour (%)	15.7
Unemployment rate (% of total labour force)	3.5
Labour force participation rate (%)	66.7
Labour productivity (GDP/employment)	3.5
Real wage per employee in manufacturing sector	0.8

Source: Economic Planning Unit, Department of Statistics

Labour supply

In 2005, the labour force comprised 11.3 million persons. Of these, 10.9 million were employed, the remaining 400,000 being officially unemployed. The size of the labour force is determined by population growth and the labour force participation rate (LFPR), while the quality of the workforce is determined by the education levels that have been attained.

There is a direct correlation between population growth and the size of the labour force, although this may be obvious only after each new generation joins the working age population (those in the 15–64 age group). For instance, the impact of declining population growth in the 1970s was felt only in the early 1990s when the annual growth rate of the workforce fell to 2.7 per cent, from 3.2 per cent in the 1980s.

The LFPR is the percentage of the working age population engaged in, or seeking, gainful employment. The overall LFPR has risen, but only marginally, especially in the 1990s. This is partly due to a fall in the male participation rate over the years, declining from 87.6 per cent in 1980 to 86.6 per cent in 2005. This decline can be attributed to the delayed entry of males into the labour market because of greater higher education opportunities.

The female participation rate experienced a slight decline in the early 1990s, but of greater significance was the marked increase which occurred throughout the 1980s. The female LFPR increased from 43.1 per cent in 1980 to 45.7 per cent in 2005, due to several factors: industrialization and urbanization; the growth of the manufacturing sector which created jobs that could be undertaken by both men and women; education, which created awareness among women of the importance of participating in the labour force; and the government policy of reducing the dependence on foreign labour. The LFPR in Malaysia is considerably higher for males than for females, unlike most industrialized countries where there is little difference between the two rates. This may be because a woman's traditional role as homemaker helps maintain social stability, or a result of lower job security and skill levels among females.

The quality of the labour force has risen. This is reflected by the increased number of workers having at least a secondary education. In 2004, 65.8 per cent of the workforce had a secondary education, compared with only 52 per cent in 1990. The creation of higher-value-added jobs suited to this pool of better-qualified workers has therefore become a priority. The attainment of higher educational levels has also influenced workers' preferences, causing them to seek better-paid employment in urban areas over low-paying jobs in rural areas. Such transitions have not always been smooth, with temporary unemployment resulting whenever there is a lack of an effective system linking potential workers to suitable employment opportunities. Recognizing this, the Ministry of Human Resources launched an Electronic Labour Exchange (ELX) in May 2002.

Labour demand

Between 1991 and 1996, due to buoyant economic conditions, employment opportunities expanded at a much faster rate than labour force growth. Some 1.5 million new jobs were created during this period, compared to 1.1 million between 1985 and 1990. Most of them were in the manufacturing and services sectors, and very few were in the agricultural sector. The resulting structural changes in employment by sector thus reflected the structural changes in the overall economy.

From an occupational point of view, the labour market underwent equally significant changes following Independence. The manufacturing sector generated a massive demand for production and operation jobs, with workers in this field exceeding the total number of workers in the agricultural sector in 1992. Professional and technical workers, as well as those in the production field, are expected to dominate future manpower requirements.

Demand for labour in the industrial sector has also led to greater female participation, albeit in jobs which involve laborious activities such as the assembly of electrical and electronic components and the sewing of textiles. In 1982, 43.1 per cent of total manufacturing workers were female. By 2004, this had increased to 54.8 per cent. Male workers dominated in areas requiring physical strength, such as construction, mining and quarrying,

Job hunters registering at the Great Malaysian Job Hunt, 2005. The two-day fair offered an estimated 3000 job opportunities from over 60 Multimedia Super Corridor (MSC) and ICT companies.

and accounted for more than 95 per cent of the workers employed in these industries.

Equilibrium and disequilibrium

Between 1980 and 1985, unemployment rose from 5.7 per cent to 6.9 per cent. This increase was due to an economic slump caused by a worldwide depression and the rate subsequently declined to 2.5 per cent in 1997. In 1998, unemployment rates were 5.2 per cent as a result of the Asian financial crisis. After this, the economy recovered, and the ensuing labour shortage in low-productivity sectors forced employers to import foreign labour from neighbouring countries, particularly for the plantation, construction, and distributive sectors, as well as to work as domestic helpers. While this solved the problem temporarily, it was feared that too great a dependence on foreign labour could in the long-term adversely affect the social and political stability of the country.

Alternative measures to increase the labour force have been considered, including extending the retirement age from 55 to 56. In the long term, however, the only viable solution lies in the greater use of labour-saving devices and in the intensification of human resource development in the form of education, training and retraining. With Malaysia's past economic advantages—ample natural resources and cheap labour— rapidly being eroded, a new competitive edge must be developed out of knowledge and skills. The Ministry of Human Resources has developed a human resource strategy that places great emphasis on the creation of a pool of technically and technologically trained workers. It has also encouraged industries to switch from labour-intensive to capital-intensive production methods, and to restructure their organizations for greater adaptability to competition and change.

Developing human resources

The Human Resource Development Fund scheme (using levies collected from employers) was implemented in 1993 to provide funds for training and skills upgrading programmes by employers. In 2004, the Institute of Bankers Malaysia and the Malaysian Insurance Institute introduced training schemes for unemployed graduates. Other employers have offered training to unemployed graduates under the double taxation incentive in the 2004 Budget to support government efforts to improve the employability of graduates.

Women in the economy

Traditional roles and transitions

Before Independence, women were mainly involved in sectors such as subsistence agriculture, traditional handicrafts, rubber tapping, tin mining, construction, and the selling of farm produce. However, female participation in the labour market has risen substantially since then. As of 2005, there were approximately 3.5 million women active in the workforce.

Three factors contributed to the greater economic involvement of women after Independence. First, a more progressive attitude among parents towards education for women and the expansion of education facilities enabled women to pursue higher levels of education. Indeed, the number of women studying at universities has increased from 37.2 per cent of the student population in 1990 to 66.6 per cent in 2005. Second, the structural shift from agriculture to manufacturing—in particular the growth of labour-intensive jobs in the electrical and electronics and textiles sectors—created many new job

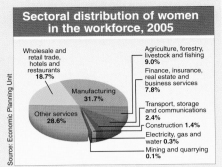

Sectoral distribution of women in the workforce, 2005

- Wholesale and retail trade, hotels and restaurants 18.7%
- Manufacturing 31.7%
- Other services 28.6%
- Agriculture, forestry, livestock and fishing 9.0%
- Finance, insurance, real estate and business services 7.8%
- Transport, storage and communications 2.4%
- Construction 1.4%
- Electricity, gas and water 0.3%
- Mining and quarrying 0.1%

Source: Economic Planning Unit

opportunities for women. Third, the New Economic Policy, which aimed to eradicate poverty and create an equitable society, provided the impetus, facilities, and encouragement for women to venture into business and management.

Organizations and policies

Despite the increased participation of women in the labour force, the number of self-employed women remains small, due to a lack of technical skills, difficulty in obtaining financing, and family commitments. Nevertheless, organizations such as Peniagawati, Usahanita, Women's Skills Institute of Malaysia (Institut Kemahiran Wanita Malaysia or IKWAM), Women's Institute of Management (WIM), and the National Association of Women Entrepreneurs of Malaysia (NAWEM) promote the interest of women in business, provide credit facilities, business training, and opportunities for networking among women entrepreneurs and organizations at both national and international levels.

Participants in a symposium during the Women's Institute of Management (WIM) launch, 1994. As of 2006, WIM has organized 405 training courses for over 15,000 businesswomen.

Flow of labour

Following Independence, foreign labour entered the country to work primarily in the agricultural and construction sectors. In 2005, there were 1.8 million foreign workers (15.7 per cent of the total employed) compared to 751,000 in 2000 and 136,000 during the early 1980s. The majority were from Indonesia, Nepal and India. Expatriates (foreign individuals who have made Malaysia their place of residence) comprised two per cent of foreign workers and were largely in the services sector.

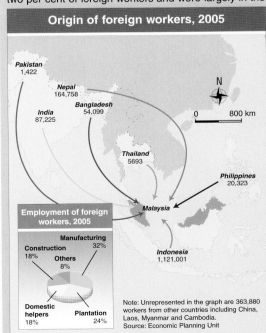

Origin of foreign workers, 2005

- Pakistan 1,422
- Nepal 164,758
- Bangladesh 54,099
- India 87,225
- Thailand 5693
- Philippines 20,323
- Malaysia
- Indonesia 1,121,001

N

0   800 km

Employment of foreign workers, 2005

- Manufacturing 32%
- Construction 18%
- Others 8%
- Domestic helpers 18%
- Plantation 24%

Note: Unrepresented in the graph are 363,880 workers from other countries including China, Laos, Myanmar and Cambodia.
Source: Economic Planning Unit

In 2005, regulations regarding recruitment of foreign semi-skilled and unskilled workers were amended to reduce dependence on them, particularly in the service sector. In addition, as of 2004, foreign workers were allowed to work a maximum of eight years only compared with ten years previously.

Over time, there has been an outflow of Malaysian citizens to the industrialized nations. To address the shortage of skilled workers, in 2001 the government implemented an incentive scheme to attract Malaysians abroad to return home (see 'Professional services'). As of July 2005, applications from 300 Malaysian experts working overseas in fields such as information technology, medicine and health, finance and accounting, had been approved.

Industrial relations

Governed by legislation and institutions, industrial relations have been shaped by the right of employees and employers to form unions and associations and by the prohibition of certain forms of industrial action. Industrial relations have undergone three phases: voluntarism, transition, and the current compulsory phase. While there has been a growth in in-house unions, and public-sector union membership is comparatively high, the overall percentage of unionized workers is low.

Minister of Human Resources Datuk Wira Dr Fong Chan Onn (left) and Prime Minister Dato' Seri Abdullah Ahmad Badawi (second from left) with award recipients at the 2004 Labour Day celebrations.

Suara NUBE (Voice of NUBE), the quarterly publication of the National Union of Bank Employees.

Unions and employers' associations

The Employment Act 1955, Trade Unions Act 1959, and Industrial Relations Act 1967 provide for the right of workers to form and join trade unions. However, despite the growth in the number of persons employed since Independence, there has not been a corresponding growth in union membership. In 2005, the percentage of employees who were registered as trade union members was roughly seven per cent, among the lowest in the world. In China, for example, over 90 per cent of employees are registered with trade unions.

Unions are permitted to form affiliations with other bodies within the country. The Malaysian Trades Union Congress (MTUC) provides support and advice to its 265 member unions (as of 2005), and represents them at both national and international levels. The Congress of Unions of Employees in the Public and Civil Service (CUEPACS) brings together public sector trade unions in Peninsular Malaysia.

Employers, too, are entitled to form unions, usually known as associations. In 2005, there were 14 employers' associations. The Malaysian Employers Federation (MEF) unites employers' associations.

The evolution of industrial relations

X. E. Nathan, the first secretary of the Malaysian Trades Union Congress, established in 1949, addressing the union members during the silver jubilee celebrations.

Voluntarism (pre-World War II to 1965)

This period was characterized by an approach modelled on the British method of resolving trade disputes through voluntary, direct negotiations between employer and employees. Third-party intervention by the government was not compulsory, and Industrial Court awards were not legally binding. In the absence of effective and responsible trade unions on one hand, and responsive and enlightened management on the other, disputes were likely to end in unproductive strikes or lockouts. In Malaysia, however, this system worked reasonably well until the 1960s. The period also saw the introduction of the Employment Act 1955 and the Trade Unions Act 1959.

The Tamil edition of the National Union of Plantation Workers' (NUPW) newsletter. NUPW was formed in 1954.

Transition (1965–1967)

Economic development in the 1960s led to a remarkable growth in the number, variety and membership of trade unions.

The early 1960s were marked by a period of industrial unrest, with a series of threatened and actual strikes in both the private and public sectors. From 1964 to 1965, during the Indonesian Confrontation, the government took action to ensure that national security and economic stability would not be undermined by disputes in the provision of essential services. In May 1965, temporary regulations were introduced under the Emergency (Essential Powers) Act 1965, prohibiting all forms of industrial action among government employees, and empowering the Minister of Labour to proscribe industrial action in both private and statutory bodies. In September 1965, these regulations were replaced by the Essential (Trade Disputes in Essential Services) Regulations, which established the Industrial Arbitration Court.

These developments introduced an element of compulsion into labour-management relations. The Minister of Labour was given the discretionary power to refer any industrial dispute in essential services to the Industrial Arbitration Court; once he intervened, no strike or lockout could take place or continue. Further, the Court's award was final and binding. The system of voluntary arbitration was maintained, however, for sectors deemed to be non-essential. For a while, the voluntary and compulsory systems of arbitration existed side by side.

Port Swettenham Harbour Workers Union members decide to 'work-to-rule' after stevedoring firms rejected their claims, c. 1964.

Newspaper workers supporting the proposal for a minimum wage during labour day celebrations in 2000.

The compulsory phase (1967 to present)

The Industrial Relations Act 1967 nullified all previous Regulations, and made way for the establishment of the present Industrial Court. With that, all vestiges of voluntarism disappeared, and the current compulsory system, or paternalism, was adopted.

Since the implementation of the Look East Policy in the early 1980s, there has been a tendency for workers to establish in-house unions (unions formed by the employees of one company) as opposed to national unions (formed by the workers of various companies in the same industry, trade, or occupation). In the early 1980s, two-thirds of the unions in Malaysia were national unions. By the early 1990s, however, about two-thirds of registered unions were in-house.

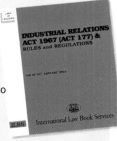

The Industrial Relations Act 1967 provides protection against unfair dismissal.

Panellists at the National Union of Journalists' (NUJ) forum on press freedom. Formed in 1962, NUJ is the sole authority that negotiates and determines the rates of remuneration and other terms and conditions of employment for journalists.

Legislation

Three key Acts of Parliament govern industrial relations. First, the Employment Act 1955 outlines minimum benefits for specific categories of workers (those earning RM1500 or less a month and manual workers) and sets out the rights of the employer and employee. The Department of Labour assumes quasi–judicial functions under this Act and empowers labour officers to hear disputes such as termination and maternity benefits, overtime payments, sick and annual leave pay.

The Trade Unions Act 1959 provides the legal framework for the formation and functioning of trade unions in both private and public sectors. It stipulates the need, but not the criteria, for the registration of a trade union. The Act also gives the Director-General of Trade Union Affairs the discretionary power to refuse or cancel registrations, and to suspend a union or one of its branches, in the interest of either the workers concerned or public order and security. Once a union has been recognized by the employer, it can initiate collective bargaining and sign collective agreements. Upon registration with the Industrial Court, these collective agreements acquire the same legal status as awards of the court. Thereafter, either party can seek redress from the court for non-compliance.

The Industrial Relations Act 1967 shaped private-sector industrial relations in three ways. First, it stipulated trade union rights and protection against acts of interference and victimization by employers. Second, it introduced provisions for trade dispute conciliation by the Director-General of the Department of Industrial Relations, his officers and the Minister of Human Resources. Third, it established the machinery of the present-day Industrial Court to which the Minister may refer disputes. Awards made by the Industrial Court are final and binding.

Selected indicators

	2001	2002	2003	2004
Trade disputes	378	431	378	321
Number of strikes	13	4	2	3
Workers involved	2,209	506	57	279
Working days lost[1]	6.0	2.0	0.1	3.0
Industrial accidents[2]	9.0	8.3	7.5	7.0

[1] per 100 workers [2] per 1000 workers
Source: Ministry of Human Resources, Economic Planning Unit

Public sector industrial relations

Members of the police, prison service, armed forces, professionals and those in managerial, confidential or high security positions are not allowed to unionize. Other employees may form trade unions, with the permission of the Yang di-Pertuan Agong.

With one million employees in 2005, the government is the single largest employer in Malaysia. In 2005, 36 per cent of unions registered in Malaysia were public sector unions, and 36 per cent of public employees were union members, in contrast to only six per cent in the private sector. The high degree of unionization among public employees is attributable to their relatively higher educational level, awareness of the benefits of trade unions, and homogeneity.

Workers picketing to demand a new salary scheme for artisans, 1985.

However, public sector unions are generally passive and inactive because their negotiating powers are greatly compromised. Under the Industrial Relations Act 1967, the public-sector unions can only strike once they have fulfilled the requirements set out in the Trade Unions Act 1959. There has been no strike in the public sector since the action taken by the Airline Employees Union against Malaysian Airline System (MAS) in 1979.

Public sector unions express their opinions to the government through their representatives in the National Joint Council, but terms and conditions of employment in the public sector are centrally determined by the Cabinet Committee. Prior to 1976, they were determined by the Salaries Commission. Industrial relations in the public sector are thus set and regulated through executive and administrative orders.

July 1966 edition of *Suara CUEPACS*, the official publication of the Congress of Unions of Employees in the Public and Civil Service.

The Public Service Department is the central personnel agency of the Federal Government. It plays a key role in public-sector industrial relations. Anomalies that arise during implementation of Cabinet Committee recommendations on salaries and employment were dealt with by the Public Services Tribunal until it was disbanded in January 2000. Issues of salary and allowances are now dealt with by the Director of the Salaries and Allowances Division within the Public Service Department itself. Other trade disputes or grievances are settled in either a civil court or the Industrial Court.

Ministry of Human Resources

The Ministry of Human Resources (MOHR), formerly known as the Ministry of Labour and Manpower, formulates labour policy and implements and enforces labour laws. Departments under its purview include: Manpower, Industrial Relations, Labour (Peninsular Malaysia, Sabah and Sarawak), Trade Union Affairs, Industrial Court, and Occupational Safety and Health.

The Industrial Court was set up to hear and decide disputes referred to it by the Minister of Human Resources or disputing parties. The Court also recognizes collective agreements which have been jointly deposited by the employers and unions. In 2004, 3406 cases were referred to the Court and 324 collective agreements were given cognizance. Decisions of the Industrial Court are final and conclusive and cannot be challenged on their merits.

The MOHR also oversees the National Labour Advisory Council, Occupational Health and Safety Council, Wages Council and National Vocational Training Council.

MTUC President Datuk Zainal Rampak (second from left) heading a picket outside the Ministry of Human Resources in 2000.

The Industrial Court in Kuala Lumpur. It has branches in Penang, Ipoh, Johor Bahru, Kota Kinabalu and Kuching.

Health and education

Two factors significantly affect the quality and productivity of human resources: health and education. While an educated and trainable workforce has enabled Malaysia to attract foreign direct investment and undertake major industrialization programmes, high-tech industrialization has required changes in the curriculum, notably the added emphasis on science, technology and technical skills. Health and education were the domains of the public sector until the 1990s when the private sector began playing an increasingly active role.

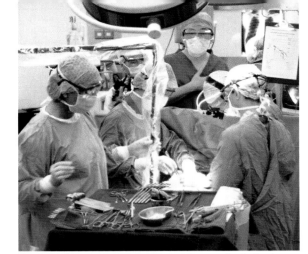

Transmyocardial revascularization heart surgery at an operating theatre of a private hospital in Penang, 2002.

Major contributors to nation building

Education is regarded as a catalyst to achieve social and economic development. Under the New Economic Policy (see 'New Economic Policy: 1971–1990'), education was a vital tool in attaining national unity. The goal of the national education system was to produce trained manpower to meet the demands of the labour market as well as produce a responsible, disciplined society with high moral values. To achieve the above goal, it is crucial for the country to have a healthy and productive society. Under the Ninth Malaysia Plan, the allocations for education (including training) and health are RM45.1 billion and RM10.3 billion respectively. The bulk (36 per cent) of the first sum is for tertiary education, while 53 per cent of the latter sum is for building new hospitals, upgrading and renovation.

In 2004, the output of the local pharmaceutical industry was RM772 million and RM4.6 million was earned through the export of medical devices.

Healthcare

The public healthcare sector

The objective of health development programmes is simply to improve the health of the population. During the Seventh Malaysia Plan (1996–2000), the allocation was RM3.73 billion, and during the Eighth Malaysia Plan (2001–05), it increased to RM5.5 billion. A major portion of this allocation went to the construction of new hospitals and the upgrading of old hospital buildings and rural health facilities. The implementation of these programmes ensured nationwide availability of health centres, mobile dental and medical units, which brought health education and treatment to the public through visits to schools, workplaces, shopping centres and other community meeting points in both urban and rural areas.

Since the early 1990s, information technology (IT) has been used extensively by the Ministry of Health, especially for non-medical, administrative purposes such as health information management, quality control and budget performance assessment. For example, between 1990 and 1995, due to increasing operational efficiency, the facility-to-population ratio improved, making it possible to

Public health facilities, 2005

	Number of units	Facility to population ratio
Community clinics	1919	1 : 13,615
Health clinics	809	1 : 32,296
Patient care services		
Hospitals[1]	128	1 : 204,122
Total beds[1]	34,761	1 : 751
Dental units[2]	3407	1 : 7668

Notes:
[1] includes medical institutions.
[2] refers to dental chairs.
Source: Information and Documentation System Unit, Ministry of Health

reduce the number of public health facilities while increasing the number of people who benefited from them. During those five years, the facility-to-population ratio for rural health clinics improved from 1:5320 to 1:4580, while for health centres it improved from 1:21,386 to 1:15,405.

With the greater availability of healthcare personnel and facilities, as well as health education programmes, the life expectancy of men and women has increased (70.6 and 76.4 years respectively in 2005), while infant mortality and crude death rates reduced to 5.1 per 1000 live births and 4.4 per 1000 people respectively in 2005.

The private sector in healthcare

To further improve efficiency, and lighten the government's financial burden, some medical and non-medical services have been privatized. These include the National Heart Institute (1992), the government's general medical store (1993) and non-medical hospital support services such as laundry and general maintenance (1995).

The private sector is playing a more active role in complementing the government's health programmes, particularly in the urban areas. The first private hospital was established in 1881. The number of private hospitals rose from 161 hospitals with 6256 beds in 1955 to 222 hospitals with 10,794 beds in 2005.

Health tourism has increased in importance in recent years. In 2004, private hospitals treated 174,189 foreign patients, earning RM105 million.

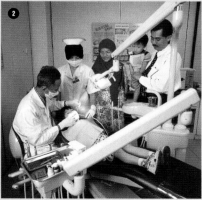

1. A nurse lecturing young mothers about the importance of a balanced diet, c. 1970s.

2. A public sector dentist at work.

3. The RM772 million Serdang Hospital in Selangor commenced operations in 2005. The 620-bed hospital contains 20 operating theatres and 19 wards.

Growth in education

The goal of education—in the economic sense—is to produce trained manpower able to meet labour market requirements and fuel growth and development. The changes in education since Independence are shown not merely by the increasing rate of enrolment or the number of schools built, but in the variety of educational options available.

In 1956, the Report of the Education Committee (known as the Razak Report) made Malay the national language, and in 1961, the Report of the Education Review Committee (known as the Rahman Talib Report) emphasized technical and vocational education at the secondary level. In the 1980s, the school curriculum was revamped (KBSR and KBSM systems) and the focus was on reading, writing and arithmetic.

From the 1990s onwards, two significant developments occurred: the rapid growth of private sector involvement in education in the early 1990s, and the gradual emphasis on science, technology and technical skills to meet the demands of industrialization and a K-economy (see 'Towards a knowledge economy'). In 2005, the Report by the Committee to Study, Review and Make Recommendations Concerning the Development and Direction of Higher Education in Malaysia emphasized the role of the tertiary education system in elevating the country to fully developed nation status by 2020.

Selected education indicators

Indicators	1990	2000	2005
Literacy rate (%)	85.0	93.8	95.1[1]
Enrolment			
Primary school (%)	99.8	92.8	96.0
Lower secondary school (%)	83.0	83.7	85.0
Upper secondary school (%)	49.1	72.6	72.5
Tertiary (%)	2.9	6.6	29.9
Pupil–teacher ratio			
Primary pupils	21.4	19.0	17.2
Secondary pupils	20.2	17.6	16.3

Note: 1 refers to 2004.

Source: Economic Planning Unit

The 2005 report by the Ministry of Higher Education.

Science, technology and technical education

Education and training content has evolved in response to economic needs. In 1971, when agriculture was a mainstay of the economy, Universiti Pertanian Malaysia (now Universiti Putra Malaysia) was established as a centre for agriculture-related education, formed from the merger of the College of Agriculture Malaya and the Faculty of Agriculture, Universiti Malaya.

The increasing shift from agriculture to manufacturing, however, created a need for a workforce skilled in industrial activities. Skills training programmes are generally conducted by the public sector and by training institutions established and run with the collaboration of foreign countries such as Germany, France, and Japan. The German–Malaysian Institute, established in 1991, offers advanced skills training in production technology and industrial electronics. The Malaysian–France Institute, established in 1995, provides training in automated mechanical systems, electrical equipment and welding technology.

At university level, efforts to produce a sufficiently skilled and technologically literate workforce to meet the needs of a knowledge-based economy have been made through the establishment of Universiti Sains Malaysia, Universiti Teknologi Malaysia and the Multimedia University at Cyberjaya.

Another significant development was the adoption of information technology (IT) at all levels of the education system. In the early 1990s, the Ministry of Education (MOE) implemented several IT-based projects. In 1992, 60 rural secondary schools were selected to participate in a pioneer project that introduced the concept of computer-aided education. In 1994, 15 rural primary schools in Selangor were chosen by the MOE to take part in a Pilot Project on Computer-Assisted Teaching and Learning for English and Mathematics. In 1996, computer literacy was made a compulsory subject in teacher training colleges. A pilot smart school project was introduced in 1999. Smart schools are equipped with computers and extensive multimedia resources which are used to enhance teaching and learning. The pilot project concluded successfully in 2002, and one additional smart school was established in 2003. As of 2004, there were 80,354 students in 88 smart schools.

From 2003, mathematics and science at all levels began to be taught in English, in order to improve competency in the language and enable school leavers to participate better in the global economy where dialogue, particularly on scientific and technical subjects, is primarily conducted in English.

Students training to be technicians and engineers at the German–Malaysian Institute, founded by Majlis Amanah Rakyat (MARA) and the Malaysian German Chamber of Commerce and Industry.

Established in 1997, Universiti Tunku Abdul Rahman (UNITAR) is the nation's first e-learning, Multimedia Super Corridor-status and ISO 9001:2000 certified private university.

The private higher education industry

Apart from a few notable exceptions, such as Goon Institute (1936), Stamford (1950) and Taylor's (1969) College, the private higher education industry truly flourished in the 1980s, driven by a new breed of academics-turned-businessmen ('edupreneurs'). The industry grew rapidly by increasing the number of places and choices for higher education. Originally established to provide tuition support for individuals with professional and semi-professional foreign qualifications, private colleges such as INTI, KDU, Metropolitan, PRIME, HELP, Sedaya and Sunway began to run pre-university, distance, twinning and transfer programmes with foreign partner institutions. Public listed companies began to invest, and three colleges (INTI, SEGi and Stamford) became listed companies.

In the early 1990s, the government intervened, enacting legislation to regulate the industry and establish measures for quality control. Foreign campuses and private universities were established, and a National Accreditation Board (LAN) was set up. Students were able to complete all three years of a foreign degree in Malaysia with the introduction of '3+0' programmes. Another development was the franchising of local university programmes to predominantly Bumiputera private colleges. Professional associations representing the education industry, such as the Malaysian Association of Private Colleges and Universities, (MAPCU) emerged.

From the mid-1990s onwards, local private universities such as UNITAR have been targeting the growing demand for e-learning. Government-linked companies such as Tenaga Nasional, Telekom and PETRONAS, have also developed universities. The new millennium saw the upgrading of private colleges, some of which were awarded university college status. In 2005, the Ministry of Higher Education oversaw 11 private universities, 12 university colleges, five foreign university branch campuses and 537 private colleges, serving around 312,000 local students and 27,000 foreign students.

Universiti Teknologi PETRONAS is a wholly-owned subsidiary of PETRONAS.

International students having a group discussion at Sunway College in Kuala Lumpur, 2006.

Foreign students

In 2005, Malaysian institutions hosted 50,380 international students, of whom 82 per cent were in institutions of higher education. Nearly 54 per cent of these students were from China and Indonesia.

Housing

Housing is both an economic and social issue. Objectives of the national housing policy include the provision of adequate housing for all citizens, increasing home ownership among Bumiputera, and ensuring that housing not only creates safe living environments, but also promotes national unity. The construction of housing for the poor was once a government-led initiative, but is now largely private sector driven. Upcoming challenges include the provision of low- and medium-cost housing, and addressing the squatter problem in urban areas.

	House construction targets and achievements (units)					
	PUBLIC SECTOR			**PRIVATE SECTOR**		
Period	Target	Achieved	% of target	Target	Achieved	% of target
6MP 1991–95	174,000	84,542	49%	399,000	562,918	141%
7MP 1996–00	230,000	121,624	53%	570,000	737,856	129%
8MP 2001–05	312,000	188,669	61%	303,000	655,374	216%
9MP 2006–10	197,805	-	-	511,595	-	-

Source: Sixth to Ninth Malaysia Plans (MP)

A medium-high-cost terraced house development in Petaling Jaya.

High-cost houses on Bukit Jambul in Penang.

Objectives of housing policies

In 1976, the government promulgated a 'home-owning democracy' with the aim of enabling all citizens to own their own homes. While home ownership for all strata of society is the long-term goal, government policies also seek to create a safe and decent living environment with adequate infrastructure and social facilities in housing schemes.

Malaysia has largely succeeded in achieving this objective because of political stability, an effective free market economy, and the availability of various financial facilities for both bridging- and end-financing purposes.

Commercial banks have long been required by government regulations to allocate about 20–30 per cent of their annual lending to the housing industry, namely purchasers and developers. With the enactment of the Housing Development Act in 1966, the government approved a unique payment scheme between the developer and purchaser which allowed the developer to receive instalments from purchasers as construction progresses. This progressive funding of housing development projects has enabled developers to finance and construct more housing than they would have otherwise been able to.

Since the New Economic Policy (NEP) (see 'The New Economic Policy: 1971–1990'), housing policies have sought to increase home ownership among the Bumiputera. Regulations have required housing developers to give special discounts to Bumiputera purchasers (five to ten per cent of the sale price) and to set aside a quota (30 per cent) for sale to them, in order to promote integration among the various ethnic communities. The discounts are cross-subsidized from sales of other houses in a particular development.

The private sector

As of 2005, there were approximately 3.5 million units of housing in Malaysia. The various five-year development plans (see 'Economic planning and growth') set specific housing targets for both public and private sector developers. Private sector housing developers have often exceeded the targets under the Malaysia Plans, especially since the Sixth Malaysia Plan.

Issues and challenges

In highly urbanized centres such as Kuala Lumpur, Penang and Johor Bahru, there is still a portion of the urban low-income population who cannot afford even low-cost urban houses. Out of necessity, they often resort to 'squatting' or building their own houses on vacant, usually government, land (see 'Urbanization'). The government provides basic amenities such as piped water, health services, educational facilities and electricity to selected squatter settlements.

The shortage of local construction workers since the early 1990s has led to a heavy dependence on foreign workers who compound the problem of squatters. These workers often lack

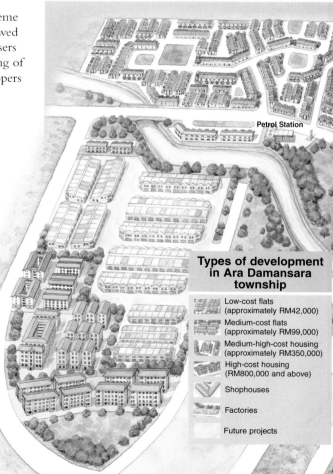

Petrol Station

Types of development in Ara Damansara township

- Low-cost flats (approximately RM42,000)
- Medium-cost flats (approximately RM99,000)
- Medium-high-cost housing (approximately RM350,000)
- High-cost housing (RM800,000 and above)
- Shophouses
- Factories
- Future projects

the requisite skills to build quality homes (see 'Construction').

The incidence of abandonment of housing projects was low in 2005, at between one to two per cent per annum. However, it continues to be an important issue as the life savings of citizens are at stake. The recession of the mid-1980s saw the setting up of the Abandoned Housing Project Fund.

Future challenges include meeting housing targets set by the government. High-cost houses are expected to continue to cross-subsidize low-cost housing, but high-cost houses constitute only about 32 per cent of targeted units under the Ninth Malaysia Plan (2006–10). At the same time, special discounts given to Bumiputera purchasers mean an additional subsidy element must be factored into the price structure of high-cost houses.

Costs have also increased because better infrastructure and amenities, such as improved transportation and sewerage systems, are being implemented through privatization. In 1970, public services constituted only 25 per cent of the gross land area of a development. By 2005, this had increased to 55 per cent.

Against this scenario of rising costs and expectations for a higher quality of life, government regulators and the private sector housing industry have had to carry out a fine balancing act of fulfilling targets and delivering affordable houses to the masses, and at the same time ensuring that housing development is still a viable enterprise.

Low-cost double-storey terrace houses built by a private developer in Desa Ilmu, Sarawak.

Low-cost housing

Besides meeting the housing needs of the nation at large, providing housing for the lower income groups has been an integral part of national policy throughout all the five-year plans of the country starting from the First Malaysia Plan (1966–70). Since the Fourth Malaysia Plan (1981–85), the government has adopted a strategy of direct intervention in the form of low-cost housing programmes implemented by state governments with loans from the Federal Treasury. Initiatives are coordinated at the national level by the National Housing Department of the Ministry of Housing and Local Government.

In 2005, low-cost housing in Malaysia was defined as accommodation of at least 650 square feet in built-up area, selling at a price not exceeding RM42,000. In general, families with incomes of less than RM1500 per month were eligible to purchase low-cost houses.

Low-cost housing was provided largely by the public sector until the 1970s, when new regulations required the private sector to participate in the building of low-cost houses; for housing development projects to qualify for approval, 30 per cent of all units built had to be of low-cost housing. The low prices are made possible through cross-subsidies from sales of other properties developed by the private sector. The private sector performed well during the prolonged economic boom of the early 1990s. Under the Seventh Malaysia Plan (1996–2000), the private sector constructed 68 per cent of the total 190,597 units of low-cost housing completed. The balance were constructed by state governments and State Economic Development Corporations (see 'The Federal, state and local governments in the economy').

In 2004, squatters were resettled into these flats at Jalan Cochrane, Kuala Lumpur under the Citizens' Housing Programme.

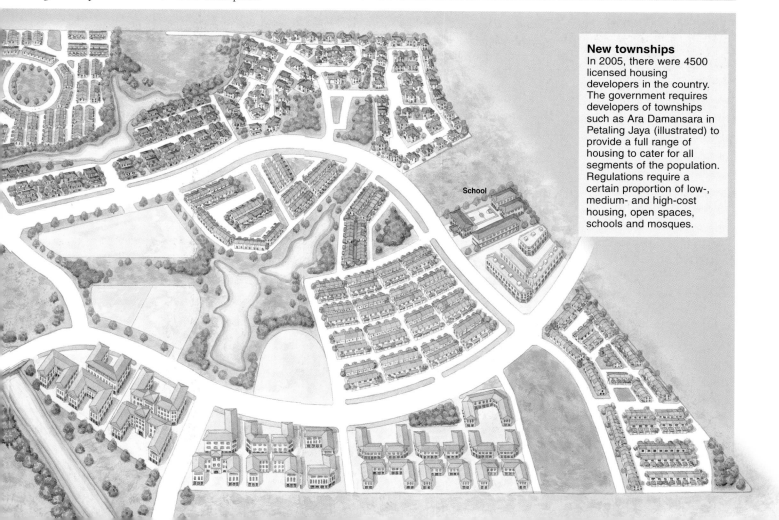

School

New townships

In 2005, there were 4500 licensed housing developers in the country. The government requires developers of townships such as Ara Damansara in Petaling Jaya (illustrated) to provide a full range of housing to cater for all segments of the population. Regulations require a certain proportion of low-, medium- and high-cost housing, open spaces, schools and mosques.

Urbanization

With the industrialization of the country in the 1960s, industrial estates and satellite towns were developed. By 2005, nearly 63 per cent of the Malaysian population was living in urban areas. In addition to better opportunities for employment and business, urban dwellers enjoy more options in terms of education, health, infrastructure and entertainment.

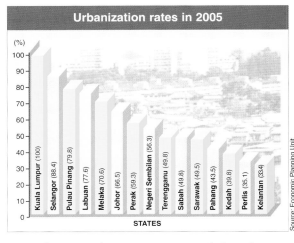

Urbanization rates in 2005

Source: Economic Planning Unit

An aerial view of Petaling Jaya, Selangor, the first 'satellite' town, c. 1960.

Petaling Jaya was granted city status on 20 June 2006.

The emergence of urban centres

Urbanization is attributable to several factors, of which urban economic activity is the most influential. This economic activity continues to provide the main reason for rural-to-urban migration, and in earlier times led to the development and growth of large urban centres. Melaka and Penang originated as trading ports in the 15th century and late 18th century respectively, while Ipoh and Kuala Lumpur were mining towns established in the late 19th century. In Sarawak and Sabah, cities such as Kuching and Sandakan were centres for trade. Many of these early urban centres eventually became government administrative centres.

In the post-Independence years, another development in urbanization arose as a result of the industrialization drive of the 1960s, which saw the establishment of industrial estates and the growth of so-called 'satellite' towns near the older urban centres. Petaling Jaya was the first such town (see 'Industrial areas'). Other satellite towns that emerged during this period include Sungai Buloh and Rawang in the Klang Valley, Perai and Gelugor in Penang, and Pasir Gudang and Skudai in Johor.

Transport was another key factor in urbanization. To facilitate the growth of the rubber and tin industries, a network of railways and roads was built, beginning in the mid-1880s. It branched out from early urban centres such as Kuala Lumpur and Ipoh, and connected them to minor ports along the coast. By enabling the free movement of goods and people, this transportation network opened the way for commerce and industry and encouraged rural-to-urban migration.

In the 1950s, the government resettled rural people, mainly Chinese, into new villages, some of which had easier access to main roads. These villages later developed into small urban centres or townships around Kuala Lumpur such as Jinjang, Salak and Kepong.

As a result of the large-scale resettlement schemes, such as FELDA, undertaken by federal and state economic development authorities, a number of townships emerged in rural areas, for example Jengka in Pahang (see 'Rural and regional development'), Gua Musang in Kelantan and Perda in Penang.

Growth and expansion

By 1980, there were 67 towns defined as urban, and 4.75 million people living in them. A redefinition in 1991 increased the number of towns to 129, and the urban population to 9.47 million. The percentage of the Malaysian population living in urban areas increased from 34.2 per cent in 1980 to about 63 per cent in 2005. Rural-to-urban migration in pursuit of better economic opportunities and a higher standard of living remains one of the principal causes of increasing urbanization. At the same time, new urban centres are emerging as a result of policies encouraging entrepreneurs and investors to locate their operations in less developed areas, such as the east coast of Peninsular Malaysia, Sabah and Sarawak.

There are some notable examples of planned areas. For example, to ease urban congestion in Kuala Lumpur, the Federal Government's administrative centre has been moved to Putrajaya, a new town in the Multimedia Super Corridor. Putrajaya and its neighbouring town, Cyberjaya, have been earmarked as world-class garden areas that will serve as models for Malaysia's future urban centres (see 'The Multimedia Super Corridor').

The quality of urban life

Compared with the rural population, urban dwellers generally enjoy access to a wider range of economic activities, educational opportunities, medical facilities, infrastructure and entertainment. Urban income levels are also higher. For instance, between 1999 and 2004, the average monthly income of rural households in Peninsular Malaysia increased at the rate of 1.9 per

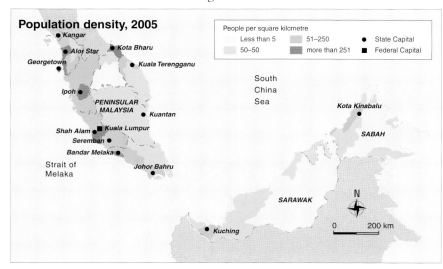

Population density, 2005

People per square kilometre

Less than 5	51–250	● State Capital
50–50	more than 251	■ Federal Capital

Kangar
Alor Star
Kota Bharu
Georgetown
Kuala Terengganu
Ipoh
PENINSULAR MALAYSIA
Kuantan
Shah Alam
Kuala Lumpur
Seremban
Bandar Melaka
Strait of Melaka
Johor Bahru
South China Sea
Kota Kinabalu
SABAH
SARAWAK
Kuching
N
0   200 km

Urbanization of several Malaysian cities

Kuching

Kuching was granted city status in August 1988. Governed by two local authorities, the Kuching North City Hall and the City Council of Kuching South, the city covers 431 square kilometres and has expanded to include adjacent areas under the Padawan Municipal and Samarahan District Councils. The city's population increased from 53,392 in 1963 to 511,352 in 2004.

Kuching has undergone low-density development with decentralized newer townships established in suburbs around the Central Business District. Most development projects in Kuching have a density of not more than 20 units per hectare, with few high-rise buildings. In the 1970s, housing estates such as Kenyalang Park were within a three to five kilometre radius of the city centre. However, by 2004, residential properties such as Semariang, Rampangi, Stutong and Mile 13 were established within a 20–25 kilometre radius of the city centre. Growth has occurred in both newer townships such as Batu Kawah as well as established areas such as Tabuan Jaya and Kota Sentosa.

Kuching's Main Bazaar fronting the Sarawak River.

Kota Kinabalu's waterfront.

The pioneer industrial estate built was the Pending and Bintawa Industrial Estate of the 1970s. The Demak Laut Industrial Park (Phase I) and Sejingkat Industrial Park were developed in 1988, followed by the Samajaya Free Industrial Zone in 1992 and the Demak Laut Industrial Park (Phase IIA) in 2002.

Kota Kinabalu

Kota Kinabalu began as the small fishing village Kampung Api-Api, which was renamed Jesselton by the British North Borneo Chartered Company in 1899. As the terminus of the North Borneo Railway and close to the deepwater Gaya Bay Harbour, the city has been an important port since its founding. Razed during World War II, it was quickly rebuilt and land reclamation projects along Gaya Bay's foreshore have ensured the availability of land for development, with most of the city centre built on landfills. Jesselton replaced Sandakan as Sabah's capital in 1947, and in 1968 was renamed Kota Kinabalu after Mount Kinabalu. It achieved city status in February 2000 with a population at that time of 354,153.

The city limits have been expanded northwards to encompass the Kota Kinabalu Industrial Park (KKIP). Many new housing estates such as Kingfisher Park and Taman

The Sultan Salahuddin mosque and its surroundings, Shah Alam.

Indah Permai—as well as two unversity campuses—have been developed between the city centre and KKIP. To the south of the city there is a new township, Dongonggon.

Shah Alam

Shah Alam is the administrative centre of the state of Selangor. It was established in 1963 at Sungai Renggam, an oil palm plantation also referred to as Batu Tiga on pre-Independence maps. The township was bestowed the name Shah Alam in 1978 by the Sultan of Selangor when it became the capital of Selangor. Initially occupying 41.69 square kilometres, its boundaries were expanded in 1997 to encompass 290.3 square kilometres. In October 2000, Shah Alam was awarded city status with a population of 319,612. By 2005, its population had grown to 509,943.

Located between Kuala Lumpur and Port Klang, Shah Alam has seen a constant stream of development projects carried out in its five industrial areas and 15 residential zones. The city's planners have eliminated early problems of imbalanced development and the existence of shanty towns at the city's borders. The Shah Alam City Council administers the city and oversees the welfare of its population.

---

cent per annum. In contrast, the rate of increase for urban households was 5.1 per cent per annum.

The government is improving the quality of life of people in urban centres by resettling squatters, building affordable low- and medium-cost housing, introducing projects to improve traffic flow and controlling the prices of essential items such as rice and sugar. In Kuala Lumpur, a policy utilized since the 1970s has aimed to disperse the urban population to satellite towns, and industry to the less-developed regions of the country.

While transportation promotes rural-to-urban migration and the growth of cities, it is also a key factor in dispersing the population away from congested cities. In recent years, improved transport infrastructure has made it easier for people working in Kuala Lumpur to live further away, in neighbouring towns and even states. To reduce the number of cars that are driven in the city every day, the inter- and intra-city public transport systems have been upgraded. Kuala Lumpur's inhabitants now have at their disposal a Light Rail Transit (LRT) system, a monorail system and a commuter train service, in addition to a bus network (see 'Roads and railways'). Special lanes on key roads have also been created to enable buses and taxis to bypass peak-hour traffic jams.

The central Kuala Lumpur skyline. In 2005, approximately 1.4 million people inhabited Kuala Lumpur, making it the most populous city in Malaysia.

Urban and rural population

Source: Economic Planning Unit

	1957 6.3 million	1980 13.8 million	1991 18.4 million	2000 23.5 million	2005 26.7 million
Rural	73.3%	65.8%	49%	38%	37%
Urban	26.7%	34.2%	51%	62%	63%

Rural / Urban / Total population

Rural and regional development

Historically, different patterns of development in the states have resulted in an unequal distribution of income, amenities and opportunities. Poverty was a serious social problem in the early 1970s when more than half of the population resided in rural areas and more than 60 per cent of that rural population were considered poor. The government embarked on various development strategies, emphasizing the provision of physical infrastructure and social, as well as human development.

Tun Abdul Razak, Minister of National and Rural Development (seated in the middle), discussing rural development in the National Operations Room, c. 1960s.

Desa Kencana village in the FELDA Sahabat complex in eastern Sabah.

FELCRA settlers spraying fertilizer in *padi* fields in Seberang, Perak, 2001. The use of modern technology by FELCRA settlers has yielded them higher returns on their crops.

A signboard at FELDA LBJ settlement in Negeri Sembilan shows the various facilities available: office, school, clinic, police post, mosque, religious school and kindergarten.

Pre-New Economic Policy (1957–1970)

During the First Malaya Plan (1956–60), the government spent about 24 per cent of the national budget on agricultural development which was related to rural development. Rural dwellers traditionally comprised uneconomic rubber and *padi* smallholders, inshore fishermen and small gravel-pump tin miners. Key strategies included the opening up of virgin forests for agricultural activities and land development. The Federal Land Development Authority (FELDA) started 22 land development schemes and by the end of 1960, four years after its formation, nearly 30,000 acres had been cleared and planted with rubber and palm oil. Irrigation facilities boosted rice production in Perlis, Kedah, Perak and Kelantan, while drainage and protective works rehabilitated coconut and rubber lands on the west coast of the Peninsula. In addition, nine rural health care centres were established.

Under the Second Malaya Plan (1961–65), rural development aimed at providing infrastructure and employment opportunities for the rural sector. A new Ministry of National Rural Development was established in 1959 (in 2006, it is known as the Ministry of Rural and Regional Development). Under this Ministry, planning was formalized in a master plan: the Rural Economic Development (RED) Book Plan. The National Rural Development Council was formed in 1960 and thereafter, State and District Rural Development Committees were also created. At the grassroots level, development planning was centred at the District Office. This basic three-tier system of rural development planning continues in 2006.

Various institutional agencies were also established. The Federal Agricultural Marketing Authority (FAMA) was formed in 1965 to improve the marketing system and ensure that farmers obtained fair prices for their products. That same year, Bank Bumiputra was set up to provide credit and banking facilities to assist Bumiputera in commerce, industry and other economic activities. The former Rural Industrial Development Authority (RIDA) was reorganized and Majlis Amanah Rakyat (MARA or the Council of Trust for the Indigenous People) established in 1966. MARA's activities included the provision of technical and financial assistance to the Bumiputera in new or existing industrial and commercial projects. In 1966, the Federal Land Consolidation and Rehabilitation Authority (FELCRA) was established to rehabilitate alienated fringe schemes. The Malaysian Agricultural Research and Development Institute (MARDI) was set up in 1968 for public sector research on all crops except rubber, livestock, poultry and freshwater fisheries. In 1969, Bank Pertanian (Agriculture Bank) was established to provide credit facilities to farmers on reasonable terms.

The First Malaysia Plan (1966–70) sought to raise the productivity and income-earning capacity of the rural sector. Since Malaysia was then the world's largest producer of rubber and tin, efforts were made to improve their yield and production processes. A new Standard Malaysian Rubber was introduced and tin was more efficiently mined using modern dredges and gravel pumps.

The period also saw an increase in infrastructure and social facilities in rural areas. Secondary educational facilities, especially in the sciences, were greatly expanded both by the construction of schools in rural areas and the provision of residential facilities in other schools. As a result, rural schools accounted for three-quarters of the primary schools and approximately half of the secondary schools in Peninsular Malaysia.

New Economic Policy era (1971–1990)

A more concerted and coordinated effort against poverty took shape in 1971 with the introduction of the New Economic Policy (NEP) (see 'New Economic Policy: 1971–1990). All development programmes were oriented towards the two main objectives of poverty eradication and socio-economic restructuring.

During the Second Malaysia Plan (1971–75), measures introduced included programmes for double cropping, off season and inter-cropping, drainage and irrigation, improved marketing and credit, financial and technical assistance to small-scale businesses and industries, new land development schemes, fishing and forestry projects.

By the Fourth Malaysia Plan (1981–85), the focus had changed to the role of citizens and self-reliance. A 'New Approach to Village and Rural Development' (NAVRD) was introduced in mid-1984. To make agricultural ventures more economically viable, villagers' plots were combined

FELDA settlers showing off their land titles in Selangor, 1991. As of 2005, 77,287 FELDA settlers (74.9 per cent) had completed their repayments and received their land titles.

Federal Land Development Authority

The Federal Land Development Authority (FELDA) was established pursuant to the Land Development Act 1956 to reduce rural poverty and bring about a more equitable distribution of income and land ownership. Its main functions are to open up and develop forest land into agricultural smallholdings and to undertake commercial services supporting the smallholder programme. FELDA stopped accepting new settlers in 1990.

As of 2005, FELDA had relocated 104,946 settler families in 278 schemes throughout the country. The total settler population was about 750,000, and the main crops cultivated were oil palm (71 per cent), rubber (28 per cent) and sugarcane (one per cent). At the end of 2004, FELDA produced 21, 16 and 14 per cent of the nation's total palm oil, rubber and refined sugar output respectively. In 2004, FELDA spent an average of RM51,241 to emplace a

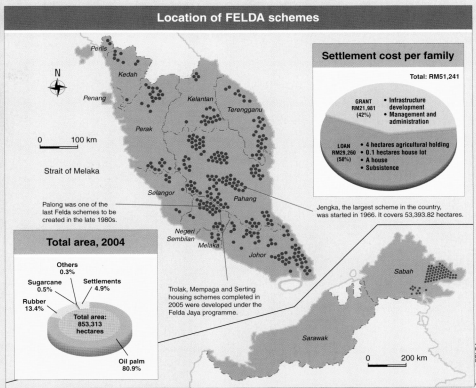

Location of FELDA schemes

Settlement cost per family

Total: RM51,241

GRANT RM21,981 (42%)
• Infrastructure development
• Management and administration

LOAN RM29,260 (58%)
• 4 hectares agricultural holding
• 0.1 hectares house lot
• A house
• Subsistence

Jengka, the largest scheme in the country, was started in 1966. It covers 53,393.82 hectares.

Palong was one of the last Felda schemes to be created in the late 1980s.

Total area, 2004

Others 0.3%
Sugarcane 0.5%
Settlements 4.9%
Rubber 13.4%
Total area: 853,313 hectares
Oil palm 80.9%

Trolak, Mempaga and Serting housing schemes completed in 2005 were developed under the Felda Jaya programme.

Source: FELDA

settler family in the scheme. A loan with interest of 6.25 per cent per annum has to be repaid within 15–20 years from the date that the crops come into production. Thereafter, the settlers own the plot of land. Settlers can also invest in the FELDA group of companies by purchasing shares in the FELDA Investment Cooperative.

As almost 60 per cent of settlers are over 60 years old, on 1 October 2005, the

government increased its loan to settlers from RM50 to RM75 per acre (0.4 hectare) to meet their rising cost of living. This loan is given until the settlers' land produces yield; 36 months for oil palm and 72 months for rubber. It has been proposed to rename settlers 'national entrepreneurs' as they no longer merely open up jungle land for agriculture but also cultivate crops.

into estates managed by experts in order to reap economies of scale. Agencies such as the Rubber Industry Smallholders Development Authority (RISDA) and FELCRA encouraged participation in this programme. In 1986, the 'Village Revolution' was implemented to oversee villages that were not part of the NAVRD. In 1987, the government reintroduced the District Development Guideline Book (Red Book II), emphasizing coordination at various governmental levels and the participation of citizens and the private sector in rural development.

National Development Policy era (1991–2000)

Increased productivity remained the primary goal in this era. Area development through replanting activities (rubber, oil palm and commercial crops), consolidation and rehabilitation of idle and uneconomic farm programmes initiated by the government in the early 1970s continued until the Fifth Malaysia Plan (1985–90).

In 1994, the Ministry launched the Second Rural Transformation and the Rural Vision Movement (RVM). Strategies continued to focus on the modernization of the rural sector and the provision of social and physical infrastructure. New land development was concentrated in Sabah and Sarawak. In addition, four Integrated

Agricultural Development Projects (IADPs) were completed during the Sixth Plan Period (1991–95).

In 1996, the Federal Government dissolved five regional development authorities (KEJORA, DARA, KETENGAH, JENGKA and KEDA) and placed them under the administration of the respective states to reduce the size of the public sector. In addition, FELCRA was corporatized.

Rural monthly household income increased from RM951 in 1990 to RM1300 in 1995, and the incidence of rural poverty was also reduced from 21.8 to 18 per cent during the same period. However, income disparity between rural and urban households widened from 1:1.7 in 1990 to 1:2 in 1995 due to the continued dependence of rural households on agricultural activities as a major source of income, limited business opportunities, capital constraints and the lack of competitiveness of rural industries.

National Vision Policy era (2001–2010)

Emphasis on the provision of quality infrastructure in rural areas, especially in Sabah and Sarawak, continues. Special attention is given to the hardcore poor, poor and vulnerable groups with the introduction of the Development of the Citizens Welfare Scheme. The government also set the target of totally eradicating hardcore poverty by 2009.

Workers manufacturing fertilizers for rubber and oil palm plantations at FPM Sdn Bhd in Pasir Gudang, Johor.

Solar-powered street lamps installed for the first time in rural Kampung Peliau near Miri, Sarawak.

Protection through the law

Malaysia's legal framework protects the rights of employees, consumers, companies and creators of intellectual property. Basic employee rights are ensured. Consumer protection, which emerged in the 1960s as a public reaction against fluctuating prices, is today enforced by the Ministry of Domestic Trade and Consumer Affairs. Company laws govern the formation and conduct of businesses, while laws relating to copyrights, trademarks and patents safeguard the rights of companies, inventors and creators of intellectual property.

Minister of Human Resources Datuk Wira Dr Fong Chan Onn (right) examining and speaking to a SOCSO beneficiary.

Employee protection

In addition to the right to form and be active in trade unions (see 'Industrial Relations'), employees are entitled to benefits in the form of financial security in old age, a safe work environment and medical benefits.

The most important of the relevant laws are the Employees Provident Fund Act 1952, the Employees Social Security Act 1969, the Occupational Safety and Health Act 1994, the Workmen's Compensation Act 1952 and the Pensions Act 1980.

Employees Provident Fund (EPF) Service Centres accept withdrawal applications, receive monthly contributions and provide advice on EPF's services.

Financial security in old age
Public sector employees are covered under the Pensions Act 1980. Upon retirement, they are entitled to a monthly income and medical benefits for life. When a married male pensioner dies, the income goes to his widow until she remarries, and to his children until they leave school.

For private sector employees, financial security is ensured by the Employees Provident Fund (EPF or Kumpulan Wang Simpanan Pekerja, KWSP). Under the Employees Provident Fund Act 1952, both the employee and his or her employer are obliged by law to make monthly

SOCSO's logo.

contributions towards the employee's EPF account. Rates are decided by law and may change from time to time. In 2005, employees contributed 11 per cent of their monthly salary, while employers contributed 12 per cent. In normal circumstances, members may withdraw up to one-third of their total credit at age 50, and the rest at age 55. However, they may also make partial withdrawals earlier to settle extraordinary medical expenses, buy a house, and to invest in approved unit trust funds. At the end of 2005, the EPF had over five million members, whose accumulated contributions amounted to RM260 billion.

Occupational safety and health
In 1969, the Employees Social Security Act established a comprehensive insurance scheme protecting all employees in the event of worksite and work-related injury or disease. The Act is administered by the Social Security Organization (SOCSO or Pertubuhan Keselamatan Sosial, PERKESO). Like the EPF, monthly contributions to SOCSO are made by employers and employees, but unlike the EPF, SOCSO is a form of insurance, under which no payouts are made unless the employee has an accident or dies. Contributions are not compulsory for those who earn RM3000 or more per month and have not previously contributed. Contributions to SOCSO schemes are therefore smaller than EPF contributions. Public sector employees are exempted from the SOCSO scheme as they have their own medical benefits under the Pensions Act. The Occupational Safety and Health Act 1994 applies to all economic sectors in Malaysia. It is administered by the Ministry of Human Resources' Department of Occupational Safety and Health (formerly the Department of Factories and Machinery). The Act provides for the safety, health and welfare of persons at work. It also protects others against risks to safety or health in connection with work. An advisory body, the National Council for Occupational Safety and Health, ensures effective implementation of the Act.

Some laws concerning the safety and health of employees cover only specific groups. The Factories and Machinery Act 1967 covers factory workers. As of July 1992, the Workmen's Compensation Act 1952 provides compensation for work-related injuries only to foreign workers earning RM500 or less per month or engaged in manual work.

Selected SOCSO statistics						
	1999	2000	2001	2002	2003	2004
Total contributions (RM million)	898.7	990.1	1,047.7	1,095.1	1,143.6	1,213.7
Registered employers	385,916	415,523	443,904	447,150	507,854	542,629
Registered employees ('000)	8,598	8,877	8,769	7,912	9,996	10,239
Reported accidents	92,074	95,006	85,229	81,810	73,858	69,132
Number of claims paid out	202,817	222,350	223,845	232,327	239,004	255,381

Source: SOCSO

Shareholders
Legal protection is available to shareholders of all Malaysian companies by virtue of the Companies Act 1965, enforced by the Companies Commission of Malaysia (or Suruhanjaya Syarikat Malaysia, SSM). The Act provides shareholders with rights in relation to approving specific corporate transactions and also prevents companies from entering into specified prohibited transactions. Shareholders are also ensured of involvement in a company's decision-making process by virtue of their right to be informed of and to attend and vote at general meetings of the company. They are further entitled to have access to corporate information, inspect the company's books and be informed of the company's financial status. Shareholders are able to sue directors for oppressive conduct and breach of duty to the company. As a last

resort, shareholders may protect their investment by winding up the company.

Malaysia operates under a common law system where case law aids the interpretation of the Companies Act. Non-compliance with certain sections of the Act may result in criminal prosecution.

Shareholders in public listed companies are provided with additional protection as a result of the Listing Requirements of Bursa Malaysia (see 'Financial markets'), guidelines issued by the Securities Commission, and the Securities Industry Act 1983. Furthermore, directors of public listed companies are subject to the Mandatory Accreditation programme monitored by Bursa Malaysia. There is also a Malaysian Code on Corporate Governance which sets out the principles and best practices in relation to corporate governance, including shareholder

protection. Organizations that further promote good corporate governance and encourage shareholder activism include the Malaysian Institute of Corporate Governance and the Minority Shareholders Watchdog Group.

Tan Sri Dato' Seri Dr Ahmad Sarji Abdul Hamid (middle), Chairman of Sime Darby, and members of the Board of Directors of Sime Darby at their annual general meeting in 2005.

Creators and inventors

The Intellectual Property Corporation of Malaysia, established in 2003, deals with all matters related to intellectual property (IP). Malaysia is a member of the World Intellectual Property Organization (WIPO), a signatory to the Paris and Berne Conventions, and the Agreement on Trade Related Aspects of Intellectual Property Rights (TRIPS) signed under the auspices of the World Trade Organization (WTO).

There are four key pieces of IP legislation. The Patents Act 1983 allows an invention to be patented if it is new, involves an inventive step and is industrially applicable. The Trade Marks Act 1976 protects registered trade marks and service marks in Malaysia. The Industrial Designs Act 1996 provides for the registration of industrial designs which can be 2D (pattern) or 3D (shape) in nature. The Copyright Act 1987 provides comprehensive protection for copyrightable works, which include computer

software. There is no registration of copyright works. Copyright protection in literary, musical or artistic works is for the duration of the life of the author and 50 years after his death. In sound recordings, broadcasts and films, copyright protection is for 50 years after the works are first published or made.

The Layout Design of Integrated Circuit Act 2000 provides for the protection of layout designs of integrated circuits based on originality. There is no registration for the layout design of an integrated circuit. The Act reassures investors in the electronics industry of their ownership in the designs and ensures the growth of technology.

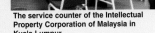

The service counter of the Intellectual Property Corporation of Malaysia in Kuala Lumpur.

The Geographical Indications Act 2000 provides protection upon registration to goods according to the name of the place where the goods are produced. Protection is applicable to goods such as wines and spirits, natural or agricultural products, or any product or handicraft or industry. 'Sarawak Pepper' is the only geographical indication to have been registered since 2001.

Intellectual Property (IP) registered in Malaysia (2005)

IP type	Applications received	Applications approved	Percentage of foreign IP
Patent	6286	2508	99
Trade mark	22,144	11,454	68
Industrial design	1116	525	61

Source: Intellectual Property Corporation of Malaysia

Consumers

Minister of Domestic Trade and Consumer Affairs Dato' Shafie bin Haji Apdal comparing products at a Carrefour hypermarket during the 'Smart Consumer Campaign' in 2005.

Consumer associations

The consumer movement emerged in the mid-1960s primarily as a public reaction against frequent fluctuations in the prices of essential goods, especially food, during festive seasons.

Public resentment intensified in late 1964 and this led to the formation of the Penang Consumers' Association (PCA), which lasted less than three months. The Selangor Consumers' Association (SCA), formed in 1965, is still active today, making it one of the oldest consumers' associations in Asia. The Consumer Association of Penang (CAP) was established in 1969, followed by associations in Sarawak and Negeri Sembilan in 1971.

In 1973, the Federation of Malaysian Consumers' Associations (FOMCA) was established in Alor Star, Kedah, to act as a national-level coordinating and consultative agency through which the various consumers' associations could interact and take collective action. FOMCA has been instrumental in initiating mandatory product tagging (price and expiry date); mediation bureaux (insurance and

banking); codes, charters, guidelines (Patient's Charter, Malaysian Code of Business Ethics, Guidelines for Guarantors, Malaysian Code of Advertising Practice); consumer legislation (Food Act 1983, Direct Selling Act 1993, Consumer Protection Act 1999); and campaigns. By 2005, over 400 consumer clubs in schools throughout the nation had been established by FOMCA as part of its consumer education programmes.

In 2005, there were 11 consumer associations affiliated to FOMCA.

Consumer rights education today is part of the national school curriculum, and some institutes of higher learning have introduced consumerism as a course. Consumer issues are frequently discussed in the mass media, which is generally supportive of consumerism.

Government efforts in consumerism

The Ministry of Domestic Trade and Consumer Affairs, formed in 1990, aims to bring about fairer trading practices, better business ethics, and greater public awareness in the following areas: prices and supply of essential goods; trade description and consumer information such as labelling; trade practices including hire-purchase and cheap sales; standards, weights and measures; and the promotion of consumerism. It is advised by the National Advisory Council for Consumer Protection (NACCP), which comprises representatives from business, government, and other organizations.

Many other ministries, such as Science, Technology and Innovation and Housing and Local Government, enforce consumer protection laws. Agencies include the Pesticides Board, the Electrical Inspectorate, and the Standards and Industrial Research Institute of Malaysia (SIRIM).

Domestic Trade and Consumer Affairs Ministry enforcement officers carrying out price checks on controlled items at the Kajang market, Kuala Lumpur.

While the laws protecting consumers date back to 1946, the term 'consumer' only appeared in Malaysian laws in 1992, when the Hire Purchase Act (Amendment) and the Direct Selling Act were passed by parliament.

Between 1990 and 1999, several laws were amended to provide for even greater protection. Regulations relating to the Trade Descriptions Act 1972 were amended to make labelling compulsory for all products, and those pertaining to cheap sales were revamped to achieve better control and supervision of these sales. The Price Control (Indication of Price by Retailers) Order 1977 was reviewed to extend compulsory price tagging to all products. The Direct Sales Act 1993 required the licensing of all direct selling companies. A Price Information Centre was established to monitor 97 essential goods in 14 towns and disseminate price information nationwide. A 'fair price shop' programme was launched, involving 856 retail outlets committed to offering fair prices.

Buletin Pengguna (Consumer's Bulletin) is a monthly publication by FOMCA and the Domestic Trade and Consumer Affairs Ministry.

The Consumer Protection Act was enacted in 1999 to provide victims of unfair dealings an efficient mechanism to seek redress. The Act also established a Consumer Claims Tribunal. Before this, disputes between a consumer and a supplier or manufacturer were heard in civil courts. This often involved protracted trials and high legal cost. The Tribunal now allows consumers to seek redress in an easy, inexpensive and speedy manner.

In 2002, the National Consumer Policy and the Housing Tribunal were established and in 2003, a National Consumer Master Plan was introduced. A Fair Trade Practices Law will be implemented in stages under the Ninth Malaysia Plan (2006–10).

The various Ministers of Finance since Independence

1. Tun (Col.) Sir Henry Lee Hau Sik (1957–59)
2. Tun Tan Siew Sin (1959–74)
3. Tun Haji Abdul Razak Hussein (1974)
4. Dato' Hussein Onn (1974–76)
5. Tengku Tan Sri Razaleigh Hamzah (1976–84)
6. Tun Daim Zainuddin (1984–91 and 1999–2001)
7. Dato' Seri Anwar bin Ibrahim (1991–98)
8. Dato' Seri Dr Mahathir Mohamad (1998–99 and 2001–03)
9. Dato' Seri Abdullah Ahmad Badawi (2003–present)

Foreign reserves of Bank Negara Malaysia

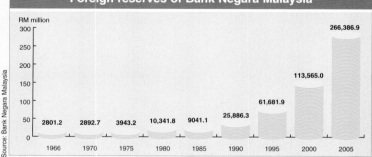

RM million

Source: Bank Negara Malaysia

Year	RM million
1966	2801.2
1970	2892.7
1975	3943.2
1980	10,341.8
1985	9041.1
1990	25,886.3
1995	61,681.9
2000	113,565.0
2005	266,386.9

1. The Ministry of Finance Incorporated building in Putrajaya. The Ministry ensures that financial and budgetary efforts help achieve steady economic growth in line with national development policies.

2. Inland Revenue Department officers sorting through income tax forms in 2005. Income tax revenue totalled RM50,789 million in 2005, accounting for 47.8 per cent of the total Federal Government revenue.

3. Freshly minted coins dropping out of a minting machine at the Royal Mint of Malaysia in 1995.

4. The first Board of Directors of Bank Negara Tanah Melayu (now Bank Negara Malaysia) in 1959: (from left) Lim Huck Aik, Dato' Dr Mohd Said, Dr Chua Sin Kah, Tan Sri W.H. Wilcock, Choi Siew Hong, Dato' A.H.P. Humphrey and R. Govindasamy.

MACROECONOMIC POLICY

Malaysia is an open economy that is strongly dependent on trade and therefore heavily influenced by global economic forces in its performance. To manage the economy, the government uses macroeconomic policy to ensure high employment, low inflation, sustainable economic growth rates and a healthy balance of payments. The key tools used to achieve these goals are fiscal policy and monetary policy.

Bank Negara Malaysia Governor Tan Sri Dr Zeti Akhtar Aziz holding a copy of the Bank's 2005 Annual Report.

Since the 1970s, policy thrusts have emphasized improvement of economic resilience, enhancement of competitiveness and the promotion of foreign private investment while keeping in mind the attainment of socioeconomic distributional objectives. New sources of growth such as high value-added and knowledge-based manufacturing and services have been developed since the 1990s.

Fiscal prudence and responsibility are the cornerstone of the nation's fiscal policy. This strong fiscal discipline has ensured that the fiscal deficit and debt levels remain sustainable and easily financed. With the Privatization Policy of 1983, the relative size of the public sector shrank. Nevertheless, fiscal deficits were common, mainly due to the government's commitments toward development and measures to counter economic slowdowns.

Government expenditure is primarily financed through taxation and borrowing. Direct—as opposed to indirect—taxation has traditionally been the major source. Revenue from import and export duties continues to decline in line with trade liberalization. Monetary policy complements fiscal policy in maintaining stable prices, stable exchange rates and a healthy balance of payments position. The trend towards domestic, as opposed to foreign, borrowing in the form of government bonds and private debt securities grew as a result of post-liberalization policies such as the centralizing of the regulation of financial markets in 1999.

Overall, Malaysia's exchange rate has been largely determined by market forces, till the Asian financial crisis of 1997–98 when a fixed exchange rate regime with selective capital controls was adopted, and the Ringgit was de-internationalized. However, in July 2005, the Ringgit was de-pegged from the US dollar and now trades within a managed float system.

Malaysia's government has also been actively using investment incentives to draw foreign direct investment as the economy industrializes. These have ranged from the introduction of Pioneer Status in the 1950s, when the focus was on promoting new industries and industrialization, to the incentives under the Multimedia Super Corridor in the 1990s which were used to draw more high-technology investments. At the same time, domestic investments have begun to grow and the role of the private sector as a source of domestic investment is expanding. The widening of the range of capital market assets available will also draw more savings from the private sector.

Monetary policy and Bank Negara Malaysia

The object of monetary policy is to influence the performance of the economy as reflected in factors such as inflation, economic output and employment. The central bank, Bank Negara Malaysia, is entrusted with maintaining the country's monetary and financial stability.

Bank Negara Malaysia's annual reports review the country's economy from the central bank's perspective.

An electronic display board showing the exchange rates outside of RHB Bank in Kuala Lumpur. Bank Negara Malaysia controls foreign exchange rates to safeguard monetary stability.

Managing the economy

In attempting to control economic variables such as growth and inflation, the government adopts two approaches: fiscal and monetary policy. While fiscal policy is concerned with taxes and public expenditure as tools to influence the economy (see 'Federal Government revenue and expenditure'), monetary policy serves a similar purpose by determining the quantity of money available in the financial system and controlling the interest rates.

Bank Negara Malaysia (BNM) is entrusted with the conduct of the country's monetary policy through the use of monetary operations and other instruments, including raising or lowering the statutory reserve ratio and administrative measures such as requesting banks to curb their lending to consumers.

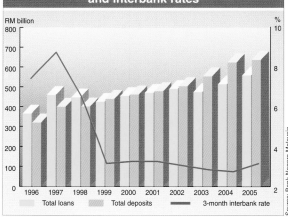

Banking system: loans, deposits and interbank rates

Source: Bank Negara Malaysia

Monetary policy objectives

The primary objective of monetary policy is to maintain price stability by ensuring low rates of inflation in order to create a conducive environment that allows the economy to expand in a sustainable manner.

BNM conducts its monetary policy by influencing interest rates that borrowers pay on their loans and depositors earn on their deposits. It has a number of monetary instruments at its disposal to inject and withdraw funds to influence interest rates in the financial system (see 'The financial sector'). Examples of these instruments include the purchase and sale of securities of BNM and the Federal Government, changes in the statutory reserve requirements and direct lending and borrowing in

Bank Negara Malaysia

The Central Bank of Malaya was established in 1959 under the Central Bank of Malaya Ordinance 1958, and was subsequently renamed Bank Negara Malaysia (BNM) in 1963. It is a statutory body wholly owned by the Federal Government. In 1959, it started with a paid-up capital of RM20 million. This was increased to RM100 million in 1977.

BNM functions on the principle that it acts only in the economic interest of the nation without regard to profit. It focuses on the three pillars of central banking: monetary stability, financial stability and the payments system (the method of transfer of funds for commercial transactions). In addition, BNM has a developmental role with respect to economic management, institutional building and the development of the financial system.

Besides its regulatory and supervisory role in the banking industry (including Islamic banking), BNM also oversees the insurance industry, money changers and development finance institutions. BNM is also the 'lender of last resort' for financial institutions in need of funds to resolve short-term liquidity problems. The bank has also been appointed as the 'Competent Authority' under the Anti-Money Laundering Act 2001. In addition, the Governor of BNM is the Controller of Foreign Exchange.

BNM's premises in Kuala Lumpur from 1959–71.

Objectives and functions

1. To issue currency and keep reserves, safeguarding the value of currency.

2. To act as banker and financial adviser to the government.

3. To promote monetary stability and a sound financial structure.

4. To influence the credit situation to the advantage of the country.

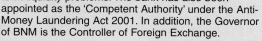

Governors

Tan Sri W.H. Wilcock (1959–62)

Tun Ismail Mohamed Ali (1962–80)

Tan Sri Abdul Aziz bin Taha (1980–85)

Tan Sri Dato' Jaffar bin Hussein (1985–94)

Tan Sri Dato' Ahmad bin Mohd Don (1994–98)

Tan Sri Dato' Seri Ali Abul Hassan bin Sulaiman (1998–2000)

Tan Sri Dato' Sri Dr Zeti Akhtar Aziz (2000–present)

Section 9(1) of the Central Bank of Malaysia Act 1958 provides that the Governor shall be appointed by the Yang di-Pertuan Agong on the advice of the Prime Minister, while the Deputy Governor is appointed by the Minister of Finance. As of 2006, there have been seven Governors of BNM.

BNM headquarters in Kuala Lumpur.

Minting money

In Malaysia, coins have been minted domestically since 1971, initially by the Mint Department of Bank Negara Malaysia (BNM). Before that, the monopoly of issuing money was given to the Board of Commissioners of Currency, established in 1897. Following the reorganization and restructuring of BNM's operations, it was decided that the minting operations of the bank be privatized.

In 2000, the Royal Mint of Malaysia was established and it now mints all coins. In March 2005, it started producing its own blanks which were previously imported from South Korea and

Europe. As of 2006, currency notes are still being printed abroad in the UK, Germany and France for security reasons.

When financial institutions do not have enough money of certain denominations, such as RM10 or RM50 notes, they will order the notes from BNM and charge it to their clearing account. When the financial institutions have more currency than is needed or safe to hold, they send it back to BNM. Torn and worn notes are removed from circulation and destroyed. Usable notes are kept in a vault until they are needed again.

1. The Royal Mint of Malaysia in Shah Alam.
2. The five denominations of Malaysian coins.
3. Blanks are subsequently turned into coins.
4. Coining dies are used to mint blanks with the appropriate designs. Each blank is minted with 100 to 150 tonnes of pressure.

the interbank market. The performance of the economy is also influenced by developments beyond its borders. To this end, BNM manages the foreign exchange reserves to ensure that Malaysia is able to meet its international obligations. Exchange control policies ensure the stability of the Ringgit and encourage the use of the country's financial resources for productive and non-speculative purposes (see 'Malaysia's innovative response to the financial crisis').

In the first decades following Independence, the aim of monetary policy was to set up sound financial infrastructure and control inflationary pressure. Then, as is the case now, monetary policy complemented fiscal policy. After financial liberalization in 1978, monetary policy reforms were implemented and the role of monetary policy was extended to promoting the highest sustainable rate of output growth, consistent with domestic price and exchange rate stability.

These objectives remained in place throughout the 1980s and 1990s, even as the Asian financial crisis prompted the pegging of the Ringgit and sharp cuts in key interest rates.

In April 2004, BNM introduced a new interest rate framework, making the Overnight Policy Rate (OPR) the new indicator of the country's monetary policy stance. With this new framework, the ceilings on base lending rates and prescribed lending spreads were removed. The new framework was aimed at making monetary policy more effective so that changes in the policy rate would be reflected in other market rates and ultimately, support key macroeconomic objectives.

In April 2005, further relaxations of the foreign exchange administration rules were made and in July 2005, the exchange rate of the Ringgit was allowed to operate within a managed float.

How Bank Negara Malaysia's monetary policy affects the economy

When monetary instability occurs, prices either rise (inflation) or fall (deflation) and this can lead to distortions which undermine long-term economic prospects.

If inflation is too high, the purchasing power of money falls. This results in demand for inflation-proof assets like property. There is less interest in investment and savings. Fixed income earners are able to buy fewer goods and services and their standard of living falls. Exports are more expensive, making them less competitive. Persistent inflation reduces the growth potential of the economy.

When deflation occurs, prices fall. Businesses find their profits shrinking, and may reduce their costs by laying off workers. Workers, in turn, have less money to spend and reduce spending, leading to a further reduction in demand for goods and services and a contraction of economic activity.

Where there is monetary or price stability, the future value of savings and investment returns is preserved. Increased investment leads to increased economic activity and new job creation, allowing the economy to expand in a sustainable manner.

The relationship between monetary policy and economic growth.

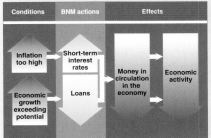
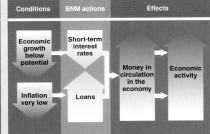

How Bank Negara Malaysia constrains the economy

When the economy is overheating, monetary policy is tightened by the withdrawal of funds from the banking system and raising interest rates. The higher interest rates encourage people to save more and spend less as it is more expensive to borrow money. This causes consumption and investment to slow down and reduces the prospect of high inflation.

How Bank Negara Malaysia stimulates the economy

When economic conditions are weak, funds are injected into the banking system and interest rates are reduced. With lower interest rates, spending and borrowing rise. The resulting increase in consumption and investment stimulates further economic activity, leading to higher income, employment and economic growth. This occurred during the Asian financial crisis.

Federal Government revenue and expenditure

From Independence to the implementation of the privatization policy in 1983, the government played an important role in the economy. The government remains the single largest employer in the country and patterns of government revenue and expenditure reflect the nature and direction of Malaysia's economic policies and development. A deficit budget has typically been implemented in order to progress Malaysia to developed nation status by the year 2020.

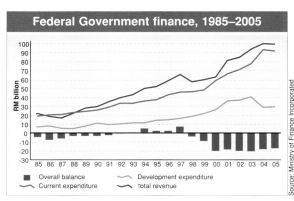

Federal Government finance, 1985–2005

Overall balance
Current expenditure
Development expenditure
Total revenue

Source: Ministry of Finance Incorporated

The main boulevard of Putrajaya, the administrative capital of Malaysia.

The public sector

The public sector in Malaysia has been an important provider of services and income, producer of goods, investor of capital, and manager of the economy. In order to finance these various activities, the revenue and expenditure of the public sector have increased. At the end of 2005, revenue totalled RM106 billion (40 per cent of GDP) while expenditure was RM125 billion (48 per cent of GDP). Malaysia has in most years experienced deficit budgets and efforts have constantly been made to manage the deficit. In the period 2001 to 2004, for example, the deficit was about five per cent of GDP.

The government budget

Both Federal and state governments have annual budgets, but the power to tax, spend, borrow and lend lies primarily with the Federal Government. State revenues are significantly smaller; in fact, the states are largely dependent on grants from the Federal Government (see 'The Federal, state and local governments in the economy'), in particular, the Ministry of Finance. States' sources of revenue (excluding Federal Government grants) and expenditure account for about a tenth or less of the Federal Government revenue and expenditure, while local governments' revenues and expenditure are about a quarter to a third of that of the state governments.

The annual budget provides a description of the Federal Government's sources of revenue and its expenditure on the provision of goods and services to the public.

Revenue

The major sources of revenue are direct taxes (such as income taxes on companies and individuals, including petroleum tax), indirect taxes (such as export duties, import duties, sales and service tax) and non-tax revenues (such as government commercial undertakings, interest and returns on investment, licences and royalties). Between 2001 and 2005, direct taxes accounted for about 45 per cent of total revenue, indirect taxes accounted for 25 per cent and non-tax revenue accounted for the remaining 30 per cent.

Expenditure

Government expenditure consists of operating expenditure (such as emoluments, debt service charges, grants to state governments and statutory bodies, subsidies and supplies) and development

The budgetary process

Prime Minister and Minister of Finance Dato' Seri Abdullah Ahmad Badawi presenting the 2005 Budget.

The budget is the government's official statement outlining its proposed expenditure and revenue for the upcoming year. Until 1968, the government employed the Line-Item Budget or Standard Object Budget system. In that year, the Programme and Performance Budgeting System (PPBS) was introduced. Under the PPBS, each programme had to have a clear objective which justified expenditure. Subsequent performance was measured and evaluated. The PPBS resulted in improvements in the organizational structure of the government machinery, but also led to instances where agencies inflated fund applications in anticipation of cuts by the Ministry of Finance Incorporated (also known as the Treasury). To overcome the weaknesses in the PPBS, the Modified Budgeting System (MBS) was introduced in 1990.

Under the MBS, several changes were made to the process by which agencies submit their expenditure proposals to the Treasury. Expenditure targets are set, and 'programme agreements', outlining the objectives, resources required, programme outputs and impact indicators are prepared for each activity of the operating agencies. At the end of the fiscal year (31 December), agencies provide the Treasury with 'exception reports' on areas where actual performance failed to meet the targets agreed upon in the programme agreements. An evaluation of all activities is conducted by agencies every time there is any change in major issues, and at least once every five years. The decision reached at the evaluation becomes the basis of a new expenditure target. Managers are held accountable for the efficiency and effectiveness of the programmes, and not just for compliance with rules and procedures.

Budget formulation process

January
Ministry of Finance issues circular calling for new year estimates

February
Government agencies prepare and submit new year estimates

March
Submissions received and Budget Relations Officers make individual studies

April
Preliminary hearing

May–July
Budget hearing

August–September
Approval of new year estimates by Ministry of Finance and Cabinet

September
Budget document printed and submitted to Parliament

October–December
Parliament debates and approves new year budget

End of December
Minister of Finance issues Warrant for Expenditure

The next fiscal year
Government agencies execute budget

☐ Responsibility of Ministry of Finance Budget Management Division
☐ Involves government agencies
☐ Involves Parliament

Inland Revenue Department officers (left) in Muar, Johor, helping tax-payers fill out their self-assessment forms in 2005.

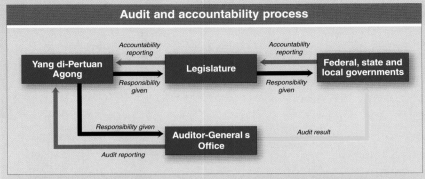

Role of the Auditor-General and National Accounting Committee

The Auditor-General (AG) is appointed by the Yang di-Pertuan Agong on the advice of the Prime Minister after consultation with the Conference of Rulers. The AG, through the Legislature, is given wide-ranging powers to audit and report on the accounts of the Federation, states, local governments and public bodies.

The National Accounting Committee (or Public Accounts Committee) is elected at the beginnning of each Parliament sitting to check that the government's accounting and fund allocation as approved by the Parliament meets the state expenditure and any accounting of national administrative bodies and other associations that handle state funds.

expenditure for various sectors (such as security, social services, economic services and general administration).

Other aspects of the budget

The budget also reflects fiscal policy, with which the government attempts to control economic variables such as growth. Decisions to lower taxes or increase public expenditure with the intention of stimulating growth are referred to as loosening fiscal policy (see 'Malaysia's innovative response to the financial crisis'). Conversely, the government tightens fiscal policy by increasing taxes or reducing public expenditure, thereby controlling aggregate demand.

The government practises deficit budget financing (expenditure exceeding revenue, mainly through borrowings) in order to stimulate aggregate demand and promote growth. Most Malaysian government borrowing is from domestic sources, through the issue of Malaysian Government Securities and the *syariah*-compliant Government Investment Issue. A surplus budget policy (revenue exceeding expenditure, thus mobilizing savings) is practised when the economy is at risk of over-heating, such as from 1994 to 1997, when Malaysia experienced full employment.

Trends in Federal Government finance

The importance of the public sector structure is manifest in the ratios of Federal Government expenditures and revenues to GDP. As a percentage of GDP, Federal Government expenditure accounted for an increasing share of total output from less than 25 per cent in the 1960s to a high of about 45 per cent in early 1980s. After that, it declined to below 30 per cent for most of the period after 1982. This decline occurred during the implementation of the privatization policy (see 'Public sector, private sector').

Still, the actual amount the government spent on both development and operating expenditure has generally been increasing. Although the government's expenditure on development continues to increase, the expenditure on each sector has changed. On average, development expenditure for economic services (agriculture, industry, public utilities, transport and communications) declined from 65 per cent in 1975 to 40 per cent in 2006, as a result of privatization, while allocation for social services (housing, health and education) increased from 15 per cent to 28 per cent during the same period. As a matter of policy, Federal Government operating

expenditure has always been financed from current revenue, so that account has almost always been in surplus.

The expansion of development expenditure has often caused the overall balance to be in deficit, but the government normally finances its overall deficits from non-inflationary sources such as domestic bonds and loans. In general, the public sector has relied mainly on its own savings and the long-term savings of the private sector, mobilized through the financial system (see 'Capital resources'). The government has also resorted to foreign borrowings as residual financing of which a significant portion is tied to project loans. In 2005, foreign borrowings made up 13 per cent of the Federal Government debt of RM228.7 billion.

Direct taxes have become more important than indirect taxes as a contributor to total revenue as individual and corporate incomes have increased. Between 2000 and 2004, direct tax revenue grew rapidly at an average rate of 16.8 per cent per annum and accounted for more than half of total revenue and two-thirds of tax revenue. The increase in collection was attributed to the increase in the number of tax payers captured by the tax system and increased compliance following the introduction of the self-assessment system for the corporate sector in 2001. Self-assessment for individuals was introduced in 2005.

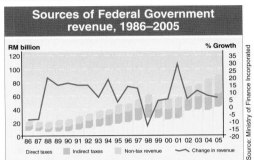

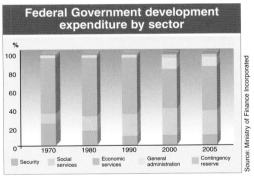

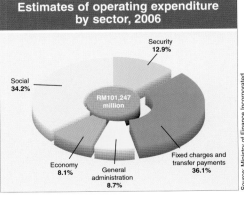

Investment incentives and foreign direct investment

The government, through its various agencies, offers a wide variety of financial and other incentives intended to encourage investors to establish businesses in Malaysia. Unlike portfolio investment, foreign direct investment involves long-term investment into plants and machinery.

Prime Minister Tun Abdul Razak at the opening of the Matsushita factory in Petaling Jaya, Selangor in 1973.

Prime Minister Dato' Seri Abdullah Ahmad Badawi (centre) in the United States with Dell executives in 2006. Dell plans to establish a technology and development centre in Cyberjaya.

Investment incentives

The government has three main forms of incentives to draw domestic and foreign investment. Tax incentives grant partial or total relief from the payment of tax for a stipulated period. Non-tax incentives provide financial support facilities such as export credit refinancing and funds for technical assistance for small and medium enterprises (SMEs) (see 'Small and medium enterprises'). The government also has non-financial incentives such as providing infrastructure, setting up free trade zones and allowing the employment of foreign knowledge workers in the Multimedia Super Corridor (MSC) (see 'The Multimedia Super Corridor').

The Pioneer Industries Ordinance of 1958 was the first tax incentive offered to encourage the growth of the electronics and electrical products industry by creating employment opportunities. Many other incentives were subsequently introduced such as those for MSC-status companies. Incentives are revised periodically, with designated 'promoted' activities, products and regional areas changing depending on policy objectives and developmental needs. Industries which have been promoted include manufacturing, agriculture, tourism, integrated logistics and IT-related industries, and activities of national strategic importance. Incentives have been used to meet broader economic objectives such as promoting export-oriented activities, SME development, research and development, high technology, and technical or vocational training.

While incentives have been used liberally to promote development in Malaysia, agreements under the World Trade Organization and the increasing call for a multilateral or regional framework may restrict the use of these measures in the future.

Foreign direct investment (FDI)

When savings in a country are insufficient to satisfy the demand for investment, FDI is a potential source of financing that can support the country's industrial growth.

Prior to Independence, foreign investment was concentrated mostly in mining, plantations, external trade and financial services. After Independence, however, the Investment Incentives Act 1968 diverted FDI to the manufacturing sector.

Investments by approved projects, 2005

Total: RM31.1 billion

Foreign direct investment 57.6%

Domestic investment 42.4%

Chemicals and chemical products 6.5%

Electronics and electrical products 63.3%

Others 39.7%

17.6% Others

18.8% Electronics and electrical products

Basic metal products 21.1%

Plastic products 3.3%

Non-metallic mineral products 3.3%

Food manufacturing 7.0%

Transport equipment 6.9%

Chemicals and chemical products 4.9%

Scientific and measuring equipment 7.6%

Investment objectives and incentives

In addition to promoting specific industries and activities such as manufacturing, agriculture and tourism, incentives have been used to address many economic issues.

The 1950s
Objective: To promote new industries and industrialization
Incentives: The Pioneer Industries Ordinance 1958 introduced the Pioneer Status and Investment Tax Allowance. With Pioneer Status, companies enjoyed varying degrees of tax exemption, while the Investment Tax Allowance, an alternative to Pioneer Status, was for projects with large capital investment and long gestation periods.

Yang di-Pertuan Agong Tuanku Syed Putra Al-Haj Ibni Syed Hassan Jamalullail (second from left) being shown a cigarette packing machine at a Rothmans of Pall Mall factory in Petaling Jaya, 1963.

The 1960s
Objective: To promote import-substituting industries.
Incentive: Tariffs on imports created an environment for local infant industries to develop and produce goods to replace imports.

Objective: To counterbalance inherent bias of existing incentives towards capital-intensive activities.
Incentive: The Labour Utilisation Relief scheme provided incentives for expansion of labour-intensive industries.

The 1970s
Objective: To promote export-oriented industries.
Incentive: The Free Trade Zone Act 1971 led to the creation of zones which were deemed to be outside Malaysia, and received special incentives.

Minister of Trade and Industry Tan Sri Dato' Khir Johari (right) presenting Pioneer Status certification to the Managing Director of National Semiconductor Electronics, 1972.

The former Free Trade Zone Act 1971 prompted many multinational corporations (MNCs) to set up manufacturing plants in the country and relocate to Malaysia, particularly in the electronics and textile industries. At that time, the country offered a large pool of low-cost, educated labour.

However, the New Economic Policy, with the objective of growth with equity, restricted foreign equity ownership to 30 per cent. Consequently, although foreign investment increased throughout the 1970s and early 1980s, the relative share of foreign capital in the total private sector fell noticeably, from 63 per cent in 1970 to 29 per cent in 2002.

The recession of the mid-1980s, accompanied by the twin problems of fiscal and external deficits, prompted the government to encourage private sector-led economic growth. The Promotion of Investments Act 1986 saw a liberalization of policies regarding foreign equity ownership, with 100 per cent foreign equity allowed subject to stipulated export conditions. Full liberalization occured in 2003 with the removal of conditions.

Consequently, FDI inflows rose from RM959 million in 1985 to RM17.9 billion in 2005.

In 2005, a World Bank report ranked Malaysia 21st out of 155 countries in terms of ease of doing business. A survey by AT Kearney in 2005 of the Asia–Pacific region rated Malaysia the third most attractive offshore location behind India and China in terms of growth potential and investment for foreign companies over the next five years.

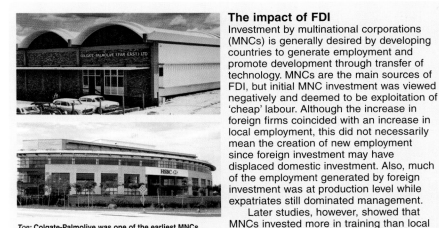

Top: Colgate-Palmolive was one of the earliest MNCs enticed by investment incentives of the 1960s. FDI at the time was focused on manufacturing.

Above: HSBC has taken up incentives to open a branch in Cyberjaya. FDI in the 2000s is primarily in services.

Promotional material produced by the Malaysian Industrial Development Authority (MIDA), the government's principal agency for the promotion and coordination of industrial development.

The impact of FDI

Investment by multinational corporations (MNCs) is generally desired by developing countries to generate employment and promote development through transfer of technology. MNCs are the main sources of FDI, but initial MNC investment was viewed negatively and deemed to be exploitation of 'cheap' labour. Although the increase in foreign firms coincided with an increase in local employment, this did not necessarily mean the creation of new employment since foreign investment may have displaced domestic investment. Also, much of the employment generated by foreign investment was at production level while expatriates still dominated management.

Later studies, however, showed that MNCs invested more in training than local employers, an important component of technology transfer, particularly when MNC employees leave to work for local firms or establish their own businesses. Another potential area for technology transfer is the procurement by MNCs of local intermediate products and components; although in the 1980s there was a high level of imported content in MNC production, local procurement has since risen, and training intensified.

High import content and the repatriation of profits have a negative impact on the Balance of Payments (BOP), as does the possibility of transfer pricing, which is a method of pricing between different companies in a group so as to maximize profits. It has been suggested that FDI may be a zero-sum game with outflow matching, or even exceeding, inflow of foreign capital. However, there is generally an 'export lag': capital and intermediate goods have to be imported before exports can be made. Furthermore, an evaluation based on the BOP alone does not take into account the non-pecuniary impact of FDI.

Top 10 FDI sources for government approved projects, 2005	
Country	**FDI (RM million)**
United States	5155.0
Japan	3671.7
Singapore	2920.0
Netherlands	1674.0
South Korea	673.6
Switzerland	563.2
India	558.9
Taiwan	430.7
Germany	387.7
Norway	303.2

American MNC Agilent Technologies Inc's chairman briefing the Penang Chief Minister Tan Sri Dr Koh Tsu Koon (second from left) on plans for the company's extension there in 2003.

The 1980s

Objective: To promote export-oriented industries.
Incentives:
- Double deductions for export credit insurance premiums and export promotion expenses.
- Export allowance, where tax was deducted based on the value of export sales.
- Abatement of adjusted income for export sales in relation to total sales.
- Export credit refinancing facilities to provide short-term credit to exporters.
- Export credit insurance and guarantee schemes to protect exporters against losses due to commercial risks such as buyer's insolvency, and political risks such as war.

Minister of Public Enterprises Dato' Seri Rafidah Aziz on the cover of Malaysian Business magazine, 1981.

The 1990s

Objective: To address issue of weak linkages between MNCs and local enterprises.
Incentive: Policy to promote local sourcing of raw and intermediate goods implemented. Electronics producers granted tax incentives had to use a minimum of 50 per cent local content by the third year of operations, with 'local content' meaning aggregate of local materials, components, or value added.

Objective: To promote small and medium enterprises.
Incentive: Industrial Technical Assistance Fund (ITAF) created.

Objective: To promote the Multimedia Super Corridor (MSC).
Incentives: Financial incentives such as tax exemption and duty-free importation of multimedia equipment, with R&D grants for SMEs. Non-financial incentives targeted skill-intensive needs of the MSC by allowing unrestricted employment of foreign knowledge workers.

The 2000s

Objective: To adapt to tight labour conditions of the late 1980s and 1990s.
Incentive: Non-labour-intensive and high-technology enterprises were encouraged and supported.

Objective: To transform the nation from a production-based economy to a knowledge-based one.
Incentive: Strategic Knowledge-based Status granted to companies that invest in knowledge-intensive activities, making them eligible for Pioneer Status and Investment Tax Allowance.

Objective: To help Malaysian brands improve competitiveness.
Incentive: Exemptions on import duty and sales tax for raw materials and semi-finished goods granted.

Objective: To promote development in specific regions.
Incentive: The Infrastructure Allowance in less developed states.

Capital resources

In formulating fiscal and monetary policies, the Federal Government promotes public and private savings so that a larger portion of national capital resources can be channelled into productive investments. This is important as Malaysia is dependent on foreign money to finance the high level of capital needed for economic growth.

Employees Provident Fund

Shoppers making enquiries at an EPF booth in a shopping mall.

The Employees Provident Fund (EPF) manages Malaysia's biggest pool of private savings, with almost five million members and assets totaling RM260 billion at the end of 2005.

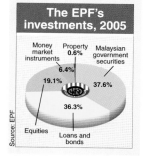

The EPF's investments, 2005

Money market instruments
Property 0.6%
Malaysian government securities
6.4%
19.1%
37.6%
36.3%
Equities
Loans and bonds

Source: EPF

Capital formation

Savings is income not spent on consumption. It is thus a source of capital funds that can be used to finance investment (i.e. capital formation), which is in turn an important factor in economic growth. In the Malaysian context there are three major sources of capital funds: public savings, private savings and foreign financing. Malaysia has a relatively high rate of savings as a result of mandatory contributions, with an average rate of 29 per cent of Gross National Product (GNP) between 1961 and 2004. In 2005, Gross National Savings (GNS) was 34.7 per cent of GNP.

The difference between savings and investment is termed the resource gap. The resource gap for the economy, also known as the overall savings-investment gap, can be a surplus when GNS exceeds Gross National Investment (GNI), or a deficit if GNI exceeds GNS. Malaysia has had a surplus resource gap, except during the 1990s when a deficit resulted in a high dependence on foreign monies.

Commodities, public sector expenditure and demographic patterns are important factors which have determined the savings pattern. The mandatory contribution by half of the labour force to the Employees Provident Fund (EPF) also explains the savings behaviour (see 'Protection under the law').

A substantial part of the capital required for development is foreign. As a result, the flow of net foreign payments have always been significant. Malaysia's GNS has consistently remained lower than its Gross Domestic Savings (GDS) by roughly five to six per cent of GNP. The gap between GNS and GDS is expected to remain for some time in the future as a result of the large number of foreign workers in the country.

Public savings

Public savings are the current surplus of revenue over expenditure (see 'Federal Government revenue and expenditure') of the consolidated public sector. The consolidated public sector encompasses the Federal, state and local governments, statutory bodies and non-financial public enterprises (NFPEs), which are autonomous or semi-autonomous entities owned or controlled by the government.

Public savings grew substantially after 1980 as a result of the large operating surplus of the NFPEs, with the main contributor being the national petroleum company PETRONAS. Other factors which resulted in improved public savings were the

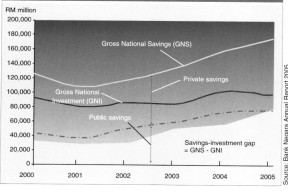

Gross National Savings and the savings-investment (resource) gap

RM million
200,000
180,000
160,000
140,000
120,000
100,000
80,000
60,000
40,000
20,000
0

Gross National Savings (GNS)
Private savings
Gross National Investment (GNI)
Public savings
Savings-investment gap = GNS - GNI

2000   2001   2002   2003   2004   2005

Source: Bank Negara Annual Report 2005

growth of the economy after the recession of 1985–86, leading to an increase in tax revenue; government downsizing and the rationalization of the NFPEs, aimed at reducing the fiscal and external deficits (or 'twin deficits'); and a shift towards private investment as the engine of economic growth.

Despite the increase in public savings, however, the negative resource gap for the public sector persisted throughout the 1980s, and peaked during the Fourth Malaysia Plan (1981–85). This was caused by the government's counter-cyclical policies and its involvement in the development of heavy industries, which led to a substantial increase in public gross domestic capital formation. It was only after 1992 that a surplus emerged. In the Sixth (1991–95) and Seventh (1996–2000) Malaysia Plan periods, the public sector resource balance recorded surpluses of 0.8 and 4.5 per cent of GNP respectively. From 2001 to 2005, the average annual resource balance decreased again to around two per cent of GNP.

Private savings

In the case of private savings, both statutory and voluntary savings play important roles in providing capital resources for the economy. Statutory savings primarily consist of contributions made to the EPF.

Where voluntary savings are concerned, a significant portion is in the form of deposits at banks and finance companies.

Beginning in the late 1970s, the capital market began to play a more important role in harnessing

Customers at the ATMs in front of Maybank headquarters in Kuala Lumpur. The household savings component (bank deposits, provident and insurance funds, and equities) of private savings has been at least twice as large as that of the business sector.

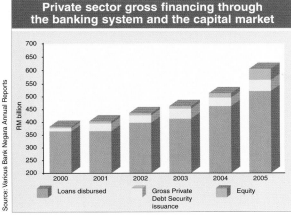

Private sector gross financing through the banking system and the capital market

RM billion

Legend: Loans disbursed | Gross Private Debt Security issuance | Equity

Source: Various Bank Negara Annual Reports

private, particularly corporate, savings (see 'Financial markets'). With the establishment of Cagamas Berhad in 1986, private debt securities or bonds became significant investment instruments for private savings. However, not all funds raised in the capital market were used to finance capital formation. In fact, many firms used the capital market to manage their liabilities more effectively and to raise working capital.

By 1980, the banking system mobilized close to half of private savings, and this proportion continued to increase. With the launch of the Financial Sector Master Plan in 2001, both the banking system and the capital market became major sources of financing for the private sector.

As with public savings, trends in private savings mirrored changes in the country's economy. Overall, the private resource gap has been positive except for the first half of the 1980s and the 1990s, which were periods of high growth in private capital formation.

Foreign financing

There are two types of foreign or external capital inflows, namely long-term capital and short-term or portfolio capital.

Long-term capital, comprising foreign borrowings and foreign direct investment (FDI) (see 'Investment incentives and foreign direct investment'), has played an important role in financing the nation's development. Inflows in the 1970s were relatively small since capital formation

was financed mainly from domestic savings, but this pattern changed in the 1980s when the government increased its foreign borrowings to finance its counter-cyclical fiscal policies of 1981 to 1982 as well as its venture into heavy industries. The subsequent escalation in the debt-service ratio then compelled the government to seek alternative ways of financing the country's development, in particular non-debt financing through FDI. As a result, foreign equity ownership regulations were relaxed. This change in policy created a significant increase in corporate net inflows after 1986. For most of the 1990s and the first half of the 2000s, net inflow of long-term capital continued to remain strong. Gross FDI in 2005 was RM25 billion or 5.3 per cent of GNP, with flows to major sectors including services, manufacturing and oil and gas.

Short-term capital consists mainly of foreign assets of banking institutions and large corporations, portfolio investments and other forms of capital reflected in the 'errors and omissions' component of the balance of payments. Before 1985, short-term flows were relatively unimportant. Since then, due to the liberal exchange policy that existed until the Asian financial crisis, Malaysia has seen bouts of large fund outflows or inflows based on expectations of gains from exchange rate and interest rate differentials. These short-term flows can be volatile, and can destabilize the economy. As such, the government has emphasized its preference for long-term flows that are sustainable and that can contribute positively to economic development.

In 2005, portfolio investments recorded a net outflow of RM11.9 billion mostly from the debt market, and to a lesser extent, the equity market.

PNB Chairman Tan Sri Dato' Seri Ahmad Sarji Abdul Hamid (left) and CEO Tan Sri Dato' Hamad Kama Piah Che Othman announcing the income distribution for Amanah Saham Bumiputera in 2004.

Permodalan Nasional Berhad
Commonly known by the abbreviation PNB, this wholly-owned subsidiary of Yayasan Pelaburan Bumiputra (YPB) (see 'New Economic Policy: 1971–1990), is an important investment vehicle.

Through PNB, YPB holds substantial, and even controlling, equity stakes in many major Malaysian corporations. In 2005, PNB held equity stakes in 29 per cent of the companies listed on Bursa Malaysia. These stakes are transferred to a trust fund and sold to individual Bumiputera in the form of smaller units. The total value of funds under the management of PNB in 2005 was RM72 billion.

A PETRONAS offshore oil platform. When it expanded its exports of petroleum products in the early 1980s, PETRONAS caused a significant increase in the current surplus of the public sector.

Outstanding external debt

RM billion

Legend: Federal Government | NEPEs | Debt/GNP ratio | Private sector | Short-term*

Note: * Excludes currency and deposits held by non-residents with resident banking institutions
p Preliminary

Source: Bank Negara Annual Report 2005

Islamic finances
Islamic financial markets in Malaysia were created in the early 1980s with the introduction of Islamic banking and *takaful* (Islamic insurance) and have since expanded rapidly (see 'Islamic financial services').

In the Islamic capital market, as in the conventional capital market, bonds and equities are two asset classes. Islamic equities include *syariah*-approved securities listed on Bursa Malaysia and Islamic unit trust funds. In 2005, *syariah*-approved securities comprised more than 80 per cent of the total securities listed on Bursa Malaysia. From three Islamic unit trust funds in 1993, there are now more than 50, managing nearly 25 per cent of total funds. The Islamic private debt market grew from a 2.4 per cent share of issuance in 1998 to more than 50 per cent in 2002.

Other *syariah*-compliant banking products are currently available, including Islamic savings accounts and term deposits.

Bank Islam advertisement.

Malaysia's contribution to multilateral organizations, 2005

Source: Economic Planning Unit

RM '000

United Nations	13,727.1
United Nations Peacekeeping	6785.6
World Trade Organization	6751.3
Regional Centre of Education in Science and Mathematics	3300.01
ASEAN	2917.6
United Nations Development Programme	2390.0
International Labour Organization	2,288.4
Organization of Islamic Conference	1,927.5
Islamic Education, Scientific and Cultural Organization	1,834.1
Food and Agriculture Organization	1,520.1
Others	22,390.2

1. ASEAN and other East Asian leaders, including Prime Minister Dato' Seri Abdullah Ahmad Badawi (second from right), joining hands after signing the Kuala Lumpur Declaration during the 11th ASEAN Summit in 2005.

2. PROTON cars ready for export at Northport in Port Klang. Malaysia's trade balance in 2005 widened to RM99.8 billion. This was the eighth consecutive year of trade surplus.

3. Dato' Seri Abdullah Ahmad Badawi (second from left), Minister in the Prime Minister's Department, signing an agreement on behalf of Malaysia. The Look East Policy of the early 1980s saw Malaysia signing bilateral agreements with South Korea and Japan.

4. Tin dredge belonging to Malaysian Smelting Corporation Bhd's Indonesian subsidiary PT Koba Tin, the fifth largest tin producing company in 2004.

5. A PETRONAS onshore platform in Pakistan.

6. United Nations Secretary-General Dag Hammarskjold (right) paying a visit to Minister of External Affairs Dr Ismail Dato' Abdul Rahman in 1959.

7. The 12,000-metric tonne Yoho integrated deck used in Sime Darby Berhad's oil and gas project in Nigeria, Africa.

MALAYSIA IN THE GLOBAL ECONOMY

Trade is recognized as an important tool for raising standards of living, ensuring full employment and developing the use of the world's resources. In 2004, Malaysia was the 18th largest trading nation in the world (18th largest exporter and 20th largest importer). In 2005, total exports amounted to RM533.8 billion while total imports were valued at RM434 billion. Manufactured goods comprised 77 per cent of exports, with electrical and electronic products constituting half of this. Similarly, manufactured products, particularly electrical and electronic goods, also formed the bulk of imports.

Malaysia has established trading links with more than 230 countries and economies. Major export markets include the Association of Southeast Asian Nations (ASEAN), USA, Japan, China and the European Union. In 2005, Malaysia's pattern of trade indicated that her trade with Asia was growing at a faster rate than that with North America or the European Union. From 1999 to 2004, total trade with Asia grew at a pace of 11.9 per cent compared with 4.6 per cent for North America, and 4.7 per cent for the 15 original members of the European Union. This pattern of trade can be expected to continue as Malaysia engages in Free Trade Agreements (FTAs) with its trade partners in Asia, both regionally or bilaterally. The first tranche of preferential market access under the ASEAN-China FTA came into effect in 2005. Trade with emerging markets, especially in West Asia, Eastern Europe, India, Russia, Latin America and Africa, continues to expand. Malaysia and the United States have begun to negotiate a FTA that is expected to be completed in 2007.

The 1997–98 financial crisis (see 'Malaysia's innovative response to the financial crisis') underscored the necessity for international and regional cooperation in order to ensure financial stability and enhance economic integration and resilience. Malaysia has therefore continued to participate actively in various regional and international forums, particularly ASEAN, the Asia-Pacific Economic Cooperation (APEC) and the World Trade Organization (WTO). Work towards achieving an ASEAN Community (in terms of security, social and economy) by 2020 is still underway.

Direct investment abroad by Malaysian companies has increased over the years, reflecting expansion strategies that enhance the synergistic capabilities of their core operations locally and access overseas markets. Most of these investments were through acquistions and joint ventures. Investment overseas has mainly been in oil and gas, services, followed by manufacturing, agriculture and construction. In oil and gas, investments in recent years have been concentrated in large undeveloped oil fields in Africa and ASEAN countries.

A promotional brochure from the Malaysia External Trade Development Corporation (MATRADE), the external trade promotion arm of the Ministry of International Trade and Industry which was set up in 1993.

Groupings, trading blocs and organizations

Malaysia's entry into the world economy predates Independence as a result of its commodity export-based orientation. As the economy became more diversified and industrialized, participation in global and regional institutional developments became crucial. Closer links with the global economy have been achieved through multilateral and bilateral measures.

Prime Minister Dato' Seri Abdullah Ahmad Badawi (left) meeting with United States President George W. Bush over bilateral trade issues in 2005.

The Malaysian–United States Trade Investment Framework Agreement (TIFA)

The United States is Malaysia's largest trade partner outside of ASEAN. In 2005, trade with the United States was valued at RM161 billion and accounted for 16.8 per cent of Malaysia's global trade. The United States was also the largest source of foreign direct investment (FDI) with total investment amounting to RM5 billion, representing 29 per cent of total approved FDI in the manufacturing sector.

Signed in 2004, TIFA's objective is to enhance economic relations, especially in trade and investment. Under TIFA, a Joint Council on Trade and Investment was formed, providing a forum for dialogue. TIFA also provides a platform toward the negotiation of a free trade agreement (FTA) with the United States. In 2006, the United States and Malaysia jointly announced the start of talks on an FTA which are expected to be completed by early 2007. The scope of the FTA includes agricultural and other goods, trades in services including financial services, investment, government procurement, intellectual property rights and the environment.

Multilateralism

Multilateralism is associated with reciprocal tariff cuts granted under the 'most-favoured nation' status by members of the World Trade Organization (WTO), formerly the General Agreement on Trade and Tariffs (GATT). Active participation in the WTO is vital to Malaysia, whose major trading partners are Japan, the United States and the European Union. Tariff reduction has become a tool to promote trade since the Uruguay Round of negotiations in 1993.

Overall, Malaysia cut unweighted tariff rates between 1960 and 2000. Malaysia has also reduced protectionist non-tariff barriers such as licensing quotas, health and safety regulations and trade prohibition. In return, Malaysia has gained better market access to other WTO countries. Other parts of the Uruguay Round agreement that Malaysia has committed to include trade-related investment measures that have resulted in the removal of regulations on foreign-produced content, trade-related intellectual property measures have caused copyright laws to be reviewed and enforced, and the General Agreement on Services which led to the liberalization of sectors such as offshore banking, insurance, the charge card business, stock, money and foreign exchange brokerage services, financial leasing, underwriting and asset management.

Bilateralism

Bilateral trade and investment agreements are a major tool for expanding trade. As of 2005, Malaysia had signed 64 bilateral agreements, mostly with developing countries, 61 investment guarantee agreements, 57 bilateral payment arrangements or agreements, and 70 agreements on the avoidance of double taxation.

As of 2005, Malaysia was a beneficiary of the Generalized System of Preferences (GSP) schemes of Australia, Canada, the European Economic Community, New Zealand, Japan and Eastern Europe.

Association of Southeast Asian Nations (ASEAN)

Economic cooperation

ASEAN economic cooperation is crucial to Malaysia's economic development. ASEAN, which began as the three member Association of Southeast Asia in 1961, became the five-member ASEAN in 1967. Further expansion occurred in 1984 (Brunei), 1995 (Vietnam) and 1997 (Laos and Myanmar). Cambodia was admitted in 1999.

To deepen cooperation, the ASEAN Industrial Project scheme, Brand-to-Brand Complementation and the ASEAN Industrial Joint Venture schemes in the private sector were established following the 1976 Bali summit. In 1995, BBC and AIP were replaced by the ASEAN Industrial Cooperation Scheme, under which Malaysia approved 54 applications for projects. ASEAN has also liberalized the services sector.

Intra-ASEAN trade expanded from US$82.4 billion in 1993 to US$221.9 billion in 2004. Intra-ASEAN trade in 1993 accounted for 19 per cent of ASEAN's global trade and increased to 23 per cent in 2004. Malaysia has benefited as an international production base from intra-ASEAN trade. Trade with ASEAN countries accounted for 25 per cent of Malaysia's global trade in 2005.

In October 2003, ASEAN leaders agreed to establish the ASEAN Economic Community by 2020. The ASEAN Economic Community is envisaged as a single market and production base with free flow of goods, services, investment, skilled labour and freer flow of capital.

ASEAN has also forged external links with the European Union, Japan, the United States, and with Australia and New Zealand through the ASEAN Free Trade Area-Closer Economic Relations of Australia and New Zealand.

ASEAN Preferential Trade Arrangements (APTA) and ASEAN Free Trade Area (AFTA)

ASEAN remains one of Malaysia's largest trading partners. High growth in trade has been attributed to reduced tariff rates for eligible ASEAN products under APTA since 1977. Malaysia initially granted APTA to 158 items in 1978; by 1992 this figure had risen to 4809 items.

To further stimulate trade, ASEAN took steps in 1992 to establish the AFTA, a single market with a proposed common internal tariff range of zero to five per cent by 2008. AFTA has integrated the ASEAN economies into a single production base and created a regional market of 500 million people. The first stage saw the implementation of the Common Effective Preferential Tariff (CEPT) scheme, through which tariff and non-tariff barriers were to be gradually liberalized. The CEPT covers all products except unprocessed agriculture products. By 2004, the government had offered 99 per cent of products for tariff concession, out of which 60 per cent could be imported without any import duty. The CEPT rate for Malaysia's products was reduced from 10.8 per cent in 1993 to 1.9 per cent in 2004.

Since 1 January 2005, Malaysia has also transferred completely built-up and knocked-down automotive products into the scheme to comply with its obligations under AFTA. The 11th ASEAN Summit was held in Kuala Lumpur in December 2005 and it saw the formation of the first East Asia Summit as a forum for dialogue.

ASEAN+3

At the ASEAN summit in 1992, the East Asian Economic Caucus (EAEC) was formed, more as a discussion forum than as a fully-fledged bloc. The EAEC involved ASEAN and Northeast Asian countries.

In 1999, ASEAN+3, comprising the members of the EAEC, was formed. In 2002, ASEAN and China agreed to form a free trade area, the world's largest, by 2012. Tariffs on more than 600 products (mainly agricultural items, constituting ten per cent of traded items) are to drop to zero.

The trade volume among ASEAN+3 surged to US$258.2 billion in 2004 from US$206.5 billion in 2003.

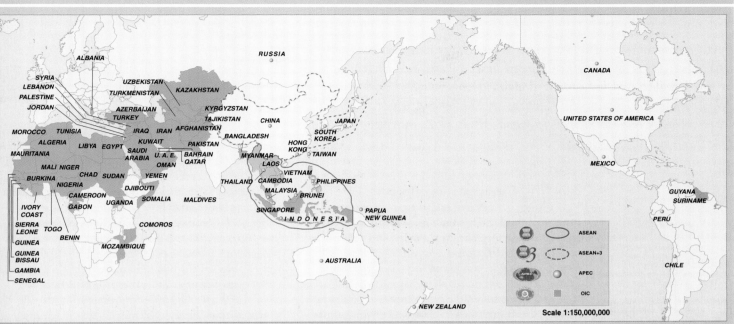

Scale 1:150,000,000

Legend:
- ASEAN
- ASEAN+3
- APEC
- OIC

1. Heads of states and governments from the 57 OIC-member countries during the OIC Summit in Putrajaya, 2003.

2. The Seventh Summit of the Group of 15 (G-15) held at Kuala Lumpur in 1997.

3. The Sixth ASEAN Finance Ministers Meeting in Yangon, Myanmar in 2002.

4. Prime Minister Dato' Seri Dr Mahathir Mohamad (left) speaking at the opening of an ASEAN meeting in Kuala Lumpur, 1997.

5. Deputy Prime Minister Dato' Sri Najib Tun Razak (second from left) launching a Non-Aligned Movement (NAM) conference in Kuala Lumpur, 2005.

6. Delegates of the APEC Summit in Busan, Korea in 2005.

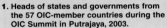

Asia-Pacific Economic Cooperation

Formed in 1989, Asia-Pacific Economic Cooperation (APEC) is the forum for facilitating economic growth, cooperation, trade and investment in the Asia-Pacific region. In 2005, its 21 member economies accounted for 57 per cent of world GDP, 45.8 per cent of world trade volume and over 44.8 per cent of the world's population. APEC generated nearly 70 per cent of global economic growth within its first ten years. Malaysia has participated significantly in trade facilitation initiatives such as customs clearance, business travel documentation, technical standards and e-commerce. Malaysia has also reduced import duties, liberalized equity policies for manufacturing, and increased aggregate foreign shareholding for financial leasing, in addition to participating in APEC Collective Action Plans, human capacity building and the Economic and Technical Cooperation. APEC aims to achieve the goals of free and open trade and investment in the APEC region by 2010 (for industrialized economies) and 2020 (for developing economies) respectively.

Organization of the Islamic Conference

The Organization of the Islamic Conference (OIC) is an inter-governmental organization which was formed in 1969. To a large extent, OIC countries are exporters of commodities such as crude oil, natural gas, petroleum products, leather and hides, and mineral products, and are importers of manufactured products and capital and intermediate goods, including foodstuffs and beverages, machinery and transport equipment, and electrical and electronic products.

Malaysia's trade with the OIC has been growing steadily. Between 1995–2004, Malaysia's trade with the OIC grew an average annual rate of 16.4 per cent, from US$6.3 billion in 1995 to US$16.2 billion in 2004, representing seven per cent of Malaysia's global trade in 2004. As for investment, foreign direct investment (FDI) inflows into the 57 OIC member countries totalled US$24.1 billion in 2004 as compared to US$19.1 billion FDI into the ten-member ASEAN grouping.

Other bodies

Malaysia has actively participated in several other groupings, forums and associations:

- The Commonwealth
- United Nations (UN)
- World Trade Organization (WTO)
- Group of Fifteen (G-15)
- Group of Seventy-Seven (G-77)
- Non-Aligned Movement (NAM)
- International Tin Council (until its collapse in 1985)
- Indian Ocean Rim Association for Regional Cooperation (IOR-ARC)
- Asia-Europe Meeting (ASEM)
- Pacific Economic Cooperation Council (PECC)
- Asian Development Bank (ADB)
- United Nations Industrial Development Organization (UNIDO)
- United Nations Conference on Trade and Development (UNCTAD)
- World Food Organization (WFO)
- Food and Agriculture Organization of the United Nations (FAO)

135

Glossary

A

Authorized capital: The nominal amount of capital that a limited company is permitted to raise.

B

Balance of Payments (BOP): The difference in value between a country's inward and outward payments for goods, services and other transactions.

Bancassurance: The combination of the business of banking and insurance within the same organization.

Base Lending Rate (BLR): A minimum interest rate calculated by financial institutions. The BLR is based on a formula which takes into account the institution's cost of funds as well as other administrative costs.

Biotechnology: Any technological application that utilizes living organisms or biological systems to make or modify products or processes for a particular use.

Bonds: Documents recording loans which specify the dates of maturity and the rates of interest to be paid.

Bumiputera: (literally 'sons of the soil') Ethnic Malays as well as other indigenous ethnic groups accorded special privileges under the Federal Constitution.

C

Capital controls: Restrictions on the movement of assets across international borders. Countries use capital controls to curb volatile inflows and outflows of capital.

Capital goods: Also known as investment goods or fixed human-made means of production. Real products used in the production of other products but which are not incorporated into the new product. They include factories, machinery, tools and buildings.

Clearing account: A temporary account containing amounts to be transferred to other accounts.

Clearing house: A central institution where banks exchange cheques or drafts. Banks maintain an account against which credits or debits are posted.

Commercial bank: A financial institution that offers a broad range of deposit accounts, including cheque, savings and time deposits, and extends loans to individuals and businesses, in contrast to invesment banks.

Consumer Price Index (CPI): A statistical index which measures the average level of prices of a fixed basket of goods and services in an economy relative to a base year.

Consumption goods: Goods that can be immediately consumed.

Corporatization: The process of registering a government entity as a company under the Companies Act 1965. It is then managed and run as a company, but the ownership still remains with the government.

D

Delisting: The exclusion of a company's shares from listing on the stock exchange. This occurs when the company fails to fulfil the exchange's rules or when the company no longer meets the listing requirements or financial specifications.

Demutualization: A conversion in which a mutually owned company becomes a shareholder-owned company, usually done in order to raise additional capital.

Derivatives: Financial instruments such as futures and options which derive their value from under-lying securities including bonds, bills, currencies and equities.

Development Financial Institutions (DFIs): Specifically set up to promote strategic sectors of the economy, they specialize in providing medium to long-term loans, equity capital and guarantees for loans. Besides financial, technical and managerial advice and assistance, they also provide consulting and advisory services in the identification and development of new projects. DFIs complement banking institutions in providing financing to strategic sectors such as agriculture, infrastructure, shipping, manufacturing and export and to SMEs.

Discount houses: Institutions which mobilize deposits from financial institutions and corporations, and specialize in short-term money market operations. They are permitted to invest funds in treasury bills, government securities, bankers' acceptances, negotiable deposit instruments, private debt securities and to accept short-term funds.

E

Economies of scale: Cost advantages associated with large-scale production.

Equity: Ordinary shares of a company.

F

Finance companies: These accept savings and fixed deposits from individuals and businesses and provide hire purchase financing, consumer financing, housing loans, block discounting and leasing transactions.

Fiscal policy: The way in which governments raise money to fund current spending and investment.

Foreign direct investment (FDI): Investment of foreign assets directly into a domestic company's structures, equipment and organizations.

Futures: Contracts to buy or sell specific quantities of a commodity or financial instrument at a specified price with delivery set at a specified time in the future.

G

Generalized System of Preferences (GSP): Preferential treatment by way of reduced or duty-free tariff rates granted by developed countries (preference-giving countries) to developing countries (preference-receiving or beneficiary countries). This preferential treatment is granted without any reciprocal obligation on the part of the developing countries. The aim of the tariff preferences is to provide competitive edge and a better market access to goods from developing countries.

Gini coefficient: The measure of income inequality. A Gini coefficient of zero corresponds to perfect equality where everyone has the same income, while a coefficient of one corresponds to perfect inequality where one person has all the income and everyone else has no income.

Gross Domestic Product (GDP): The measure of the total economic activity occurring in a country in a particular year; it can be measured in three ways: (i) production—measures GDP as the sum of all the value added by all activities which produce goods and services; (ii) income—measures GDP as the total of incomes earned from the production of goods and services; (iii) expenditure—measures GDP as the total of all expenditures made either in consuming finished goods and services or adding to wealth, less the cost of imports.

Gross Domestic Savings (GDS): The total savings by residents in the country (including those owned by foreign citizens or producers).

Gross National Investment (GNI) or Gross Capital Formation: The total capital formation or investment required by the economy.

Gross National Product (GNP): The final value of goods and services produced in an economy in a year, plus income earned by its citizens abroad, minus income earned by foreigners from domestic production.

Gross National Savings (GNS): The total savings by the citizens of a country.

I

Indices: Statistical measures of change in the economy or financial markets. A stock index, for instance, would measure change in selected stock prices.

Inflation: A rate of increase in the general price level of all goods and services and a decline in the market value or purchasing power of money.

Initial Public Offering (IPO): The first offering of shares when a privately owned company goes public.

Interest rate: Cost of borrowing, paid at regular intervals and expressed as a percentage of the total amount of credit.

Intermediate goods: Also known as producer goods. Goods used as inputs in the production of other goods, such as partly finished goods or raw materials. In the production process, intermediate goods either become part of the final product, or are changed beyond recognition.

International reserves: The assets denominated in foreign currency, and gold, held by Bank Negara Malaysia, sometimes for the purpose of intervening in the exchange market to influence or peg the exchange rate.

Internet Service Provider (ISP): A company that provides Internet access.

Investment banks: Also known as merchant banks. These banks serve corporations, and play a role in the short-term money market. Their capital-raising activities including underwriting, loan syndication, corporate finance and management advisory services, arranging the issue and listing of shares, as well as managing investment portfolios.

Investment goods: See 'Capital goods'.

Islamic banking: A system of banking which is consistent with the principles of *syariah* (Islamic law) and guided by Islamic economics.

K

Knowledge-based economy (k-economy): An economy in which knowledge, creativity and innovation are the primary engines of economic growth.

L

Labour force: The total number of people who are actively employed or have the potential to be employed in an economy.

Lending spreads: The difference between interbank lending rates and actual loan rates.

M

Malaysian Exchange of Securities Dealing and Automated Quotation (MESDAQ): Part of Bursa Malaysia, this is a separate market launched in 1997 for the listing of technology companies.

Development: Policies and Reforms, Petaling Jaya: Pelanduk Publications.

Jomo, K. S., G. Felker and R. Rasiah (eds.) (1998), *Industrial Technology Development in Malaysia: Industry and Firm Studies*, London: Routledge.

Junid Saham (1980), *British Industrial Development in Malaysia 1963–1971*, Kuala Lumpur: Oxford University Press.

Lim, David (1973), *Economic Growth and Development in West Malaysia, 1947–1970*, Kuala Lumpur: Oxford University Press.

Lim Chong-Yah (1967), *Economic Development of Modern Malaya*, Kuala Lumpur: Oxford University Press.

Lo Sum Yee (1972), *The Development Performance of West Malaysia, 1955–1967*, Kuala Lumpur: Heinemann.

Mahathir Mohamad (1970), *The Malay Dilemma*, Kuala Lumpur: Federal Publications.

—— (1988), *The Way Forward*, London: Weidenfield & Nicolson.

—— (1999), *A New Deal For Asia*, Subang Jaya: Pelanduk Publications.

Majlis Perundingan Ekonomi Negara (1991), *Dasar Ekonomi untuk Pembangunan Negara (DEPAN)*, Kuala Lumpur: Majlis Perundingan Ekonomi Negara.

Majlis Perundingan Ekonomi Negara Kedua (2000), *Dasar Pembangunan Wawasan 2001–2010*, Kuala Lumpur: Majlis Perundingan Ekonomi Negara Kedua.

Malaysian Palm Oil Promotion Council (1995), *Malaysian Palm Oil: Nature's Gift to Malaysia, Malaysia's Gift to the World*, Kuala Lumpur: Malaysian Palm Oil Promotion Council.

Malaysian Rubber Board (2000), *Milestones in Rubber Research*, Kuala Lumpur: Malaysian Rubber Board.

Malaysian Timber Council (2002), *Green Malaysia*, Kuala Lumpur: Editions Didier Millet.

Meerman, Jacob (1979), *Public Expenditure in Malaysia: Who Benefits and Why*, Oxford: Oxford University Press.

—— (1980), *Malaysia: Growth and Equity in a Multiracial Society*, Baltimore: Johns Hopkins University Press.

Mehmet, Ozay (1988), *Development in Malaysia: Poverty, Wealth and Trusteeship*, Kuala Lumpur: Insan.

Ministry of Finance, *Economic Report* (various years), Kuala Lumpur: Ministry of Finance.

Ministry of International Trade and Industry, *Industrial Masterplan (I–III)*, Kuala Lumpur: Ministry of International Trade and Industry.

Mohd. Yaakub Johari (ed.) (1991), *Urban Poverty in Malaysia*. Kota Kinabalu, Institute for Development Studies and Konrad Adenauer Foundation.

Navaratnam, R. V. (1997), *Managing the Malaysian Economy: Pitfalls, Challenges, Opportunities*, Petaling Jaya: Pelanduk Publications.

—— (2002), *Malaysia's Economic Sustainability: Confronting New Challenges amidst Global Realities*, Kuala Lumpur: Pelanduk Publications.

Okposin, S. B., Abdul Halim Abdul Hamid and Ong Hway Boon (1999), *The Changing Phases of the Malaysian Economy*, Petaling Jaya: Pelanduk Publications.

Ooi, J. B. (1976), *Peninsular Malaysia: Land, People and Economy*, London: Longman.

Osman Rani, H., Toh Kin Woon and Anwar Ali (1986), *Technology and Skills in Malaysia*, Singapore: ISEAS.

Pooi Wai Ching (2004), *The Development of the Malaysian Economy*, Kuala Lumpur: Prentice-Hall.

Puthucheary, James J. (1960), *Ownership and Control in the Malaysian Economy*, Singapore: Eastern Universities Press.

Ranjit Gill (2003), *The Making of Malaysia Inc.*, London: Asean Academic Press.

Rasiah, R. (1995), *Foreign Capital and Industrialisation in Malaysia*, London: Macmillan.

Samuel, B. O., Abdul Halim and Ong H. B. (1999), *The Changing Phases of Malaysian Economy*, Petaling Jaya: Pelanduk Publications.

Saw Swee-Hock and K. Kasavapany (eds.) (2006), *Malaysia: Recent Trends and Challenges*, Singapore: ISEAS.

Sawal, A. H. (1996), *Malaysian Privatisation Experience: Past Successes, Future Challenges and an Update on the Malaysian Privatisation Master Plan*, Kuala Lumpur: Economic Planning Unit, Prime Minister's Department.

Silcock, T. H. and E. K. Fisk (eds.) (1963), *The Political Economy of Independent Malaya*, Canberra: Eastern Universities Press.

Snodgrass, Donald K. (1980), *Inequality and Economic Development in Malaysia*, Kuala Lumpur: Oxford University Press.

Supriya Singh (1984), *Bank Negara Malaysia: The First 25 Years (1959–1984)*, Kuala Lumpur: Bank Negara Malaysia.

Tan Tat Wai (1982), *Income Distribution and Determination in West Malaysia*, Kuala Lumpur: Oxford University Press.

Tate, D. J. M. (1996), *The RGA History of the Plantation Industry in the Malay Peninsula*, Kuala Lumpur: Oxford University Press.

Teh Hoe Yoke and Goh Kim Leng (eds.) (1992), *Malaysia's Economic Vision: Issues and Challenges*, Kuala Lumpur: Pelanduk Publications.

Teh Kok Peng (1977), *Protection, Fiscal Incentives and Industrialization in West Malaysia since 1957*, Kuala Lumpur: FEA, University of Malaya.

Tin Industry (Research and Development) Board (1984), *Tin Mining in Malaysia*, Kuala Lumpur: Tin Industry (Research and Development) Board.

Wheelwright, E. L. (1965), *Industrialization in Malaysia*, Cambridge: Cambridge University Press.

World Bank (1997), *Malaysia: Enterprise Training, Technology, and Productivity*, Washington D.C.: The World Bank, UNDP and Government of Malaysia.

Young, K., W. Bussink and P. Hassan (eds.) (1980), *Malaysia: Growth and Equity in a Multiracial Society*, Baltimore; John Hopkins University Press.

Index

Picture Credits

Agence France-Presse, p.5, construction workers; p. 54, car showroom; p. 55, spare parts; p. 61, technicians at work; p. 78, investors; p. 89, airplanes at KLIA; p. 122, exchange board; p. 135, ASEAN Finance Ministers. Ahmad Sarji, p. 75, P. Ramlee. Alam Flora Sdn Bhd, p. 97, garbage truck. alt.TYPE/REUTERS, p. 100, MSC panel; p. 135, NAM conference, Dr Mahathir at ASEAN; p. 148, oil palm plantation. Arkib Negara, p. 10–11, Tunku in Melaka; p. 12, Abdul Razak, Hussein Onn; p. 18, rubber estate, Klang Gates Dam, Tunku making trunk call; p. 19, Yang di-Pertuan Agong, Abdul Razak, Subang International Airport, Tan Siew Sin, tin mine; p. 21, MARA; p. 39, Yang di-Pertuan Agong visiting refinery; p. 46, rubber factory; p. 51, Abdul Razak at opening; p. 54, first car plant; p. 57, Pekeliling flats; p. 66, Jalan Tuanku Abdul Rahman; p. 75, S.M. Salim; p. 76, printing press, Bernama launch; p. 81, OUB, Bank Bumiputra; p. 83, old stock market; p. 87, NERP cover; p. 90, Jalan Universiti; p. 110, nurse lecturing mothers; p. 114, Petaling Jaya in 1960; p. 116, Abdul Razak; p. 122, old BNM building; p. 126, Rothmans factory, Khir Johari; p. 127, Colgate-Palmolive factory; p. 130, UN Secretary General with Abdul Rahman. Associated Press, p. 1, investors cheering; p. 56, construction workers; p. 106, MSC job exhibition. ASTRO ALL ASIA NETWORKS plc, p.99, broadcast truck. Bank Islam Malaysia Berhad, p. 84, Bank Islam headquarters; p. 129, advertisement; p. 140, ATM. Bank Negara Malaysia, p. 80, clearing house; p. 120, board of directors; p. 122, new BNM building, Bank Negara Governors; p. 123, coins. Bank Perusahaan Kecil & Sederhana Malaysia Berhad, p. 59, SME bank. Bernama, p. 13, Abdullah Badawi with leaders; p.14, Abdullah Badawi at LID; p. 16, SMART

project; p. 17, fogging; p. 61, Dr Mahathir at BioMalaysia; p.62, doctors; p. 77, journalists at work; p. 78, polymer notes; p. 102, workers taking pledge, FELCRA settlers; p. 107, Great Malaysian Job Hunt; p. 110, Serdang Hospital; p. 130, ASEAN leaders; p. 132, ASEAN leaders, Malaysia fair; p. 134, Abdullah Badawi and George Bush; p. 135, OIC leaders, APEC Summit. Bursa Malaysia Berhad, p. 83, Abdullah Badawi at launch. Chai Kah Yune, p.8, stack of money; p. 36, trees; p. 37, piece of timber; p. 91, KTM trains; p. 93, cargo; p. 94, airplanes; p. 95, KLIA; p. 97, sources of power; p. 101, MSC; p. 112–113, Ara Damansara. Chang, Tommy, p. 16, SEDC building. Chang Yan Yi, p. 109, industrial court. Chin, Jackie, p. 104, people of different ages. Celcom Berhad, p. 99, advertisement. Citrin, William, p. 43, eggs; p. 61, science centre; p. 66, Metrojaya; p. 69, 1901 hot dogs. COMMEX Malaysia, p. 82, trading floor. Dell Inc., p. 25, worker. Dewan Bandaraya Kuala Lumpur, p. 17, street cleaning. DRB-HICOM Berhad, p. 52, truck assembly, die-casting; p. 56, railway construction. E. Ravinderen Kandiappan, p. 119, service counter. Editions Didier Millet Archives, p. 27, mixed plantation; p. 32, rubber estate; p. 102, water village; p. 109, CUEPACS publication. Endulgence Sdn Bhd, p. 71, Chinese advertisement. Enfiniti Productions, p. 74, filming a movie scene. Eva binti Mohd Ali, p. 36, forest products. Federal Information Department, p. 10–11, Dr Mahathir and Look East Policy; p. 12, Dr Mahathir in Korea, Dr Mahathir at launch; p. 20, Dr Mahathir and NEP; p. 22, MAPEN meeting; p. 32, rubber sheets; p. 48, soap manufacturing; p. 53, satellite; p. 108, MTUC anniversary; p. 120, Ministers of Finance; Abdullah Badawi signing agreement; p. 135, G-15 Summit.

Federal Information Department, Sabah, p.6, padi workers; p. 19, drying copra; p. 31, copper mine; p. 36, sawmill; p. 98, postmen in Sabah; p. 106, young men queuing. Federal Land Development Authority, p. 35, packaging; p. 117, manufacturing fertilizers. GD Express Sdn Bhd, p. 99, central clearing hub. German–Malaysian Institute, p. 111, engineering students, technicians. Goh, Patrick, p. 120, Ministry of Finance. Golden Hope Plantations Berhad, p. 34, palm oil mill; p. 35, oil palm estate, researcher; p. 40, picking guava; p. 137, oil and fats refineries. Globetronics Technology Berhad, p. 47, sealing lids. Guthrie Berhad, p. 10–11, rubber plantation; p. 61, researcher. Hatim Bahari, p. 7, PETRONAS refinery. Hijas Kasturi Associates Sdn, p. 17, Shah Alam Stadium; p. 78, Menara Maybank; p. 82, Securities Commission; p. 84, Tabung Haji building. HSBC Bank Malaysia Berhad, p. 78, Kuala Lumpur branch. Image Asia, p. 3, television factory. Indah Water Konsortium Sdn Bhd, workers clearing a blockage. Isma Yusoof, p. 74, The Red Kebaya. Ivy Beauty Corporation Sdn Bhd, p. 71, Natifa advertisement. Johor Port Berhad/Luqman Mohd Salleh, p.15, aerial view of port. Kannan Saree Centre Sdn Bhd, p. 71, advertisement. Koh, Deborah, p. 23, Angkasapuri building; p. 41, products; p. 65, engineers; p. 69, Bonia, Royal Selangor; p. 75, album cover; p. 98, directory, teleprinter; p. 112, terraced houses. Kuala Lumpur General Hospital, p. 102, medical team. Kulim Technology Park Berhad, p. 50–51, aerial view of park. Kumpulan Wang Simpanan Pekerja, p. 118, service centre. Lee Sin Bee, p. 139, shophouses. Leong Huo Holdings Berhad, p. 27, chicken farm. Lembaga Jurutera Malaysia, p. 57, Klang Gates Dam. Lim Joo, p. 49, manufacturing products; p. 104,

people. Lion Corporation Berhad, p. 53, steel mill. Majlis Perbandaran Subang Jaya, p. 17, playground, hawkers. Malaysia–China Hydro Joint Venture, p. 86, Bakun Dam; p. 97, hydroelectric project. Malaysia Marine and Heavy Engineering Sdn Bhd, p. 53, shipbuilding. Malaysia Microelectronic Solutions Sdn Bhd, p. 60, engineer at work. Malaysia National Insurance Berhad, p. 78, advertisement, p. 115, Kuala Lumpur skyline. Malaysian Airline System, p. 95, MAS aircraft; p. 106, Malaysia Airlines applicants. Malaysian Agricultural Research and Development Institute, p. 42, cottage, pineapple, papayas, melons; p. 43, cattle, star fruit, rain-shelter, MARDI director; p. 44, researcher. Malaysian Franchise Association, p. 69, Reliance, Marrybrown, Noor Arfa, Manhattan Fish Market. Malaysian Industrial Development Authority, p. 50, industrial estate. Malaysian Institute of Accountants, p. 64, accountant. Malaysian Smelting Corporation, p. 30, tin ingots; p. 44, smelting; p. 131, tin dredge. Malaysian Technology Development Corporation Sdn Bhd, p. 60, wafer. Malaysian Timber Certification Council, p. 37, certificate. Malaysian Timber Council, p. 23, poster; p. 37, logging machinery, monitoring trees, sawing trees. Master Builders Association Malaysia, p. 57, MBAM book cover. Maxis Communications Berhad, p. 99, advertisement. Maybank Berhad, p. 7, Islamic banking; p. 80, officer and customers; p. 128, ATMs. McCann-Erickson Malaysia, p. 71, Playstation 2 advertisement. MEASAT Satellite Systems Sdn Bhd, p. 98, satellite. MHZ Film Sdn Bhd, p. 74, Sepet poster. MIMOS Berhad, p. 10, network centre; p. 24, JARING office. Minho Berhad, p. 36, timber complex. Ministry of Health Malaysia, p. 110, dentist at work. Ministry of Science,